General Education
and
The Liberal College

BY

WILLIAM F. CUNNINGHAM, C.S.C., Ph.D.

Professor of Education, University of Notre Dame

B. HERDER BOOK CO.

15 & 17 SOUTH BROADWAY, ST. LOUIS 2, MO.

AND

33 QUEEN SQUARE, LONDON, W.C.

CUM PERMISSU SUPERIORUM

IMPRIMI POTEST:

THEODORE J. MEHLING, C.S.C.
Provincial, Indiana Province
Congregation of Holy Cross

NIHIL OBSTAT:

WILLIAM FISCHER, S.T.D.
Censor Librorum

IMPRIMATUR:

✠ JOSEPH E. RITTER
Archbishop of St. Louis

June 15, 1953

Library of Congress Catalog Card Number: 53-7148

PREFACE

WITH the advent of World War II all discussion of liberal education by members of college and university staffs was stayed for some months by immediate preparations for war. Colleges for men and particularly universities had to think of the needs of the armed forces. Then, as tension in the educational world gradually eased, the old problem revived. The wartime curtailment of annual sessions of national associations afforded opportunities for the discussion of fundamental principles, policies, and practices in regional and committee meetings, where the clarification of issues is often better attained than in large national meetings. World War II really occasioned renewed interest in liberal education even though for the moment there was no possibility of putting into operation a strictly liberal-arts curriculum.

At the regional meetings of the National Catholic Educational Association, the question of liberal education came up repeatedly, and the Executive Committee of the College and University Department began to discuss to what extent, at least after the war, the nation's preoccupation with technical education during the war would effect what looked like a sharp turn towards liberal education in American colleges.[1] This problem was first seriously considered when the Executive Committee of the College and University Department

[1] In most instances this was discussed as "general education." More general education was advocated even in the training of the military personnel. Cf. *A Design for General Education for Members of the Armed Forces,* American Council on Education, Reports of Committees and Conferences, Series I, vol. VIII, no. 18, 1944.

v

met in June, 1943. One member expressed the opinion that today Catholics have no very clear idea of what liberal education is. Challenged to substantiate this statement, he qualified his remarks, and there followed a general discussion on the meaning of liberal education and the means to be adopted to achieve the desired ends, particularly, the curriculum.

As a result of the debate the president of the department appointed a committee to redefine the aims and methods of liberal education, stressing the importance of the liberal arts in postwar education. Meanwhile individual members of the department turned their attention to the same topic. Among these was the late Father Hugh O'Donnell, C.S.C., then president of the University of Notre Dame, who expressed the fear that, unlike the effect of the war in Canada, the war in the United States would so upset "the proper balance between the liberal and technological subjects . . . as not to preserve the cultural disciplines of philosophy, history, the languages, and allied subjects." The chairman of the newly appointed Liberal Arts Committee, Father Samuel K. Wilson, S.J., then president of Loyola University, Chicago, and secretary of the department, suggested to the members of the committee that they write out their ideas on liberal education. Two members complied, and the chairman himself wrote a paper on the liberal arts.

These three reports differed so fundamentally on most points, however, that agreement seemed impossible. It was decided, therefore, that a report should be prepared establishing a core of subjects to be required in any liberal-college curriculum. Before the close of 1944 the three divergent views were published in the *College Newsletter* as a stimulus to discussion by the Executive Committee. With this publication the personnel of the committee divided into three groups, which one member labeled the reactionary, the radical, and the conservative. In this classification he claimed that the reactionaries were victims of tradition; the radicals, those carried away by new ideas; and the conservatives, those trying to strike a balance between tradition and the new ideas demanding recognition. As an outcome of this division, the Liberal Arts Committee was discharged and the secretary of the department with an editorial board of three members, including the writer, was commissioned to prepare a new report. This report was presented at the annual meeting held in St. Louis in 1946. The criticisms which it received from a panel of three (a philosopher, a classicist, and a scientist), were so severe that further study of liberal education by the department was practically discontinued. So much good work had been done, however, that the author resolved that the study should not stop there. This book is the outcome of that resolution. It is, therefore, the crystalization of the thoughts and ideas of a number of Catholic educators working for more than a decade on this problem of Catholic liberal education. It is a synthesis of the ideas of administrators and faculty members in our Catholic colleges striving to improve their educational programs and do a better job in meeting the needs of the student bodies they are serving.

The author published his first articles on liberal education thirty years ago.[2] During all these years one of his major interests has been to determine in his own thinking and in his teaching of philosophy, the principles of education, and philosophy of education, what are the outstanding characteristics of any education truly liberal, and at the same time to practice the teaching techniques proper to developing such education in the minds and hearts of students under his tutelage. His continued interest in this problem has been shown by papers presented at educational meetings and by

[2] "What is a Liberal Education?" in *America*, XXVII (May 13, 1922), 79–81; "What is a Liberal Education's Value?" in *ibid*. (May 27), pp. 126–28; and "How is a Liberal Education Acquired?" in *ibid*. (June 10), pp. 173–75.

published articles,[3] and by his *Pivotal Problems of Education,* first published in 1940 by The Macmillan Co.

Considering the origin of the present work, it is evident that it would be impossible to list here all those who have made contributions to it. Such a list would include all the members of the Liberal Arts Committee and the Editorial Board mentioned above, as well as the students in my course, Current Philosophies and Practices in General Education, in which the preparation of this manuscript was for several years a major project. The contribution of some of these collaborators has been so outstanding, however, that they must be named here. Chief among these are Rev. Samuel K. Wilson, S.J., with whom I served as co-author of the final report of the Liberal Arts Committee, "The Liberal College in a Democracy," [4] and Rev. Leo R. Ward, C.S.C., who read the complete manuscript and gave me many helpful hints for its improvement. Rt. Rev. Msgr. Julius Haun and Dr. Roy J. Deferrari turned over to me their individual reports to use as I saw fit, and continued their help through correspondence and private conferences. Among my graduate students, two have been of great assistance in bringing the work to completion: Rev. John Walsh, C.S.C., and Mr. Francis Egan. Rev. Bonaventure Schwinn, O.S.B., editor of the *American Benedictine Review,* has been most encouraging and stimulating during the preparation of this work. Several sections of the present work, previously published in the *Review,* are here incorporated with his permission.

I am deeply grateful for all this assistance and particularly for the encouragement that has come from so many when at times it seemed that it would be impossible to complete the

---

[3] William F. Cunningham, C.S.C., "The American College and Catholic Education," *Thought,* I (September, 1926), 262–78.

[4] Washington: National Catholic Educational Association, Department of Colleges and Universities, 1946.

work. I feel that whatever good qualities this book may have are due in large measure to the advice and help received from those named above. On the other hand I realize that the deficiencies and shortcomings are my own, and I carry full responsibility for them.

W. F. CUNNINGHAM, C.S.C.

ACKNOWLEDGMENTS

GRATEFUL acknowledgment is made to the authors and publishers for permission to reprint quotations from the following publications:

"What Drove Me Crazy in Europe" by Perry Miller, copyrighted in 1951 by *The Atlantic Monthly; Cooperation in General Education* by the American Council on Education, copyrighted in 1947; *The Future of the Liberal College* by Norman Foerster, copyrighted in 1938 by Appleton-Century-Crofts; *Democracy in School Administration* by G. R. Koopman, A. Miel, and P. J. Misner, copyrighted in 1943 by Appleton-Century-Crofts; "Education and the Virtues" and "The Liberal Disciplines" by W. F. Cunningham, copyrighted in 1950 by the *American Benedictine Review; Science in General Education* by Earl J. McGrath, copyrighted in 1948 by William C. Brown, Co.; *How to Educate Human Beings* by Edward A. Fitzpatrick, copyrighted in 1950 by The Bruce Publishing Co.; "Mark Hopkins, The Log and the Dollar" by Willis D. Nutting, copyrighted in 1950 by *The Commonweal; A Study of the Liberal College* by Leon B. Richardson, copyrighted in 1924 by the Dartmouth College Press; *Issues in Integration* by William E. Kerstetter, copyrighted in 1948 by the Foundation for Integrated Education, Inc.; *History of Modern Elementary Education* by S. C. Parker, copyrighted in 1912 by Ginn and Co.; *General Education in a Free Society*, Report of the Harvard Committee, Harvard University Press, copyrighted in 1945 by the President and Fellows of Harvard College;

General Education in Science by I. Bernard Cohen and Fletcher G. Watson (eds.), copyrighted in 1952 by the Harvard University Press; *Education and World Tragedy* by Howard Mumford Jones, copyrighted in 1946 by the Harvard University Press; *Christ in the Church* by Msgr. Robert H. Benson, copyrighted in 1911 by the B. Herder Book Company; *Blueprint for a Catholic University,* by Leo R. Ward, copyrighted in 1949 by the B. Herder Book Company; "Primarily for Students" by F. Edward Cranz, copyrighted in 1950 by *The Journal of Higher Education; The Nature of the Liberal College* by Henry M. Wriston, copyrighted in 1937 by the Lawrence College Press; *Teacher in America* by Jacques Barzun, copyrighted in 1945 by Little, Brown and Co.; *The Abuse of Learning* by Frederick Lilge, copyrighted in 1948 by The Macmillan Company; *Secondary Education* by T. H. Briggs, J. P. Leonard, and J. Justman, copyrighted in 1950 by The Macmillan Co.; *The New Liberal Arts Program,* Manhattan College, 1949; *Educational Problems in College and University* by John Lewis Brum (ed.), copyrighted in 1921 by the Michigan University Press; "The Challenge of Catholic Education" by John A. Elliot, copyrighted in 1949 by the *N.C.E.A. Catholic High School Quarterly;* "Disciplining Reason" by Sister Ann Gertrude, copyrighted in 1950 by the *N.C.E.A. Catholic High School Quarterly; Higher Education for American Democracy* by The President's Commission on Higher Education, The United States Government Printing Office, 1947; *Fifty Golden Years* by Hunter Guthrie, copyrighted in 1946 by the College of Notre Dame, Md.; "In Defense of the Philosophy of Education" by Mortimer J. Adler, and "The Philosophy of Catholic Education" by William J. McGucken, in *Philosophies of Education, Forty-first Yearbook of the National Society for the Study of Education,* Part I, copyrighted 1942 by Nelson B. Henry; *Humanism and America* by Norman Foerster (ed.), copyrighted in 1930 by Rinehart

Company; *Autobiography and Selected Essays* by Thomas Henry Huxley, copyrighted in 1909 by the Riverside Press; *The Teaching of Religion in Higher Education* by Christian Gauss (ed.), copyrighted in 1951 by The Ronald Press Company; *School and Society*, May 7, 1949; *The Meaning of Education* by Nicholas Murray Butler, copyrighted in 1915 by Charles Scribner's Sons; *The Faith of a Liberal* by Nicholas Murray Butler, copyrighted in 1924 by Charles Scribner's Sons; *The Meaning of Man* by Jean Mouroux, copyrighted in 1948 by Sheed and Ward, Inc.; *Liberal and Vocational Studies in the College* by Henry Waldgrave Stuart, copyrighted in 1918 by the Stanford University Press; *Education at the Crossroads* by Jacques Maritain, copyrighted in 1942 by the Yale University Press.

CONTENTS

Part III

HOW AND WHERE TO TEACH—METHOD AND ADMINISTRATION

LIST OF DIAGRAMS

INTRODUCTION

GENERAL AND LIBERAL EDUCATION

UNTIL the end of the nineteenth century the classics and mathematics, topped off with philosophy, constituted most of Catholic liberal education. One reason was that most of our early Catholic educators had first learned to express themselves in tongues other than English, and they could not be expected to extend courses in the literature of a language with which they were not altogether familiar. Another reason was that the opinion prevailed that no education could be liberal unless it were classical, for it was believed that the classics and philosophy best sharpened the minds and enlarged the hearts of free men; and freedom, somehow or other, seemed all wrapped up in the literary declarations of two ancient democracies, Athens and Rome. One writer recalls a perfect squelching he received just before the turn of the century when in all innocence he asked a teacher what classical languages Socrates and Plato had studied.[1] But whatever the reasons for this classical addiction, it remains that Catholic education looked backward rather than forward, and our heritage from the Middle Ages and the Renaissance was philosophical and classical to the core.

Early in the twentieth century, however, the study of the classics fell into disfavor in this country and the natural sciences were in the ascendant. Educators, influenced by the new scientific age, looked upon the old system of intellectual

[1] Samuel K. Wilson, S.J., *The Liberal College in a Democracy* (Washington: National Catholic Educational Association, 1946), p. 13.

1

training as definitely outmoded. But within two or three decades natural science, at least in the undergraduate field, was on the defensive, its position threatened by the extraordinary rise of the social sciences, even though in the minds of many educators some of these were hardly sciences at all, but rather a miscellany of facts from many departments of knowledge.

Of all the causes combining to supplant our traditional liberal education, probably the most effective was the elective system. This is not written by way of pleading a thesis; rather, it is a historical fact that is doubly interesting because of its recent termination. The very university which by a sophomoric enthusiasm for the elective system first administered the death thrust to the old system, was, by a study of liberal education in our own day (made almost apologetically), to arouse among Catholics a suspicion that they had acted hastily in adopting without reservation the elective system.[2]

Even before the first World War some Catholic colleges had begun to adopt the new system and to discontinue many of the old studies except philosophy and theology. When reaction against this cafeteria complex in education began to seethe in shrines of electivism, Catholic traditionalists took heart. Papers read at the annual meetings of the National Catholic Educational Association indicated this stirring, and many Catholic teachers began to examine their pedagogical consciences and to ask themselves and others to what low estate had their colleges fallen.

I. The Hutchins Blast

This movement was well on its way in 1935 when the National Catholic Educational Association introduced regional organization. For several years the Catholic institu-

---

[2] The Harvard Report, *Education in a Free Society* (Cambridge: Harvard University Press, 1945).

tions holding membership in the North Central Association
had been meeting informally on the occasion of the annual
meeting of the regional accrediting association. The year
after this practice was adopted for all regional groups, Father Samuel K. Wilson, S.J., at that time president of Loyola
University, Chicago, was elected chairman of the Midwest
Region, and he set up a Problems Committee to plan the
program for the succeeding annual meeting. Under his leadership the Committee invited Dr. Robert Maynard Hutchins,
at that time president of Chicago University, to address the
midwest group. The latter agreed to do so on one condition:
that no reporters be present. If he spoke at all to Catholic
college educators, he wished to speak frankly with no publicity in the newspapers. The following excerpts from his
speech are certainly frank enough, but that did not deter the
editor of the *College Newsletter* (Father Wilson himself)
from publishing Dr. Hutchins' speech in the first issue, May,
1937.

In brief, Dr. Hutchins accused Catholic colleges and universities of imitating the worst features of secular institutions
of higher education and of ignoring most of the good ones.
"There are some good ones, relatively speaking," he said,
"high academic standards, development of habits of work,
and research." Two of the worst features of the secular institutions which in his opinion we had adopted were athleti-
cism and collegiatism. He described the product of collegiatism as

. . . well-tubbed young Americans. They don't have much in
their heads but are acceptable as decorations of at least one
political party and make good additions to a house party.

The third bad feature of secular education is vocationalism;
that is, securing good jobs . . . for its [the college's] graduates. . . . The fourth bad feature is anti-intellectualism. If the
object of a university is to produce good athletes or well-tubbed

Americans or to secure its graduates good jobs, what is the point of intellectual training? Abstract problems have no relation at all to those aims. Consequently, intellectual training has been driven out of the curriculum until we have merely a general program of disseminating information, a program which leads to the highest degrees. All these things produce the disintegration of education.

This was a novel explanation of the disintegration of liberal education in the American college, since this is commonly blamed on the adoption of the elective system and the excessive departmentalization that accompanied it in both high school and college. But this was not the complete message which Dr. Hutchins delivered to the Catholic college administrators assembled at that meeting. He especially emphasized the great opportunities of Catholic colleges.

Now in all these respects, I believe, Catholic education is as bad as, maybe worse, than secular education. My charge, then, is that Catholic education is not Catholic enough. . . . The Catholic Church has the longest intellectual tradition of any institution in the contemporary world, the only uninterrupted tradition and the only explicit tradition; that is, it is the only institution which is conscious of its tradition. What I say is that this tradition must not be merely an ideal, but must be practiced. . . . I defy you to prove that your graduates are more proficient in these [the liberal] arts than ours, which is a serious accusation because if the products of your education are what they should be your students must excel in the liberal arts. Ours don't have to. You have a great tradition to uphold. We have, or think we have, none. . . .

In these days philosophy, in most universities, is merely one department of fifty or sixty. Any attempt to secure its rightful position in the hierarchy would be long and arduous and in a secular university would be vain. In your universities, however, it should be a success. Unless this is done Catholic education will never be Catholic enough. The best service Catholic education can perform for the nation and all education is to show that the intellectual tradition can again be made the heart of higher education.[3]

This book is at least one answer to Dr. Hutchins' challenge and will prove to be, it is hoped, an inspiration, if not a guide, to all Catholic educators working to steer the liberal college out of its present doldrums.

II. Defining Our Terminology

Before entering upon the main problems with which we will be concerned, we must clearly distinguish several types of education to be discussed throughout our study. The first of these is special education.

1. Special Education. In our use of the term, special education always means some type of occupational training, either in a trade or on the professional level. The only way that we can distinguish between these two types of specialized training is in terms of the quantity and the quality of the formal schooling preparing for them. Adequate trade training calls for little general education in comparison with the many years of general or liberal education that have always been preparatory to the so-called "learned professions." So, too, with the specialized training. The doctor or clergyman spends several years in the professional school to become adept in the professional skills of his calling and to develop an adequate knowledge of and familiarity with the sciences basic to that calling. Not so the worker on the trade level. The skills of his calling are largely manual in character, and the knowledge required for applying them effectively is, for the most part, a knowledge of material things such as wood, iron, and other metals, and this is best

[3] *College Newsletter* (official organ of the N.C.E.A. College and University Department), May, 1937, pp. 1 and 4.

acquired by working with them. But there is another distinction between technical and professional occupations. Whereas the former are concerned for the most part with things of the material world, the latter deal with human beings and their problems. The skills demanded in the professional man's calling are those of diagnosis, treatment, and counsel. This is obvious in the case of the physician in restoring and conserving his patient's health; but it is just as true of the other callings that are truly professional in character, although we do not commonly use the word "skills" when speaking of the abilities which a lawyer or the pastor of a parish must have if he is to exercise his vocation effectively.[4]

2. General Education. Turning now to general education, we first point out the appropriateness of this name for the type of education called for in any society that is truly democratic. In the first place it is general since it is the education that all the citizens of any free society should have. In the second place it is general since, if all the citizens are to play their part in preserving and promoting the freedom of that society, they must be familiar with the advancing knowledge that brought that society into being and the culture that characterizes it today. To achieve this end the curriculum of all schools concerned with general education (in this country, the elementary school, high school, and college) must offer to the student courses in all the great fields of knowledge, that are selected, graded, and continuous. The courses must be selected because knowledge has become so extensive that it is literally impossible to present all of it. Nor is this necessary. Much of the cultural inheritance is conveyed to the members of society, both young and old, by a process of social transmission. We learn what we live; and living as members of the great social institutions such as home, church,

---

[4] The term "special education" is also used by some writers to signify special schools for the physically handicapped and mentally retarded.

and community, young people soon develop the attitudes and ideals of these institutions and become familiar with their customs. The school is only the formal agency for this transmission. Here we are in agreement with Alexander Meiklejohn, who says: "In a word, education is the agent of a social, cultural intention. It has authority. Without such authority, teaching does not exist at all." [5] Later he adds:

Teaching must find its roots in some active code of behavior. It must express some authoritative pattern of culture. It must believe something. Some social group must be speaking through it, impressing its way of life. Nothing short of that is education. . . . In the midst of our shifting, uncertain, self-contradictory world, what shall we teach? That is the puzzling, baffling problem into which everyone is sooner or later plunged who sees teaching as the activity of a specific social group. It is, I think, the most significant form of the question with which the contemporary theory of education is called upon to deal.[6]

This problem will be our concern in the four chapters of Part II: "What To Teach—The Curriculum." [7]

In the second place the curriculum must be graded. The mind of the kindergarten pupil is radically different from that of the college senior. This difference is a matter of growth and development and requires another characteristic in the curriculum: it must be continuous, that is, without gaps and without overlapping. These requirements form the basis for the distinction between the psychological and the logical organization and presentation of subject matter. The former means that both content and method must be adapted to the immature mind of the child; whereas logical organization and presentation are demanded by the maturing mind

[5] Alexander Meiklejohn, *Education Between Two Worlds* (New York: Harper and Brothers, 1942), p. 92.

[6] *Ibid.*, p. 103.

[7] See below, pp. 71–187.

of the college student. This difference explains the difficult situation of the high school, which has to adapt itself to the minds of students undergoing rapid growth and development during this period of transition. Both high school and college must help students make this transition in their efforts to assimilate the fundamentals of the great fields of knowledge which constitute the curriculum on all levels of general education.

This latter phase of general education has two aspects, social transmission and individual development. Although the latter is the more important, the two must be correlative. The development of the student's mind cannot go on in a mental vacuum. It takes place through his efforts to assimilate the cultural inheritance presented in the educational program of the school, which includes the curriculum and all the activities under the direction of the staff of teachers and administrators, and those other activities which students initiate under the guidance of faculty counselors.[8]

3. Liberal Education. This description of general education brings up the question whether there is any difference between it and what for centuries has been called liberal education. These qualities of general education in a modern democracy are all characteristic of liberal education, which is the kind of education all citizens should have. Why then introduce the term "general" at all? In answer to this question I find myself in agreement with the point of view presented in the following statement from a recent book entitled *General Education in Science*.

The German influence of research and analysis has permeated graduate schools and undergraduate teaching, and as the lecture system has displaced discussion, we have practically lost what little boast to liberality we might ever have had in so-called liberal education. . . .

[8] Cf. William F. Cunningham, *The Pivotal Problems of Education* (New York: Macmillan Co., 1940), pp. 282–90.

Liberal education *should be* concerned with ideas rather than facts. But since it has so largely failed in this task, General Education has become the pinch hitter. In this sense, General Education *is* only an improved version of liberal education—or should be if it is to have any claim to permanence. In fact, this is its only reason for existence and it is altogether possible that it may one day become indistinguishable from liberal education, should liberal education again assume its true function of teaching students to deal with ideas. . . .

I would put first in any General Education program in science the objective of learning to reason critically, imaginatively, and constructively about problems in science. . . . Clearly there is in this connection a need for careful coordination with General Education courses in other fields than science.[9]

When students ask me, "What is the difference between general and liberal education?" I always answer by basing the distinction on a difference of school levels. Traditionally the college has been spoken of as the agency for liberal education. Its name, "the liberal college," indicates this usage, and thus the term is used in the Harvard Report: "If one cling to the root meaning of liberal as that which befits or helps to make free men, then general and liberal education have identical goals. The one may be thought of as an earlier stage of the other, similar in nature but less advanced in degree." [10] Today, however, some authors are using the term "liberal education" for the general education received in high school, though not for that received in the elementary school.[11] But there is danger that this use of the term will

[9] Sydney J. French, "General Education and Special Education in the Sciences" in *General Education in Science,* ed. by I. Bernard Cohen and Fletcher G. Watson (Cambridge: Harvard University Press, 1952), pp. 24 f.

[10] *Op. cit.,* p. 52.

[11] "In these chapters on 'interests,' the terms 'higher education' and 'liberal education' are not used in the limited sense as applying only to collegiate and higher education, but in a broader and more generic sense as applying to all of education above the level of mastery of fundamental facts

result in confusion worse confounded. In English-speaking countries the term has always been applied to the education received in university colleges. Thus Newman uses it in his frequently quoted description of the product of liberal education in the colleges of Oxford University.[12] Thus we also shall use it here.

In the proceedings of the first workshop conducted by the Foundation for Integrated Education, the terms "general" and "liberal" seem to be used interchangeably. In the section called "Supplementary Papers Issued for the Workshop," the selections carry no authors' names. Here we find the following: "Liberal education in the sense of intellectual emancipation and the attainment of maturity, implies wisdom and insight, culture, integrity. For this kind of education conceptual cross-connections are indispensable." [13] On the other hand Dr. Judson Butler, dean of the General College at Boston University, gives this statement of the goal of his institution:

General education, as we use the term, is the antithesis of academic isolationism, of separatism, of narrow specialization, and of educational atomism generally. It is concerned with giving all students, regardless of the later area of specialization, a basic understanding of the sciences, social sciences and humanities—including the ability to deal logically and informatively and imaginatively with novel problems as they may arise in living. Later, as the student specializes in some one area he may weave his advanced knowledge into the pattern of his

---

and skills, i.e., as applying to the secondary school as well. As the highest institution of formal education which the majority of the American public attends, the secondary school must aim at the cultivation of men and women, who, within the limits possible, are liberally educated in the best sense of the term" (T. H. Briggs, J. P. Leonard, J. Justman, *Secondary Education* [New York: Macmillan Co., 1950], p. 11 note).

[12] This quotation from Newman is given below, pp. 57 f.

[13] First National Workshop of the Foundation of Integrated Education, *Issues on Integration,* IX (1948), 84.

generalized understanding, and follow the ramifications suggested by his special interest, into neighboring fields—thus his concentration on a specific subject, in addition to making him a competent specialist, will add further to his "general education." Furthermore, the means of general education is integrated study, and the end is integrated knowledge and understanding. It has the function to teach not mere facts, but to utilize facts and principles wherever found as the means for fuller understanding.[14]

This surely is a good description of liberal education at its best, though the term "liberal" does not occur therein. Another term, however, is used in the phrases "integrated study" and "integrated knowledge" which we will be using continually.

4. Integrated Education. For us integrated education is an education characterized by a quality that all education should have. Everyone knows the difference between an integral and a fractional number. Any education that is fractionized, that is, broken up into parts instead of being a unified whole, is not a good education. The difficulty with the term, however, is that in most discussions of its meaning, it has been applied solely to the curriculum. And here too often it has meant no more than selecting pieces or parts of traditional courses, fitting them together to form a new course, and calling the labor involved in this procedure "integration." The early survey courses were products of this type.

But a little reflection reveals that integration as a goal, if it is realized at all in any education, is something that takes place in the mind of the student. L. T. Hopkins, a professional consultant among those working on the reconstruction of the high-school curriculum, stresses this point in his book which is entitled *Integration*.[15] Further, inte-

---

[14] *Ibid.*, p. 12.
[15] New York: Appleton-Century, 1937; cf. chaps. 1 and 2.

gration must characterize the mind of the teacher if it is to be developed in the mind of the student. The teacher cannot give what he does not have. With this interpretation of the term we see that a curriculum truly integrated is no more than a tool which student and teacher both use to produce this effect in the mind of the student. We may go further and add that integration should characterize the activities of the administrative staff as well as those of students and teachers, all working together to bring about the achievement of the goal which integration signifies. This is just as true in special education as it is in general and liberal education. Special education aims at the perfection of an individual's powers in respect to an occupation. But behind the specific skills of any calling are the liberal arts, the intellectual arts, and the arts of language. The specific skills of any occupation cannot be learned effectively unless the learner is already in command of these fundamental arts; but with a masterly command of these arts, specific skills are learned quickly and easily and function effectively when occasion calls for them.

Integration is a quality that all education should have. If it is not integrated, that is, if it is not a unified whole within the student's mind rather than a hodgepodge of unrelated bits of knowledge, it is simply not good special education or good general education, and certainly not good liberal education.

In summary, then, special education is occupational training on any level in high school, trade school, or professional school of the university. General education is that of the elementary school and the high school, although it is continued in college and should be continued all through life. Liberal education is the particular concern of the college; it is broader, deeper, and more intensive than general education, and for most college students culminates their education as far as formal schooling is concerned. Integrated education is a quality that should characterize all education.

Our concern is with the college as the formal agency of liberal education. We now inquire what are the goals of any education that is truly liberal; but since our special concern is the Catholic college, our inquiry carries us forward in the search for those ends and means that make a liberal education truly Catholic.

PART I

WHY TEACH—EDUCATIONAL GOALS

CHAPTER 1

LIBERAL EDUCATION IN AMERICA

WE USE the term education to describe the bringing forth or the maturing of the intellectual powers of man rather than the pouring in of factual information, although information is a necessary product of any system of mental development. The term liberal is commonly used to describe the kind of discipline by which, during the era of Hellenic splendor, leaders of Greek society were educated. These leaders, *liberi,* as the Romans called them, were the only free citizens of the republic, and they alone were deemed worthy to receive a liberal education. The term is also employed with reference to a system of education which frees, or liberalizes, the individual from narrowness of vision, shallowness of thought, the inhibitions of prejudice, and from the enslavement of the passions. The ancients themselves understood this significance, as Epictetus declares: "Rulers may say that only free men should be educated, but we believe that only educated men are free." [1] We shall combine both meanings and use the term to denote a system of education which, as far as possible, liberalizes all citizens of a democracy, all of whom are *liberi.*

Traditionally we are inclined to think and speak not of the end, which is the educated man, but of the means, which are the arts and sciences. Since the time of Plato and Aristotle the phrase "liberal arts" has been used with reference to the means of liberal education. These are not the only means, of

[1] *Discourses,* II, chap. 1.

course, for certainly the teacher and the administrator have their place in all considerations of the means of education. Nevertheless, because the arts and sciences remain the primary tools by which the individual is educated, a large portion of this investigation will deal with problems of the curriculum. The phrase "liberal arts" as used here, then, will commonly include not only the traditional liberal arts, but also the liberal sciences. Indeed, some contend that today the sciences are a greater factor in liberalizing the individual than are the ancient arts.

In its Attic sense, liberal education is limited to a relatively small element of society which did not need to engage in commerce or gainful labor. A pagan philosophy or a materialistic philosophy may legitimatize this situation in which a class that does not earn its own living is supported by a larger class that does. But in a democracy all men are free and equal, and each should contribute his services to society that in return he may receive the means of supporting life and advance his position in society. Yet it would be unjust were we to condemn, hastily and unreservedly, the philosophy which made Greek culture effective then and inspiring now. We must remember that the *liberi* were not free from all work, but gave a great deal of their time and effort to the service of society through the direction of their government and, when occasion demanded, its defense.

I. LIBERAL EDUCATION IN A DEMOCRACY

The type of schooling open only to a privileged few is inimical to democracy, where all men are free and all must work. Nevertheless the American people need the kind of education which prevailed among the relatively few *liberi* in ancient Greece and Rome. If for no other reason, we need liberal education because in freeing or liberalizing the mind it prepares the individual to discharge the duties of his citizenship intelligently and thus serves as a safeguard of our democracy.

History has proved that liberal education has conferred remarkable benefits on the qualified few who were able to secure it. Likewise we must admit that the liberal education of the Greeks and Romans made their governments strong and their society so effective that today we participate in the cultural advantages these early leaders procured for posterity. It behooves us, therefore, to seek some of these advantages directly for ourselves. In our democracy no free man or woman who can profit by a liberal education should be deprived of its benefits because of poverty.

1. Liberal Education in the Ancient and Medieval Worlds

We have pointed out that the liberal arts in Greece constituted a system of education which was developed for the ruling class and we have urged that the best features of this system are applicable to the education of all citizens of a democracy, each of whom, through helping to form public opinion, participates in governmental rule. Now we must turn our attention to an analysis of the curriculum used by the Greeks and their predecessors. The most widely pursued and intellectually effective of their disciplines was the study of philosophy, the inquiry into the nature and the ultimate causes of all physical and human phenomena. Apart from that their interests lay in what today we call the science of government and the science of society. Thus liberal studies from the beginning were professional, at least in part.

The Romans, influenced by Greek culture, adopted a similar kind of education. As long as the republic lasted, the Roman citizen was actively interested in the progressive organization of his government, and this political consciousness focused attention on the study of law and of rhetoric, or the art of pleading before the courts. The tradition persisted even after the republic had given place to the empire.

In medieval times the chief liberal subject pursued was also philosophy, and the studies of the clergy were largely professional inasmuch as the clergy were being prepared for work in ecclesiastical and civil courts, or for the teaching and preaching of theology. In these three epochs of liberal education the background of all study was an inquiry into the nature and ultimate causes of things, and philosophy in its various divisions was the core curriculum followed by Greek statesmen, Roman legalists, and medieval clerics. Thus, during these three periods of world history, the principal studies were concerned with occupational or professional pursuits.

2. Liberal Education in the Modern World

As we have seen, the term "liberal" was not always used in its passive or static significance. Even from early times it has had, at least occasionally, a dynamic meaning, although this meaning has come into general use only in contemporary discussions. American writers stress the concept of freedom or the freeing from ignorance and passion as implied in the dynamic sense of this term. It is a freedom that differentiates man from the brute animal, a freedom with which man can choose his ultimate goal and the numerous preliminary means leading to that goal.

To achieve all this man must possess a mature mind. He must have knowledge, not a superficial knowledge of isolated facts, not merely a penetrating acquaintance with one area of knowledge which, because it is narrow, is grotesquely distorted, but a comprehensive view of all that concerns human living. He must also have a disciplined will, which implies strength to keep his appetites in check and to conquer the opposing forces of environment. He must possess a trained body, not necessarily a robust body or the muscular type sought by athletic coaches, but one that can support the intellectual and moral dictates of the mind. The ancient Greeks have been criticized for their worship of the strong and beautiful body. From the Christian, even from the purely rational, point of view, this censure is partly deserved. But the very writers who decry this worship of the body are themselves in favor of physical training by a more or less rigorous discipline. Finally, at least in a large proportion of cases, it is necessary to provide some training by which body and soul can be kept fittingly together.

We close this section on "Liberal Education in a Democracy" with what is perhaps the most eloquent description in the English language of the product of liberal education, the liberally educated man. It is that by Thomas H. Huxley, and all true humanists, Catholic and non-Catholic alike, enthusiastically endorse it.

That man, I think, has had a liberal education who has been so trained in youth that his body is the ready servant of his will, and does with ease and pleasure all the work that, as a mechanism, it is capable of; whose intellect is a clear, cold, logic engine, with all its parts of equal strength, and in smooth working order; ready, like a steam engine, to be turned to any kind of work, and spin the gossamers as well as forge the anchors of the mind; whose mind is stored with a knowledge of the great and fundamental truths of nature, and of the laws of her operations; one who, no stunted ascetic, is full of life and fire, but whose passions are trained to come to heel by a vigorous will, the servant of a tender conscience; one who has learned to love all beauty, whether of nature or of art, to hate all vileness and to respect others as himself.[2]

II. Catholic Liberal Education in Our Democracy

The ultimate purpose of the Catholic college of liberal arts and sciences, as of every social agency under Catholic auspices, is to bring souls closer to God with the aid of His grace,

[2] Thomas Henry Huxley, *Autobiography and Selected Essays* (Cambridge: Riverside Press, 1909), p. 43. His essay, "A Liberal Education," is also published in *Science and Education* and *Lay Sermons, Addresses and Reviews*.

and to assist them in fulfilling the purpose of their creation. Without such a motive it is unlikely that Catholics would have made the sacrifices they have made to develop in the United States our present system of education. The proximate purpose of the Catholic college is to prepare its students to become contributing citizens in a democracy. Education of the individual for his proper place in divine and human society is both the ultimate and proximate reason for the existence of colleges. Catholic administrators, however, must not confuse these two objectives of the Catholic college. They must not over-emphasize the salvation of souls and neglect the thorough training of the mental and physical powers of the student. The full duty of the Catholic college is not discharged unless determined efforts are made to secure the proximate as well as the ultimate goal. Nor may the Catholic college substitute a high level of morals for a low level of intelligence. All too often intelligence is found divorced from morality. The Catholic educator cannot condone such a state of affairs; for the Catholic college, since it is a college, must be concerned not merely with the spiritual but primarily with the intellectual purpose of its existence, and if adequate efforts to achieve both ends are made, a satisfactory degree of attainment in both may be expected.

1. European Origins of Catholic Education

No exact count has ever been made, but in all probability the majority of Catholic colleges and universities in this country have been founded by religious congregations. Almost all of these congregations have European origins and, in some cases, fairly recent European traditions. On the other hand, most of the colleges and universities founded by different States and by non-Catholic religious groups have such a remote old-world background that any European influence that entered into their organization and functioning was introduced long after the American tradition had been firmly established. Originally in the colonies, it is true, college foundations were distinctly British. Such was the case, however, with only a few, Harvard, for instance, William and Mary, King's (now Columbia), and Rutgers, the last colonial school founded. Even in colonial days most American foundations took their spirit and their organization not directly from Europe, but from existing American foundations, particularly from Harvard, the very first.

A statement of these facts is almost a necessary preface to several observations to be made in this study. In our present political situation it is no longer true, as it was when George Washington wrote his Farewell Address, that "Europe has a set of primary interests which to us have none or very remote relations." In the field of education, however, the United States, isolationist if you will, has developed its own system and its own procedures. American education, at least in one important aspect, a single system for all citizens, is very different from the European system, which before World War II was determined by the existence of a peasantry or proletariat. Our system and our procedures have grown out of our democratic way of life, and the demands of a democratic society must be taken into account in making suggestions for improvement on any level of American education. Accordingly, with regard to the curriculum of Catholic colleges of liberal education in the United States, our attitude may be summarized in two points: (1) liberal education is the best possible type of general education for those intellectually equipped to profit by it; and (2) democracy demands that as far as possible the liberal studies shall be enjoyed even by those who are economically handicapped.

2. Catholic Liberal Education in the Twentieth Century

We now live in a period very different from the nineteenth century, when the classical humanities were considered to be the very essence of liberal education. We have seen that the Greeks in the time of Socrates, and the Scholastics in the time of Albertus Magnus, did not consider that the essence of a liberal education lay in the classical humanities; this notion came only with the Renaissance. In modern times the natural sciences have replaced the classics in the position of pre-eminence. May not our immediate future witness a further veering toward an emphasis on the social sciences? Whether or not the trend will be in this direction, an inquiry into the implications of human activity will always remain a notable factor in any system of liberal education, because the mind of man will always remain essentially the same, and the ultimate relationship of the human mind to the First Cause and to secondary causes as evidenced by his desires and longings, will continue unchanged while man is man.

As far as we can foresee, men in a democracy will always have to work in order to live. Liberal education, as most will admit, does not prepare the student directly to earn a livelihood. If it is followed by extensive professional training, there is no doubt that, granting student aptitude and application, results are most satisfactory. National medical groups have been advocating a more thorough preparation for professional medical study by a longer course in general education. Engineering groups have expressed similar opinions. Our difficulty is that many students are economically unable to continue their education through the many years demanded by such prolonged study. What, then, shall be done? Shall we restrict the benefits of liberal education to a select few whose families have the means to provide for many years of formal training? The alternative is to offer to these students economically handicapped, professional training which will directly prepare them to earn a living, and at the same time give them as much of the cultural value of liberal education as possible.

Let us state what most Catholic educators agree upon: namely, that for those possessing the required talents, a purely liberal education is by far the best. If students must be prepared not only for living but also for earning a living, let the proportion of professional courses to those in the purely liberal arts be as small as the purpose of taking professional courses at all will permit. In either event the courses given should be the best possible courses in the field. Not to aim at, and at least partially succeed in this high purpose, is to render vain the sacrifices men and women have made to establish Catholic colleges and universities in America.

3. Divergent Views of the Curriculum

While the ultimate aim of Catholic colleges and universities must necessarily be spiritual, immediately the Catholic college exists to prepare the student for this life, since he is not only a creature of God but also a human being living in a civilized society. This objective has been variously described and two somewhat opposing opinions have been voiced. The first holds that while the proximate purpose of the Catholic college is to develop the power to attain truth, choose the good, and appreciate the beautiful, a development of the power to earn a living must also be included in the program. In any group of college students a considerable proportion will have to earn their living beginning with Commencement Day. If these economically underprivileged students, often more talented than their more prosperous classmates, cannot take courses preparing them to earn a living, they must forego most of the advantages of a liberal education to the loss not only of the unfortunate students themselves but also of society and of the Church.

A second opinion would exclude from the curriculum of liberal education any professional preparation. This point of view expresses the traditional theory of liberal education and proceeds on the assumption that the four-year college course is all too brief to cultivate such important powers as the ability to grasp truth and avoid error, to appreciate the beautiful rather than find satisfaction in the ugly, to choose the good and reject the morally evil. Such a theory excludes from college work any economic advantage to be derived from professional courses and will tolerate the cultivation of bodily powers only when such cultivation is necessary to the well-being and development of spiritual powers. There is much to be said for the traditional opinion, which upholds a kind of intellectual training whose achievement is described by Foerster:

The liberal college is nothing more or less than a place which renders possible the growth into maturity of free men and women, not wage slaves or salary slaves, nor slaves to the sense and passions. Its aim is not to train the masses for cheap power and service, but to send into society enough thoughtful and high-minded persons whose works and deeds possess a courage and truth to which others will be tempted to rally. Let the scoffer say what he will, society has a conscience, a capacity for response to what is obviously right and enthusiasm for nobility, which is again and again duped and perverted by demagogues and mass insanities (this being a world of evil as well as good), but is ever waiting to reassert itself when spurred by the right word or deed.[3]

No one will deny that in many instances the education given by so-called liberal colleges has been anything but liberal. In spite of the adulteration of higher education by the credit complex and the elective system, colleges of the liberal arts have clung to their title even when they could be called "liberal" only through an extension of extraordinary courtesy.

These divergent opinions find expression in two conclusions about the liberal-arts curriculum. Realists, admitting the excellence of liberal studies, wish to give all students, at least those who must discontinue their formal education after four

[3] Norman Foerster, *The Future of the Liberal College*, p. 80; used by permission of Appleton-Century-Crofts, Inc., New York (1938).

years at college, as much cultural training as possible while they are being prepared to earn a living. Traditionalists contend that the introduction even of a few professional courses into the liberal arts program inhibits the strength of intellect and will which liberal education is designed to intensify and thus prevents that student from acquiring the intellectual excellence which this type of education should develop.

Because of a conviction that this type of education best represents the Catholic tradition, almost all Catholic colleges call themselves colleges of liberal arts, or, using a more precise term, colleges of liberal arts and sciences. Although the name was retained, many of them have failed, as non-Catholic colleges have failed, to follow the tradition in practice. For this reason many have suggested that the term "liberal arts" or "liberal education" should be redefined. As the traditional definition stands, the term is applicable to only a few of the nonuniversity colleges if we consider the amount of professional training that has invaded the curriculum of most of them.

We are in sympathy with a statement made in what we believe is one of the best studies of this problem of liberal and vocational education. Dr. Henry Stuart, Professor of Philosophy at Stanford University, after saying that it is not his purpose to discuss in detail the elements of liberal education, continues: "That is a task by itself, which must be repeated for each well-marked period in the life of a changing society."[4] Certainly many are the changes that have taken place in our society during the three decades and more since he wrote, and now after World War II we are in one of those "well-marked periods." Keeping in mind the ultimate goal of Catholic colleges, the educational system of which they are a part, and the requirements of the demo-

[4] Reprinted from: *Liberal and Vocational Studies in the College,* Leland Stanford Jr. University Publications, University Series, by Henry Waldgrave Stuart, with the permission of the author and of the publishers, Stanford University Press, p. 23.

cratic society for which the Catholic college in the United States prepares its students, we submit this redefinition: Liberal education is that type of education which is designed to develop the abilities to attain truth, appreciate the beautiful, and choose the good; to foster bodily and mental health, and maintain temporal well-being through economic preparedness.

All that follows in this study will attempt to explain this definition and establish its validity.

III. Our Educational Goals

In order that education as we have described it (that is, education that is truly liberal and truly Catholic) may be brought to an increasing number of the faithful in this country today, let us determine what educational goals our colleges should adopt to achieve this end. We distinguish these goals on three levels: the immediate, the mediate, and the ultimate. By the immediate goals we mean those fruits of learning which every teacher in every classroom should be striving to develop in his students; they are common to all fields and to all subjects within a field. Anything we have ever learned in our lives or will learn, is either new knowledge, a new attitude, a new ability, or the improvement of an old one. These changes that take place in students as they grow and develop should be encouraged by the teacher and directed toward proper goals. But knowledge, attitudes, and abilities do not function in a vacuum. They are always knowledge *of* something, attitudes *toward* something, or abilities *to do* something. What are these "somethings"?

1. The Seven Life Careers

The answer to this question may be stated in a general way in terms of what Snedden calls the "seven careers"[5]

[5] David Snedden, "Toward Free and Efficient Liberal Colleges" in *Journal of Higher Education,* June, 1935, pp. 311 f.

that each person is following more or less all the time if he is awake to his opportunities and aware of his obligations as a contributing citizen in a democracy. Everyone, as far as he is able, should be striving to be (1) a rational human being, (2) a healthy animal, (3) a loving child or parent, (4) an efficient producer of goods or services, (5) an enjoyer of wholesome leisure, (6) a loyal citizen, and (7) a faithful believer in God, loving and serving Him.

As society has evolved, it has produced the great social agencies the purpose of which is to advance these careers in the lives of its members. Each of these agencies has as its own specific, essential function, the promotion of one of these human needs (for example, economic security through the economic order); but all have supplementary or "instrumental" functions to perform, as Newman calls them, through which they assist the other agencies in achieving their specific aims.[6] This fact is particularly true of the school. As an intellectual agency its purpose is the developing of minds; but if it well accomplishes this purpose, it is making its best possible contribution toward the achievement of the goals of the other agencies. In the matter of health, for example, if it develops within the pupil a knowledge of health, wholesome attitudes towards health, and sound habits of health, it will have done all it can as an intellectual agency for promoting the health of the pupils, which, of course, is conditioned primarily by heredity and secondarily by the sanitary environment of the home and the community in which they live.

In Figure 1 (p. 30) we have presented the "seven careers" as human needs, for each of which there is a social agency with the primary responsibility for meeting the need. All persons experience all of these needs, and their "careers" in life are what they do in meeting them. When we speak of these

[6] John Henry Newman, *Idea of a University*, Discourse VI, "Knowledge Viewed in Relation to Learning."

Figure 1. THE HIERARCHY OF EDUCATIONAL GOALS

Philosopher's Level	Human Needs	Integration of All Levels Below (philosophical synthesis)			Social Agencies
	Supernatural Needs	Ultimate Goals (theological analysis)			Supernatural Agencies
Theologian's Level	2. Salvation (next life)	Union with God Hereafter (man's supernatural destiny)			Communion of Saints
	1. Divine grace (this life)	Union with God Here and Now (supernatural means for that destiny)			Catholic Church
	Natural Needs	↑ Mediate Goals ↑ (sociological analysis)			Natural Agencies
	7. Divine security (religious life)	↑	↑	↑	7. Church
	6. Civic security (civic life)	↑	↑	↑	6. State (community)
	5. Leisure (recreational life)	↑	↑	↑	5. Recreational agencies
Sociologist's Level	4. Economic security (vocational life)	↑	↑	↑	4. Economic order
	3. Human companionship (family life)	↑	↑	↑	3. Home
	2. Health (organic life)	↑	↑	↑	2. Health conserving agencies
		Immediate Goals (psychological analysis)			
Teacher's Level	1. Education (mental life)	Knowledge (facts and meanings)	Attitudes (ideals and appreciations)	Abilities (habits and skills)	1. School

needs as "our educational goals," we are using the word "educational" in its broadest meaning, which includes the changes that all the social agencies bring about in the young as they come under their influence. Education in the narrower meaning is the specific function of the school, the agency of formal education. The vertical arrows in the diagram indicate the contribution the school should make to the other six agencies in terms of knowledge, attitudes, and abilities, that will help them achieve their goals.

These seven life careers that are common to all in a democratic society and the social agencies that are primarily concerned with each having been determined, the pragmatic approach would be to introduce into the curriculum courses planned to impart to students the knowledge which makes secure successful living in the other six careers. Our contention is that such planning of the curriculum is anything but intelligent. It is the typical American pragmatic approach of short cuts and "get wise quickly" solutions. Thus, for example, since the decision young people make in preparing to establish their own homes is (for Catholics at least) perhaps the most important decision they will ever make in their lives, why not introduce into the curriculum a course on choosing a mate? Reports in the press from time to time indicate that some colleges, in their worship of the "practical," are doing this. Nothing could be more unintelligent. Life is too fortuitous for anything like that. There are no such simple solutions to the intricate problems of human relations in a society that has grown as complicated as ours today. The problem of marriage and the family is undoubtedly one of the most important topics for study by college students approaching adulthood, and it should be studied from two points of view: as the social institution that is the foundation of all society (the family) on the one hand, and as a sacrament of the Church on the other.

We believe that the best way to make these two points of view meaningful to students is to present them together in the same course, carefully keeping before the students the distinction between the sociologist's scientific approach and the theologian's religious approach. Such a course is a good illustration of what we mean by integration—distinction without separation—with the desired result, a deepened understanding. When such a course is offered, it should be described in the college catalogue in both departments, sociology and theology, and it may well form a part of the field of concentration in either department and likewise be open to all students in the upper biennium, if not required of them. There would also be a distinct advantage if the course were taught by one illustrating precept by practice through living a truly Catholic family life, instead of by one vowed to celibacy, since the students would then feel that the teacher was speaking from actual experience. But in any event the teacher should be one thoroughly grounded in both sociology and theology.

Since we are writing for the Catholic college, we must consider briefly another of these educational goals or human needs, divine security. On the sociologist's level we are here considering religion as a purely natural phenomena in the evolution of human culture. Certainly religion is one of the dominant factors in human history, and no presentation of the humanistic sciences can be adequate without careful consideration of the part religion has played and will always play in the life of man. Any college that is endeavoring to instill in the members of the rising generation a belief in God and a recognition of their obligation to live a life that leads to God as the Author of their being, cannot ignore this part of the cultural inheritance. This would be just as true for a Mohammedan college if there were such an institution in this country. The tax supported institutions, State universities and State and municipal teacher colleges, have a special obligation here. Iowa State University, with its provision for representatives of the three dominant religious groups in this country, Jewish, Protestant, and Catholic, as fully recognized members of the faculty presenting courses in their respective religions, has taken the leadership here; but not many colleges are following its example. Security here may not mean much more than the testimony of a good conscience, the feeling on the part of the individual that everything is right between him and his Creator; but such a mental attitude is impossible without an honest effort to lead a good life, which effort will bear fruit in terms of the moral virtues.

For the Catholic and for those believing in revelation, divine security, as the highest natural goal in this life, leads to the theologian's level, in which the supernatural element of God's grace comes into play. This help from on high to lead a truly Christian life influences the performance of all one's duties, not only those that are religious (faith, works, and worship), but also duties within the other six areas of social living. Such a life leads to the first goal in the theologian's level, Christian perfection. Even the saints never achieve this goal perfectly; but it is the one all of us should be striving for, and our success in this endeavor, even though limited, is the only guaranteed way of achieving the second ultimate goal, life with God hereafter.

It should be noticed that the top level of the educational hierarchy is labeled "Philosopher's Level." Here we are using the word "philosophy" in its broadest meaning, including the sciences which for a supernaturalist are the foundations of the science of education now coming into being: psychology, sociology, and theology. The philosophy of education welcomes and embraces all knowledge from all fields that bear on education; and revelation, that is, supernatural theology as one of these, makes an important contribution in both ends and means. In this use of the word, therefore, philosophy is not propaedeutic to theology; rather, it embraces it as it does the other two sciences which make contributions to education as a science: psychology in the learning and teaching process, sociology in the living process.

The integration of all three levels into one synthetic whole is the work of the philosopher of education.

2. What College is Not

The following conclusion to our discussion of this problem may impress some readers as a compromise in determining the goals of education in general and the specific goal of the school as school, so we emphasize that we do not view it in this light at all. Rather we insist that the school has a positive obligation to help other social agencies achieve their specific functions. The residential college particularly must keep in mind that in addition to being the formal agency for the education of older adolescents, it is at the same time home, church, and community, in which its students are living—except during vacation periods—what are perhaps in their own formation the most important years of their lives. The principle is easy to state: first things first. We positively place first the part the Catholic college, as the agency for formal education, should play in preparing youth for life in a free society, and then consider its obligations in relation to the other social agencies, with emphasis on the negative aspect.

1. As an intellectual agency the specific, essential function of the Catholic college is to bring about the intellectual, emotional, and volitional development of its students as contributing citizens in a free society and apostolic members of the Church. In addition to this, however, the college as a community has supplementary functions to perform, through which it aids other community agencies achieve their specific functions. Here the important things to be kept in mind is that the college is

2. *not a clinic or a hospital,* though it will safeguard the health of its students and promote vigorous living on the campus as the best guarantee of health in later life;

3. *not an orphan asylum or a home,* but it will manifest

paternal solicitude for the well-being of its students and exercise a fatherly care in all spheres of life;

4. *not a farm or factory, nor a store or office,* but it will give a fundamentally broad training that will prepare its students to become efficient producers of goods or services;

5. *not a park or country club,* but it will have a well-planned program of social activities and physical education (including both intramural and intercollegiate athletics) giving its students in their leisure hours relief from their work, which is study;

6. *not a police station or a penitentiary,* but it will have a student council which will share the obligation of making, keeping, and enforcing rules and regulations necessary for the welfare of a student community; and finally it is

7. *not a monastery or a church,* but it will have a vital religious program which, in addition to the development of the intellectual virtues through the curriculum, will develop the moral virtues through a life of Christian self-denial on the campus, and the theological virtues through private devotion and public worship with active participation in the liturgy of the Church.

In the following chapter we now give special attention to this last goal, the achievement of which makes a college truly Catholic.

CHAPTER 2

EDUCATING THE WHOLE MAN IN A
WHOLE WORLD

CATHOLIC education, like the Catholic faith, requires the whole man. The distinguished non-Catholic theologian, Mr. Karl Barth, who should know that no part of a man's life lies outside his relation to God, has recently criticized Catholic theology for its claim to the whole man. Barth sees the Catholic way of life as totalitarian. Actually it was Christ Himself who set the pattern for our faith when He said, "Thou shalt love the Lord thy God with thy whole heart and with thy whole soul and with thy whole mind." [1] The Catholic way of life is comprehensive and integrated; it is not totalitarian. The man made whole in baptism has no right to be a half-hearted or part-time Catholic. Yet, far from denying the freedom of the individual, the Catholic Church fashions and develops that freedom. Freedom is the right to do what is right.

In another sense Catholic education, in the widest meaning of the term, makes man whole. The Catholic ontologically constituted a whole Catholic at baptism, becomes, so to speak, wholly whole through the process of Catholic education. There is a perfect analogy in the natural order. The newborn baby is already a person; he is essentially a man. The process of education in no way changes his essence, but it does make

[1] Matt. 22:37.

him more perfectly and fully a man. If education is the process by which man's potentialities are actualized, then education which is specifically Catholic attempts to do this in a specifically Catholic way, that is, according to the whole man, body and soul. Catholic education strives to make man integral and unified; it strives, too, to unify and integrate the world in which man lives.

I. THE WHOLE WORLD: NATURAL AND SUPERNATURAL

The philosophy of education applies the principles of philosophy to the field of education. Its first duty is to define terms. What is Catholic education? Traditionally Catholic education has been defined by means of the four Aristotelian ultimate causes: efficient, material, formal, and final. A definition of this kind would, no doubt, be most precise. It would also be unwieldy and heavily academic, and for that reason modern authors tend to epitomize and describe rather than to define by genus and specific difference. Pope Pius XI has written:

Since education consists essentially in preparing man for what he must be and for what he must do here below, in order to attain that sublime end for which he was created, it is clear there can be no true education which is not wholly directed to man's last end, and . . . there can be no ideally perfect education which is not Christian education.[2]

Catholic education may be defined in terms of the progressive realization of the three basic potentialities in man.

It is the process of growth and development whereby the natural man baptized in Christ, under the guidance of the teaching Church (1) assimilates a body of knowledge derived from human effort and divine revelation, (2) makes his life ideal the person of Jesus Christ, and (3) develops the ability with the

[2] Encyclical, *The Christian Education of Youth.*

aid of divine grace to use that knowledge in pursuit of this ideal.[3]

Maritain defines education as "any process whatsoever by which man is shaped and led toward fulfillment." [4] For Maritain and for all Catholic educators the idea of complete fulfillment is sought in vain outside the Catholic Church. Similarly Father McGucken quotes Father Timothy Corcoran's definition of education which, though not specifically Catholic, is a definition acceptable to all scholastic humanists: "Education is the organized development and equipment of all the powers of a human being, moral, intellectual, and physical, by and for their individual and social uses, directed towards the union of these activities with their Creator as their final end." [5]

Although these four definitions of Catholic education differ slightly in emphasis, the important point is their complete consensus on the goals of Catholic education. To put it philosophically: Catholic education is primarily interested in the ends of education; it is only secondarily interested in the means of education. Doctor Brubacher has clearly seen this fact. In making the distinction between philosophies of education which are predicated primarily on the nature of reality and those which are predicated primarily on the nature of knowing, he rightly places Catholic education in the first category.[6] The distinction is basic and most important. The Catholic philosophy of education is much more concerned

[3] William F. Cunningham, *The Pivotal Problems of Education* (New York: Macmillan Co., 1940), p. 567.

[4] Jacques Maritain, *Education at the Crossroads* (New Haven: Yale University Press, 1943), p. 2.

[5] William J. McGucken, "The Philosophy of Catholic Education" in *Philosophies of Education* (Forty-first Yearbook of the National Society for the Study of Education, Chicago University Press, 1942), p. 255; quoted by permission of the Society.

[6] John S. Brubacher, "Comparative Philosophy of Education," in *ibid.*, p. 301.

with what we know and what we do, than it is with how we attain our knowledge.

The nature of truth and of reality are at stake in this distinction. For the Catholic philosopher of education reality is an objective order completely independent of its being known. For the subjectivist philosopher reality is only what one's knowing of it makes it to be. Catholic philosophers define truth as the conformity of the mind with reality; the subjectivists reverse the process, defining truth as the conformity of reality with the mind.

Though Catholic education is primarily oriented to the nature of reality and only secondarily to the nature of knowing, the good philosopher of Catholic education carefully checks the sources of his knowledge about reality. These sources are ultimately two: reason and revelation. The philosopher of Catholic education will study and verify, in so far as that is possible, the psychological processes by which the mind apprehends reality. But he is much more interested in the metaphysical and historical proofs about the validity and reliability of reason and the fact of revelation. The demonstrations of scholastic epistomology concerning reason itself and of Catholic theology concerning revelation are presupposed in this presentation.

It suffices here to mention that reason is a trustworthy interpreter of reality. Viewed in itself, the human intellect is an unerring guide informing us about the physical universe, about ourselves, and, to some extent, about God. God has also chosen to assist human reason and to illuminate it and give it its highest possible perfection by His revelation. St. Augustine's famous *Credo ut intelligam,* "I believe that I may understand," indicates the proper relation between faith and reason. Reason attains a new and higher certitude through faith, and faith is more meaningful and more profound when it is well-rooted in reason. God has revealed much to us. Included in that revelation are many truths of the natural order, many truths the essence and the existence of which are known to us only by revelation, and many truths the existence of which we now know but whose essence, hidden in God, will be known to us only in the beatific vision. All that we know about either the natural or the supernatural order we have come to know through reason and revelation.

Before we can truly understand man, the central figure and the subject of all educational philosophies, we must know how he fits into the whole cosmos of reality. To ask where man belongs in the scheme of creation is really to ask what is the nature of man. As Father McGuken has so well said, "every theory of education hinges on the precise nature of the educand." [7] A contemporary author, Jean Mouroux, in a single paragraph which is both philosophically exact and almost poetically inspired, has properly located man in the universe:

Man is a creature destined to live in two worlds. He is surrounded first by the realities of this world, he lives among things and plants and animals and in the society of other persons like himself, and is active among them in thought and work and love. On the other hand, he is called to live with divine realities. Christ is present in the world and in the depths of his soul to introduce him to the society of the Divine Persons and to achieve his consummation in God. Thus he has simultaneously to breathe an eternal and a temporal air. [8]

The first postulate of Catholic educational philosophy is simply this: Man is a creature living with a purpose in a created world. Composed of both body and soul, man is the bridge, the transition between pure spirit and simple matter in the hierarchy of being. Holy Scripture speaks of man as having been created only a little lower than the angels. In man

[7] *Op. cit.*, p. 262.
[8] Jean Mouroux, *The Meaning of Man* (Copyrighted Sheed and Ward, Inc., New York, 1948), p. 1.

a substantial body and a substantial soul unite to form the human person. Both his dignity and his destiny arise from the union of these two elements. For his soul, created in the image and likeness of God, can work out its salvation only in union with the body which, having shared the time of trial on earth, will also share the eternity of reward in heaven.

In addition to our knowledge of man's nature and purpose we must also know something of man's condition before we can come to grips with the Catholic philosophy of education. We must also understand the import of these words of Pope Pius XI: "Every method of education founded, wholly or in part, on the denial or forgetfulness of original sin and grace, and relying on the sole powers of human nature, is unsound." [9]

Catholic theology teaches that man's present condition is the result of two world-shaking historical realities: original sin and redemption. The account of man's fall from original justice is contained in the third chapter of Genesis. The story of man's redemption by the Son of God and his elevation to the supernatural life is told in the New Testament. Foreshadowed throughout the Old Testament, the Redeemer appears in the fullness of time. His personality and His mission are revealed to us particularly in the four Gospels.

When the Holy Father warns educators against the denial or forgetfulness of original sin, he has special reference to the twofold result of original sin which has made the use of the word "wounded" traditional in explaining man's present condition. Through original sin man's intellect was darkened and his will was weakened. The relation of education to man's wounded nature is immediately evident. If original sin had not befallen the human race, there would be no need for education as we know it. Even those educators who deny the doctrine of original sin realize that their educational prob-

[9] *Op. cit.*

lems all point to some underlying human obstruction or disinclination which renders the pursuit of truth arduous. Education requires effort of both intellect and will.

When the Holy Father warns against the denial of grace, he has direct reference to the fact that, by reason of Christ's redeeming love of mankind and by reason of the sacrament of baptism, man has the opportunity to live, as an adopted child of God, the life of charity in union with God. This life of grace establishes a special relationship between God and the justified person enabling him effectively to overcome the wayward inclinations of his will and the dullness of his intellect. In redeeming and elevating man, God has given him a richer life than he ever had before. The life of grace is the beginning of the life of glory.

II. THE WHOLE MAN: HIS FOURFOLD DEVELOPMENT

Early in life a man becomes aware of the reality of his own person and of the world in which he is a part. His limitations as well as his powers and possibilities soon make themselves felt. The scholastic adage that all that is is the adequate object of the human intellect, is repeatedly verified in man's attempt to synthesize and unify the realities with which he comes in contact. Perhaps one of man's earliest philosophical insights is the fact that he meets reality on four different levels. (1) He knows that his body is a physical, tangible object; (2) he knows that the realm of ideas is different from the things he can see and touch; (3) he knows that his relations with other people are different from his relations with animals and inanimate objects; and (4) he knows that his thoughts of God, of immortality, of right and wrong, of prayer, are realities. Man's education, then, since he is an organism composed of body and spirit, is a concomitant development on the physical, the intellectual, the social, and the religious levels. These same four levels do, in fact, comprise all that is.

The task of education is to enable man to make the best possible use of all that is, in order that he may achieve his ultimate goal, union with God, the one Being whose essence is to be. Though the process is a simultaneous one, and though because of the intrinsic unity of human nature there is much overlapping of the levels, the process of education can be clearly seen taking place on each of these four levels, as we shall attempt to show.

The process of education, viewed as a growth or as the gradual actualizing of potentialities, permits of the threefold division indicated in the author's definition of education.[10] Education is a development from ignorance to knowledge, from capacities to abilities, and from impulses to ideals. Catholic education is most interested in the kind of knowledge, abilities, and ideals toward which the process of education is directed. It is interested in the process of education only to the extent that one process is better or worse than another for achieving the desired result. Obviously if the process is entirely wrong, as it would be were original sin and grace left out of the educational picture, then the result could never be entirely right. As long as it is a moral and a psychologically sound method, any method is a Catholic method.

The work of the Catholic philosopher of education is laid out for him. He must point out the formal object of the three outcomes of learning on each of the four levels of man's development. At many points the Catholic philosophy of education is no different than any other common-sense philosophy of education except that it adds its own supernatural motivation and direction. Bishop Spaulding, perhaps the greatest of the American Catholic educators, has masterfully summarized the objectives of Catholic education in this statement:

[10] See above, p. 37.

The greatest service we can do a human being is

to give him a right education	that no child of God may live with
(1) physical	(1) an enfeebled body, or
(2) intellectual	(2) a darkened mind, or
(3) moral (social)	(3) a callous heart, or
(4) and religious . . .	(4) a perverted conscience.[11]

1. Physical Development

On the physical level the well-educated Catholic is expected to know as much as possible about the material world in which he lives. Apart from the dignity which the facts of the physical sciences have in their own right, they are important as the foundations of philosophy. And the facts of the material world, including the human body and all creation inferior to man, manifest in all their designs the wisdom of God and contribute to His greater external glory. The world is an instrument at the service of man. Knowledge of the material world, though necessary, is always subordinated knowledge because of its proximity to sensible and physical reality.

In the realm of physical abilities and skills it is difficult to state the Catholic objective precisely. The ability to use the neuromuscular system with the utmost coordination is important. Certainly, too, every man is called to be an artist, a maker of things, in some degree. Perhaps the most applicable general principle is that all capacity, including even that of the most unintellectual manual skill, is a gift of God and should be developed fully for that reason. On this level, as well as on any other, to bury a talent reflects a faulty education. The objective of Catholic education on this level is to make every workman a craftsman and to combine right rea-

[11] John Lancaster Spaulding, *Religion, Agnosticism and Education* (Chicago: McClurg, 1902), pp. 151 f.

son with manual dexterity in either the fine arts or the useful arts.

The ideal toward which Catholic education moves on the physical level is the formation of a man of sound body who knows and masters the world in which he lives, who adapts and applies physical things for the purpose of better living; who works to advance material standards of living in order to achieve higher spiritual standards of living; who, seeing the entire temporal and material order as a means to an end, uses and enjoys the beauties and the richness of the physical world without becoming dependent on it or attached to it.

2. Mental Development

On the next level, that of reason and intelligence, Catholic educational philosophy seeks to perfect the intellectual virtues, especially that most priceless of all learned virtues, wisdom. In writing of the intellectual virtues of the speculative order (understanding, science, and wisdom), St. Thomas says that understanding considers principles in themselves, science demonstrates conclusions from principles, and wisdom obtains the highest place since it uses both understanding and science. "For it contains beneath itself both understanding and science, as judging both the conclusions of science and the principles on which they are based." [12]

The intellectual abilities at which Catholic education formally aims are: the ability to reason clearly and cogently; the ability to analyze, to discriminate, to abstract, and to evaluate. The virtue of prudence, defined as right reason about things to be done, applies alike to the operations of the speculative and of the practical intellect. It is a vitally important intellectual ability and, regardless of the disputed question whether prudence can be taught by direct instruction, it is one of the aims of Catholic education. To quote St. Thomas again:

[12] *Summa theol.*, Ia IIae, q.57, a.2 ad 2.

To that which is suitably ordained to the due end, man needs to be rightly disposed by a habit in his reason, because counsel and choice, which are about means ordained to the end, are acts of the reason. Consequently an intellectual virtue is needed in the reason to perfect the reason and make it suitably affected towards means ordained to the end; and this virtue is prudence.[13]

And in another place St. Thomas says that prudence is "good counsel about matters regarding man's entire life, and the last end of human life." [14] Prudence enters into every phase of life. It contains within its concept the ability to see an existing problem, to evaluate it, and to apply right principles in solving it as accurately and as objectively as possible.

The intellectual ideal of Catholic education is the humility, freedom, and unity which results in man from what Maritain calls "the freeing of the child's and the youth's intuitive power." [15] As Maritain says, "What matters most in the life of reason is intellectual insight or intuition." [16] This intuition is the most sublime form of wisdom and reaches its culmination on the third level of abstraction in which simple being, that is, being stripped of all sensible qualities, even quantity, is grasped by the intellect. In the words of Maritain:

Education and teaching should never lose sight of the organic unity of the task to be performed, and of the essential need and aspiration of the mind to be freed in unity. If a man does not overcome the inner multiplicity of his drives and especially of the diverse currents of knowledge and belief and the diverse vital energies at play in his mind, he will always remain more a slave than a free man.[17]

13 *Ibid.*, a.4 ad 3.
14 *Ibid.*, a.5.
15 *Op. cit.*, p. 43.
16 *Ibid.*, p. 43.
17 *Ibid.*, p. 47.

Mouroux, speaking of human freedom as such rather than of the freeing of the intellect, helps to clarify the intellectual ideal of Catholic education:

The root of liberty is the reason. Man is free because he is intelligent, capable therefore of judging between good and evil, of apprehending ends and means as such, and so of deciding his own destiny. A certain effort after mental lucidity is therefore the root of liberty; and all ignorance or error about the conduct of human life will be an obstacle in its way and a danger.[18]

3. Social Development

Passing now to the social level, the focus of Catholic education turns outward rather than inward; it turns from man himself to man's relation with his fellow men. The formal object of man's intellectual education on the social level is the notion of natural law, of justice, and of rights and duties. The various units of society would all function harmoniously if the rights and duties of each were clearly defined and respected. To achieve this end requires more than knowledge, but it does require knowledge: knowledge of the origin and purpose of society, knowledge of the relation between the person and the common good, knowledge of jurisprudence, knowledge of psychology, knowledge of the various contemporary social sciences which purport to analyze man's economic and political life.

In what abilities on the social level is Catholic education principally interested? The ability to cooperate and communicate; the ability to carry on political, recreational, business, and cultural associations with a minimum of friction; the ability to choose wisely one's state in life and, once adopted, to measure up to its responsibilities; the ability to appreciate and work for the realization of the social values of a democracy; the ability to make some worthwhile con-

[18] *The Meaning of Man* (Copyrighted Sheed and Ward, Inc., New York, 1948), p. 152.

tribution toward the improvement of contemporary living standards: these are some of the goals of Catholic education on this level. And they might all be summarized in the ability to make sacrifices in adapting oneself to the greater good of society.

The ideal toward which Catholic education strives on the social level is the formation of the man of character. Rudolph Allers has defined character as "the complete realization of all the positive potentialities [values] inherent in the person." [19] Character is both the result of action and the principle from which action flows. The goal of Catholic education is to direct and deepen the social tendency inherent in every person and to ensure this tendency its proper expression in the major social relationships: the family, the state, and the Church. Maritain thus outlines the premises for any truly humanistic character formation:

What will assume full importance for the man of tomorrow are the vital connections of man with society, that is, not only the social environment but also common work and common good. . . . Education must remove the rift between the social claim and the individual claim within the man himself. It must develop both the sense of freedom and the sense of responsibility, human rights and human obligations, the courage to take risks and exert authority for the general welfare and the respect for the humanity of each individual person. [20]

In a word, life in conformity with all the moral virtues is the ideal of Catholic education on the social level.

4. Religious Development

It is on the specifically religious level that Catholic education functions most fully in the growth of knowledge, ideals,

[19] Rudolph Allers, *Psychology of Character* (New York: Sheed and Ward, 1943), p. 207.
[20] Jacques Maritain, *op. cit.*, p. 89.

and abilities. The knowledge par excellence in which all other knowledge, including metaphysics, culminates is the knowledge of the height and the breadth and the depth of the love which is in Christ Jesus our Lord. This knowledge integrates all knowledge; real consent to it suffices for salvation. The well-educated Catholic will proceed to an ever greater love of Christ through his knowledge of the commandments, the sacraments, and the history and the liturgy of the Church. The complete Catholic life is knowledge for the sake of love.

There is a vast difference between knowing the faith and living it. The ability to make Catholicism a way of life is not wholly dependent either on man's effort or his education. God's grace is an integral part of the pattern. The ability to be vitally and dynamically a Catholic is an ability, however, that every man can master in his own degree with the help of grace. The man who tries has already succeeded, for in the effort is the intention to please God.

On the religious level the ideal of Catholic education is sainthood. But obviously no saint is a saint on the religious level alone. Every phase of life contributes to the making of the saint, and every phase is elevated by the saint's contact with it. Sainthood is the perfection of life; it is the supreme goal of Catholic education. Reduced to its essentials, sainthood is conformity to the will of God in loving God and our neighbor.

But saints are saints in proportion as they are Christlike. Christ is the model, the ideal exemplar of Catholic education. Most Catholic educators, following the lead of Pope Pius XI, see the fourfold development of the Christ child—physical, intellectual, social, and religious—summarized in the text of St. Luke: "And Jesus advanced in wisdom and age and grace with God and with men." [21] Pius XI wrote:

[21] Luke 2:52.

By His example He is at the same time the universal model accessible to all; especially to the young in the period of His hidden life, a life of labor and obedience, adorned with all virtues, personal, domestic, and social, before God and men. . . . The proper and immediate end of Christian education is to cooperate with divine grace in forming the true and perfect Christian, that is, to form Christ himself in those regenerated by Baptism.

III. The School's Part: The Training of Minds

The word "education" has been used in this chapter in its widest possible meaning. When we define it as the bringing about of changes in the individual, it is evident that the term embraces activity in every phase of life in which learning takes place. It includes every sense experience, every operation of the mind, every conversation, every mistake and every success, every law of the land, of nature, and of God, every association at work and at play, every experience at home, in church, and in the community. It begins at birth and it does not cease until the life of reason is supplanted by the life of beatific vision.

It is this meaning of the word "education" which Pope Pius XI had in mind when he wrote in his masterful encyclical on The Christian Education of Youth: "It must never be forgotten that the subject of Christian education is man whole and entire, soul united to body in unity of nature, with all his faculties natural and supernatural, such as right reason and revelation show him to be." Nevertheless this particular statement in the encyclical has led to some confusion of thought among Catholic educators. Coming as it did at a time when the concept of the function of the school was in transition, many read into this statement an endorsement of the position that the task of educating "man whole and entire" devolves solely upon the school. In reality, however, such an interpretation runs counter to the spirit and to the very text of the encyclical, throughout which the Holy Father makes it clear that the school is not the only educative agency and that total educational responsibility does not rest on the school alone. Education is also the function, as well as the right and duty, of the family, the Church, the community (that is, the State), and other great social agencies. Each agency has a contribution to make to the integral education of the individual person.

Each of the great social agencies has a specific essential function to perform, and the essential function of the school is formal education. Each agency is brought into being by society (or in the case of the Church, by God) to carry out its own specific function, but in addition the school is commonly employed as an instrument (to use Newman's word) by other agencies to help them achieve their specific functions.[22] In performing these instrumental functions, however, it should preserve the safeguard never to allow itself (except in time of great emergency, like the recent war) to become so engrossed in the performance of these supplementary functions that it fails to carry out satisfactorily its own proper function. The specific function of the school as the agency of formal education, is the intellectual formation and development of the young. Its job is the making of minds. The school is not merely a socially contrived stopgap in which youngsters, while awaiting adulthood, spend a certain number of happy and harmless years playing at the "reconstruction of experience." The concern of the school is the growth and development of ideas and the training of the mind. The development of the intellectual virtues gives the school its first purpose, its direction, and its stability.[23]

If the school does well its proper duty of developing the

[22] "A University, taken in its bare idea, and before we view it as an instrument of the Church, has this object" (John Henry Newman, *Idea of a University*, Discourse VI [Chicago: Loyola University Press], p. 145).

[23] Training in the virtues, intellectual, moral, and theological, is discussed in chapter 10, "The Student Community."

mind of the pupil, it will have done much. It will have abundantly repaid society for its expense and the pupil for his effort. But if administrators and teachers so divert their attention to nonintellectual concerns (the social and recreational activities of the school's program) that they neglect the intellectual formation of the pupil, both the individual and society will suffer. Further, what right, indeed, what excuse does the school have for taking on activities and functions which properly belong to the family, to the Church, and to the other social agencies to the extent that it becomes neglectful of its own purpose? If the school fails to perform its own function properly, not only does it fail here, but at the same time it interferes with other agencies that can perform their own proper functions much more efficiently than can the school.

It is true that the human intellect cannot be isolated and developed independently of the human person. Man is a psychosomatic unity, and pupils do not became pure intellects when they step into the classroom. An emotionally upset child, especially a fearful or a rejected child, will have great difficulty in studying and learning. Neither is the child who is hungry or sick or debilitated in the right frame of mind for intellectual work. Nor is the moral delinquent apt to be a good student, no matter what the origin and nature of the delinquency may be. Often the personal problems of the pupil must be taken care of before the proper work of the school can effectively go on. Nonetheless, the school has its proper work, and it must perform that work. Educators who contend that we must teach students and not subjects would be much more correct if they recalled that the verb "to teach" takes two objects. We teach pupils something, and determining this "something" is one of the prime obligations of the school, which cannot be passed on to immature pupils. If the school's responsibility is primarily the training of the mind, does it have no responsibility for the development of virtue and character? Maritain answers this question in the way that most Catholic philosophers of education would answer it:

The main duty in the educational spheres of the school as well as of the state is not to shape the will and directly to develop moral virtues in the youth, but to enlighten and strengthen reason; so it is that an indirect influence is exerted on the will, by a sound equipment of knowledge and a sound development of the powers of thinking.[24]

To say that the school's primary goal is the training of the intellect is not to say that this is its exclusive objective. But the school must never become so engaged in health or social education and character formation that it turns out superficially enlightened intellects.

The relation between the formation of the mind and the formation of the whole man in the Catholic school becomes a special problem for the philosopher of education. The school has its own intellectual function; it is also an instrument of the Church and as such is much concerned with spiritual and moral development. Father Ward thus resolves the difficulty for the Catholic college and university: "Intellect and its values for the personal and social body are the goal of the University. The good of disciplined intellects is the end, and in the Catholic university the good of intellects disciplined as Catholic." [25] And when he speaks of the "intellect disciplined as Catholic," Father Ward insists that Catholic theology, "the highest theoretic Christian wisdom, in all its profound perspectives," makes a school a Catholic school. Catholic theology as a science, not as religious practice, must hold the primacy among all subjects because it is theology that forms the integrating and unifying principle. As

24 Jacques Maritain, *op. cit.*, p. 27.
25 Leo R. Ward, *Blueprint for a Catholic University* (St. Louis: Herder Book Co., 1949), p. 176.

Father Ward says: "In other words, the Christian mind, the Christian scholar, Christian learning, and the Christian school should get their being through their relationship to a science based on the Gospel." [26]

[26] *Ibid.*, pp. 97–99.

CHAPTER 3

LIBERAL EDUCATION IN THE COLLEGE

HISTORIANS of education in the United States are repeatedly pointing out that the first schools in this country were transplanted from Europe and were ill-adapted to meet the needs of the pioneer culture taking form and through the years developing as the settlers pushed westward. This condition was true, of course, not only of the schools but also of two other social institutions intimately affecting youth, namely the home and the church. The pilgrim fathers were fleeing from a government they could not tolerate, and much effort was needed to create a form of government that would make a free society possible. When the eight-grade elementary school was first established a little over a hundred years ago, it was an importation from Germany, and the same can be said of the American university as it first came into being. Research and professional training were its chief aims. But the earliest secondary school, which was the Latin Grammar school, and the college came to us from England, one preparatory to the other. In this present study the college is our particular concern.

In the chartering of Harvard College in 1636 the influence of the University of Cambridge was dominant. This English influence continued throughout the history of the colonial colleges. The old English universities of Cambridge and Oxford with their college or hall accommodations for both students and tutors stood in sharp contrast to the universities on the continent. English colleges furnished more than merely living quarters and chapel; each one was complete in itself with teaching staff and students. This arrangement was "domestic instruction" since each college had lecture-rooms and library to facilitate teaching and study.

These colleges, in their administration, were largely autonomous under a master or provost, all under the Chancellor of the University. The undergraduate students were hardly more than boys, and many of the tutors were young bachelors going on for their master's degree in Arts or doing work in the "superior faculties" (medicine, ministry, or law). The undergraduate part of this "domestic instruction" was described by Cardinal Newman a hundred years ago in his classic, *The Idea of a University*. This English college education stands in sharp contrast to that of our typical State universities. These latter seem to regard themselves as service institutions and will introduce the teaching of any subject demanded by the people of the State which brought the institution into being. These subjects may include anything from atomic research to zinc welding.

All the colonial colleges and many of those that were founded later and that developed into universities, were established in the English tradition that the completion of liberal education is the best preparation for any life career or for advanced study in the various fields of knowledge. Harvard has from the very first demanded that students complete the work for the bachelor degree before they enter any of the specialized schools. Only a war emergency succeeded in turning Harvard away from its traditional policy; with the war over, it made operative again this requirement. Newman's concluding paragraph of Discourse VII, "Knowledge Viewed in Relation to Professional Skill," is an eloquent account of what liberal education can do to produce the ideal man of the world. Since Newman is speaking of education within the colleges of the English universities, his use of the word "university" in this connection often leads to confusion in the American mind, because we distinguish sharply between college and university training. Hence in presenting the following selected sentences from that famous passage, I have dropped Newman's word "university" and substituted for it in brackets the word "college."

I have confined myself to saying that that training of the intellect, which is best for the individual himself, best enables him to discharge his duties to society. . . . If then a practical end must be assigned to a [college] course, I say it is that of training good members of society. Its art is the art of social life, and its end is fitness for the world. . . . [College] training is the great ordinary means to a great but ordinary end; it aims at raising the intellectual tone of society, at cultivating the public mind, at purifying the national taste, at supplying true principles to popular enthusiasm and fixed aims to popular aspiration, at giving enlargement and sobriety to the ideas of the age, at facilitating the exercise of political power, and refining the intercourse of private life. . . . It prepares him to fill any post with credit, and to master any subject with facility. It shows him how to accommodate himself to others, how to throw himself into their state of mind, how to bring before them his own, how to influence them, how to come to an understanding with them, how to bear with them. He is at home in any society, he has common ground with every class; he knows when to speak and when to be silent; he is able to converse, he is able to listen; he can ask a question pertinently, and gain a lesson seasonably, when he has nothing to impart himself; he is ever ready, yet never in the way; he is a pleasant companion, and a comrade you can depend upon. . . . He has the repose of a mind which lives in itself, while it lives in the world, and which has resources for its happiness at home when it cannot go abroad. He has a gift which serves him in public, and supports him in retirement, without which good fortune is but vulgar, and with which failure and disappointment have a charm. The art which tends to make a man all this, is in the object which it pursues as useful as the art of wealth or the art of health, though it is less susceptible of method, and less tangible, less certain, less complete in its result.[1]

I. THE OUTCOMES OF LIBERAL EDUCATION

This moving passage leads the reader to hesitate before making any selection of the qualities that liberal education should produce in turning out the ideal man of the world. Yet it is fitting at this time, in our survey of the American scene, that we pick out certain qualities that are called for in a special way in our American setting and in the world at large, and fix our attention on certain purposes as the special concern of the liberal college at this juncture in the world's history.

1. Leadership

The primary function of the liberal college from its very origin has been recognized as training for leadership. Now that mass education has been extended to the high school and to the first two years of college by the Report of the President's Commission, *Higher Education for American Democracy*, with its advocacy of the community college, training for leadership in this country is held by some to be the function of all schools. Thus we have the following statement in the very first sentence of a textbook for courses preparing teachers: "The primary and proper business of organized education in American democracy can be summed up in a single word: Leadership." [2] This statement reminds one of the *Führer* principle of pre-war Germany's National Socialism, in which the leader was paramount, and the obligation of the German people (as well as of the subject

[1] John Henry Newman, *op. cit.*, pp. 196 f.
[2] James L. Mursell, *Education for American Democracy* (New York: W. F. Norton & Co., 1943), p. 9.

peoples, the "inferior races") was to follow the *Führer* by doing what they were told to do. Criticism of the leader or his henchmen led to a concentration camp or worse, liquidation through a purge, and this penalty was meted out to the members of the Party, as well as to the people at large, if either were rash enough to express ideas at variance with the *Führer's* mandates.

What we mean by leadership in this country is well brought out by the distinction between training for jobs and for careers. Of the more than sixty million employed persons in this country today, the vast majority, of course, are engaged in jobs calling for various types of manual and mental skill; but above these are the higher executives whose vision and power for planning and carrying into execution the designs of that planning, have lifted the living standard of this country far above anything known in the world before. This organization of higher and lower executives, with foremen and workers following their directions, is what we call the new profession of "management," and it is the secret of our success in practically all fields. But this success would never have come about without another characteristic of American life.

2. Followership

American schools, liberal colleges as well as elementary schools and high schools, have something else to do besides developing leaders. In our notion of democracy intelligent followership is as important as dynamic leadership, for the simple reason that the prime responsibility of democratic followership is, by intelligent use of the ballot, the election of able and dynamic leaders resolved to employ their energies for the general welfare. These leaders must be intelligent enough to plan wisely and determined enough to actualize their plans for the advancement of the community which they are serving and of the country as a whole. This is a cooperative endeavor in which leaders and led are striving for mutual benefit, "each one learning from the other and in turn teaching him." [3]

3. Fellowship

But if the development of leadership and followership so interpreted is essential in the idea of the American school, it is not enough. Another quality is needed, which must characterize both leaders and followers in any cooperative community, and that quality is fellowship. Without this quality of fellowship, cooperation of one group with another and of individuals with their neighbors is impossible, and no community can be truly democratic. Direct instruction can do little for the development of this quality which makes a cooperative society possible, though the disciplines of theology and philosophy as well as of the humanistic sciences (such as history, psychology, and sociology) should make some contribution here. The school as a community under the guidance of inspiring teachers can exert a powerful influence in developing within child and youth those habits of thought and action and attitudes of consideration for others which characterize the good citizen. If the school fails to do this, it is no longer a democratic institution. Its failure is complete since power developed without this attitude of responsibility to the community, may result in producing *Führers* or members of a politburo who will control society for their own purposes. At best the school that operates without developing in its students this attitude of fellowship will be training clever manipulators who will prey upon their fellows wherever they are able to do so.

The liberal college, dealing as it does with a select group of later adolescents fast approaching maturity, is particularly concerned with developing the qualities that give promise of effective leadership in a free society, along with an intelligent

[3] St. Augustine, *Confessions,* I, chap. 8.

but not subservient followership, and a fellowship that binds leadership and followership together for the good of the whole. For many years, in my course in Philosophy of Education, I had been teaching that these qualities are the outcome of any education that is truly liberal; and recently I came across an article by Dean Brown of Princeton University that confirmed me in the opinion that my analysis was correct. The title of the article is "Education for Leadership." The words "followership" and "fellowship" do not occur in it, but a glance at Dean Brown's "essentials" reveals that those ideas are at least implied. He approaches the problem from the point of view of the teacher rather than from that of the student in whom these outcomes are to be realized, but the desired qualities are the same though expressed in strikingly different terms. He first makes the statement in italics that *"Liberal Education is the most effective means yet discovered to develop God-given talents of leadership."* [4] Then he presents this analysis:

> The three great essentials of an effective liberal education for leadership are:
> 1. The good teacher
> 2. The good student
> 3. A close relationship between them.
> These essentials may appear simple, but they are far from easy to attain.[5]

As we interpret Dean Brown's analysis, the good teacher furnishes the leadership, the good student the followership, and the close relationship implies what we have called "fellowship." Another way of expressing the quality which should characterize the relations between student and teacher is: companionship in the pursuit of knowledge. The college

---

[4] J. Douglas Brown, "Education for Leadership" in *Association of American Colleges Bulletin*, December, 1950, p. 564.

[5] *Ibid.*, pp. 564 f.

that provides this essential along with the other two is the ideal that all liberal colleges should be striving to become.

In Newman's description of the ideal man of the world we can hardly expect to find anything other than the English gentleman, since Newman was raised in the stratified and individualistic society of England during the first half of the last century. But, like the great Protestant educator, Bishop Comenius of the Moravian Church, Newman was deeply religious; and in the development of his educational theory, like Comenius, he could not help but include therein the fundamental concept of Christianity, that all men are equal before God and sharers in the fruits of Christ's redemption. On this basis all men should have equal opportunity to develop themselves as far as their God-given capacities will enable them. For us today this equality of opportunity is the chief characteristic of democratic education. If the question were put to Newman and Comenius, they would see this equality as the logical conclusion from the Christian idea of life, which is the only stable foundation for true democracy. Hence we are not surprised to find in Newman's description of the ideal citizen as the product of liberal education those qualities that we have identified as essentials in a free society. Thus in the passage quoted above we have liberal education "facilitating the exercise of political power." Of course, such education is not limited to that function. Liberal education, as he describes it, shows the man thus educated "how to influence" others and develops the power of leading in all the spheres of life: in the home, in business and industry, and particularly in those important civic enterprises that call for intelligence and wisdom. So too with followership: liberal education "shows him how to accommodate himself to others, how to throw himself into their state of mind, how to bring before them his own, . . . how to come to an understanding with them." And as for fellowship, the liberally educated person "is at home in any society, has common ground with every class; he knows when to speak and when to be silent; . . . is a pleasant companion, and a comrade you can depend upon." The education that does all this for anyone is surely something worth pursuing.

II. THE HUMANITIES AS MEANS TO THIS END

Dean Brown says that Princeton stands for "liberal education in depth" and not merely a smattering of general education preliminary to professional training. He says further: "At the core of liberal education in depth lie the humanities. Without that core, the social sciences would dry up; the natural sciences would become the master and not the servant of man." [6] Today what do we mean by the humanities? Fifty years ago I entered a secondary school and began my study of the classics, at that time, Latin and Greek. Soon I learned that these were the humanities; the dictionary still gives this meaning to the word when it is used in the plural. But during the past fifty years we have given a far different meaning to that word. When we turn to Good's *Dictionary of Education,* we find as his first definition of "humanities": "a term used today by many colleges in the United States to designate new comprehensive courses in literature, language, art, philosophy, religion, and history, thus distinguishing the *humanities* from social science." According to this definition the term "humanities" includes all branches of knowledge except the social and natural sciences.

We all know that during the recent decades the social sciences have not kept pace with the natural sciences in their advancement. Therefore we may rightly question whether advancement in the social sciences is not of greater importance for humanity than advancement in any other field

[6] *Ibid.,* p. 565.

of knowledge. For this reason I prefer the term "humanistic sciences" to "social sciences" since the word "humanistic" connotes all branches of knowledge concerned with a man as an individual (psychology and biography) as well as those concerned with a man as a political animal—to use Aristotle's phrase—(such as social psychology, sociology, politics, and economics). But even more, living now as we are in a scientific age with the findings of the natural sciences applied through technology not only to transportation and communication but to almost every phase of our lives, we find that these applications influence man at every turn. Everyone would draw the line at speaking of the advances of technology as humanistic. Yet acquaintance with the major findings of the natural sciences and general familiarity with the scientific method which has developed so extensively in their advancement, is an integral part of liberal education today. Hence the most appropriate name for the liberal college is the "liberal college of arts and sciences," namely, the arts and sciences that free man from ignorance of the three worlds in which he lives: the world of nature, the world of man (society), and the world of God (the spiritual world). In university colleges, at least, this is the common interpretation of the term "liberal," including therein the study of the natural sciences on the undergraduate level, leaving to the professional and technological schools the application of their findings to the particular fields with which these schools are concerned.

But even if we do not include within the humanistic sciences the natural sciences as well as all the social sciences, no intelligent person will question the validity of Dean Brown's thesis that the "humanities" (the liberal and fine arts, and the philosophical and humanistic sciences) form the core of any education that is truly liberal and must remain the chief instrument of the liberal college for training a man with an informed, cultured, and disciplined mind. The outstanding characteristic of today's world is thrown into relief when one reflects that Robert Maynard Hutchins has been one of the most ardent advocates of this thesis that the humanities are the core of liberal education, and yet he finished his career as Chancellor of Chicago University with a top scientific staff which developed a perfected technique for making the atomic bomb.

1. Training for Jobs or for Careers

When speaking of leadership we distinguished between training for jobs and for careers. The world today has become so complex in industry and business, in labor and agriculture, in the professions and public service (i.e., local, state, and federal government) that there is a demand for men with the ability to organize, who can plan the multiple phases of our corporate enterprises and, in their understanding and handling of human relations, can make people under them more productive. We can see what has been happening in some of the technological institutes today when we learn from the press that Professor Weller B. Embler, head of the Department of the Humanities at Cooper Union, New York, addressing the American Society of Mechanical Engineers, said that it would be "morally wrong" for him to advise the reading of the literary classics in this fast-moving age. The pragmatism of the professor was revealed when he said that one should read for the purpose of making practical use of what one reads; for improving the world about us rather than polishing one's mind like a jewel. He suggested that if his auditors tried reading a classic, they would grow restive and might better engage in some activity more consistent with their daily environment—going to the movies, listening to the radio, or looking at television. There is a hopeful sign, however, in the fact that one of our great metropolitan dailies reacted editorially to that news item in these words:

We feel that those counsels represent total surrender to the doctrine that great external forces, invariably troubling in nature, govern everyone in everything he does, and that the individual no longer counts for anything. It is true that something like a crisis of civilization exists, but that crisis prevails principally, if not only, because men are losing the capacity to think. . . . That is what primarily ails the world today. People are not thinking, and most of them are not even interested in developing the capacity to think. No wonder a world reflecting this general state of mind is footless and feckless.

The editorial also declared that if Karl Marx were still living, he might say that television is the opiate of the people since "it is so much easier to buy a rotating television chair and dope off in front of a TV screen than try to develop a capacity for reflection."

Another sign that the situation is not quite so dark as pictured above, is given to us in the inaugural address of Dr. Rettaliata, the new president of one of the most progressive technological institutes, Illinois Institute of Technology. As stated in the press he declared:

A gap is said to exist between our technological advances and those of the social sciences. Admittedly, emphasis should be put on intensified development of social and humanistic areas. As a nation we must become more adept at handling the social problems that confront us. The gap between our respective accomplishments in social and technological fields should be reduced, and not by diminishing our achievements along scientific lines.

If engineers as well as business men and industrialists are going to receive an education that will make them "more adept at handling the social problems that confront us," there is real promise that leaders will be developed to carry our country forward in this atomic age. But the problem remains: how can this be done?

2. Education for Occupational Careers

In discussing educational goals in the first chapter we presented one section under the title, "The Seven Life Careers." [7] Here we are concerned with only one of these, the occupational career, through which one supports himself and those dependent upon him, and makes his contribution to the community of which he is a member. The classified telephone directory of any of our great metropolitan centers gives some idea of the thousands of occupations among which the leaders in any community today are distributed. In the face of this fact, Robert D. Calkins, formerly dean of the School of Business, Columbia University, now director of the General Educations Board, urges high school and college students to "resist and fight and rebel" against what he calls "occupational predestination." [8] He presents as one of the great characteristics of the American system the fact that no one can predict the future of any individual after his school days are over if that individual has driving energy and what Nicholas Murray Butler called a "broadly educated mind sharpened to a point." This fact was brought home to me at the last alumni reunion I attended. One of the old graduates, now an executive in a large electrical company, told me his experience as a freshman engineer. Out of a possible 100, he received a grade of 16 in mathematics and 17 in an engineering course, and as a result of this poor showing was dropped by the School of Engineering. Transferred to the College of Liberal Arts, he never lost his interest in the developments going on in electricity and after graduating made it a point to locate in a firm that was well established and had good promise of a future. Today he is one of its top executives.

Service veterans brought a new tone to higher education

[7] *Supra.*, pp. 28 ff.
[8] *Association of American Colleges Bulletin*, June, 1950, p. 334.

when they were crowding our colleges. As an outcome of their war experiences some of them displayed a maturity of mind that was certainly refreshing to college instructors long worn down by the immaturity of the typical freshman student. Calkins, in the article referred to above, calls attention to the fact that "to those already in middle life there is fortunately a limitless possibility for self-education." [9] To those still in college his advice is, "Learn how to think rigorously. Learn to analyze complex problems involving many variables. . . . Learn how to express yourself, orally and in writing." [10] Then he tells college students to read history and literature, speculate on philosophy, and study art and music and religion. Finally, he concludes the article with this exhortation:

Acquire a comprehension of the physical world and the methods of science and of what is involved in seeking truth. Come to understand the meaning of evidence and how to test hypotheses. Acquire a comprehension of organization of social life and its practices not only in our times but also in earlier times. Study man's efforts to improve his lot and discover the reason and inspiration for doing what you can to create here a better life for men of your time and for those who come after you.

He closes the article with this statement: "All this is the essence of liberal education." [11]

This study is concerned primarily with determining in some detail the contribution Catholic liberal colleges should make in developing in youth entrusted to their care the qualities mentioned above, leadership, followership, and fellowship. Part I has been concerned with determining the ends of Catholic education, which include these three qualities. In Part II and Part III we will analyze the means to be used in achieving these ends.

[9] *Ibid.*, p. 333.
[10] *Ibid.*, p. 334.
[11] *Ibid.*, p. 335.

PART II

WHAT TO TEACH—THE CURRICULUM

CHAPTER 4

A PHILOSOPHICAL APPROACH TO THE CURRICULUM

THE AIM of education is the attainment, through a process of growth and development, of the greatest perfection of human personality that a man's native capacities make possible. The process is dual in nature: individual growth and development on the one hand and social transmission of our cultural heritage on the other. These two aspects of the educative process are not conflicting; on the contrary, they are complementary. One cannot go on without the other. The process itself consists in bringing about changes in the newborn babe, the child, and the adolescent as he grows and develops to maturity. These changes are threefold: (1) from ignorance to knowledge, the intellectual phase; (2) from innate capacities to developed abilities, the operational phase; and (3) from domination by animal impulses to motivation by human ideals, the ethical phase. Even the extreme naturalists (professed materialists) make no objection to this analysis of the most important changes involved in the educative process. But when we substitute "Christian ideals" for "human ideals," we bring into relief the outstanding characteristic of Catholic education: the teaching and inculcation by every possible means of the positive obligation on the part of every person who has a knowledge of Christ to strive all his life to make of himself another Christ. No lower goal should be the aim of the Catholic. To aid every person to achieve this goal by bringing this message to everyone throughout the world, "whether Jews or Gentiles, whether bond or free" (I Cor. 12 : 13), without distinction of race or color, is the purpose for which the Church was established by God. For this purpose it uses every means available, and prominent among these is the school.

When we examine carefully the three changes listed above, we see at once that the school is paramount in only two of them. It makes a contribution also to the third since it is a social agency; but it is in the life lived in the home, the community, and the Church that life ideals have their beginning. Here the school can only be a supplementary agency, for of its very nature it is an intellectual agency, and its specific and essential function is the training of the mind. For this purpose have schools been established, and only in a time of emergency should it so concern itself with the functions of the other great social agencies (the home, the community, and the Church) that it ceases to perform its proper function in an adequate way. Thus in time of epidemic the school might well become a clinic or hospital, but when the emergency has been met, the school should return to its own specific function, the intellectual training of its students. Nevertheless, as we said above, the school also is a community. Hence it too plays a part in the development of the life ideals of the pupil, though it does so indirectly.

In this chapter we take the viewpoint of the philosopher, whose aim is always to see as a whole whatever he may be considering. In this synoptic view there is, of course, both analysis and synthesis, the latter following the former. Our immediate purpose, therefore, is to make an analysis of human knowledge as it has been advancing through the centuries, comprising today what we call our cultural heritage. What are the great fields of knowledge in which this accumulated wisdom of the world may best be arranged for assimilation by the maturing minds of the young?

Before attempting to answer this question, we must answer another question about man himself: What makes man a man, standing in a class by himself in contrast to all the other creatures of the animal kingdom? The answer can be given in one word, rationality. Man is a rational animal. Someone has stated that the very purpose of education is to make him more rational and less animal. As a rational animal there are two powers which distinguish him from all other species of the animal kingdom: the power of thought and the power of expression, both of which play an important part in the discovery and in the transmission of knowledge. The lower animals, whose sense experience is manifested in their instinctive behavior, sometimes have sense powers more highly developed than those of man himself; but the exercise of none of these reveals what we commonly call rational thought, that is, thinking with concepts or universal ideas made possible by the power of abstraction. Similarly, animals of the higher orders are able to communicate by some forms of expression, but here again there is nothing that we would dignify by the word "language." In regard to the products of their instinctive behavior, again there is nothing that we would classify as fine art or applied art, although many of these products are truly beautiful and useful, such as the nest of the bird and the honeycomb of the bee. We see these as products of those impulses planted in their nature by God Himself and fixed in their mode of performance without progress or improvement. In the case of man, however, the chief characteristics of his planning are freedom and progress in improving the creations that come from his mind and hand. Herein lies his rationality.

I. The Great Fields of Knowledge

The curriculum of any school on any level is an attempt to select the most worth-while portions of the racial inheritance accumulated through the ages and make them available to the mind of the child according to its capability. In the university this accumulated knowledge is organized and presented according to the nature of the subject matter itself, since here we are dealing with the mature mind. The first division into which this accumulation of human experience falls is a simple one, namely, the sciences and the arts. By "sciences" we mean those facts and insights which man has accumulated through the ages about the world in which he lives; by "arts" we mean those practices and procedures, skills and techniques, that he has developed through the ages to make his living more comfortable and more elevated, so that he can live the life of a truly civilized person.

1. The Sciences

The sciences are placed in the curriculum to provide those materials with which the mind of the child or adolescent is to be concerned so that his powers of thought and expression may reach the fullness of their capacity. What do we wish students to think about? The answer to this question is simple: we wish them to think about the three worlds which man has always been thinking about, the worlds in which students are living their own lives as they grow and develop and in which they will continue to live until death: the physical world, the human world, and the spiritual world. We classify the knowledge that man has accumulated about these three worlds as (1) the natural sciences, dealing with physical nature and the living creatures below man; (2) the humanistic sciences (more commonly spoken of as the social sciences), dealing with human nature, that is, with man as an individual and as a member of society; and (3) the philosophical sciences, dealing with God and man's relations with God; this is the world of high ideas and spiritual ideals treated in philosophy and theology. (See below, Figure 2.)

2. The Arts

Turning now to the arts, we have another threefold classification. First of all, there are the arts of communication, which, of course, are for the most part the language arts, since these are the principal means for the communication of ideas; but mathematics also must be included as the language of quantity. The second group is the fine arts, in which man's endeavor is to produce and enjoy what is beautiful. Here he uses every medium available for this purpose dealing particularly with the two senses that play so important a part in this life: the sense of sight (the visual arts, or the pictorial and plastic arts) and the sense of sound (music). Finally we have the applied arts, in which man endeavors to create and enjoy what is useful: those things that are essential for life on earth (the products of the arts of agriculture and so forth) and those that make his living in this world more comfortable and convenient (the products of the industrial arts). (See below, Figure 2.)

Figure 2. THE GREAT FIELDS OF KNOWLEDGE

A Philosophical Approach to the Curriculum in General Education

The Two Human Abilities	Man's Worlds and Man's Works	The Great Fields of Knowledge	Butler's "Spiritual Inheritance"	The Academic Divisions
I The Sciences Thought about the	physical world, human world, spiritual world	1. natural sciences 2. humanistic sciences 3. philosophical sciences	scientific inheritance institutional inheritance religious inheritance	mathematics & natural sciences history & social sciences theology & philosophy
— and —				
II The Arts Expression of	the true, the beautiful, the good (i.e., the useful)	4. language arts 5. fine arts 6. applied arts	literary inheritance aesthetic inheritance	language & literature visual arts & music occupational training

Nicholas Murray Butler made an often quoted summary of what he called the "Spiritual Inheritance" which must be the possession of every well-educated person:

If education cannot be identified with mere instruction, what is it? What does the term mean? I answer, it must mean a gradual adjustment to the spiritual possessions of the race, with a view to realizing one's potentialities and to assisting in carrying forward that complex of ideas, acts and institutions which we call civilization. Those spiritual possessions may be variously classified, but they certainly are at least fivefold. The child is entitled to his scientific inheritance, to his literary inheritance, to his aesthetic inheritance, to his institutional inheritance and to his religious inheritance. *Without them all he cannot become a truly educated or a truly cultivated man.*[1]

It will be noticed that this fivefold classification does not include the applied arts. Since even a simple mechanical invention such as the wheelbarrow (said to have been invented by the universal genius, Leonardo da Vinci) is an idea put to work, it involves an intellectual insight. In this case it is the law of the lever in the wheel. If it is intellectual, it is certainly not a material entity but a spiritual one. It is difficult to explain, then, why the application of these insights that have made the industrial revolution a reality is not part of the spiritual inheritance of mankind. The inventions (that is, these insights put to work) that have brought about the technology of today are surely part of the social inheritance to be passed on to our youth. But these inventions are so multitudinous and so many of them are useless for the vast majority that it would be absurd to say that all should be taught by the school even if this were possible. The vocationalists are now beginning to recognize this fact and in courses in the industrial arts they now em-

[1] Nicholas Murray Butler, *The Meaning of Education* (New York: Scribners, 1915), pp. 25 f. The italics are the author's.

phasize general skills in woodwork, ironwork, electricity, and so forth, that find applications in many types of employment rather than specific skills that have application in only a few. These skills, largely manual, have never been grouped among the liberal arts; but this statement leads us into the controversy between the vocationalists and the culturalists which we will treat in section III of the following chapter (p. 121 ff.). Our concern now is with the liberal arts.

II. THE LIBERAL ARTS

Since we are writing especially of the liberal college, it is eminently appropriate that we devote a special section to the liberal arts. As their name indicates, these are the arts that make man free. From what does training in the liberal arts free man if it is effective? First of all it frees him from ignorance. Through the assimilation of the cultural heritage he becomes familiar with the principal findings in the three great fields of science: the natural, humanistic, and philosophical sciences. In the second place it frees him from undeveloped capacities as he exercises those two abilities that make him man, the ability to think and the ability to communicate his thoughts to others and in turn receive their own. Finally, it frees him from the domination by animal impulses to act under the motivation of human ideals, or as the Christian tradition phrases it, he is freed from the slavery of animal passions to live in the pursuit of Christian ideals.

1. The Intellectual Arts

Thus interpreted the liberal arts fall into two groups, the intellectual arts and the arts of communication. The development of the intellectual arts comes through training in careful observation and reflective thinking. With these two as bases the student's imaginative powers are stimulated, and such stimulation has lead to those great inventions, the products of the mind of man, that have made our civilization. We are not using the word "invention" here as applying only to the natural sciences and their applications in the applied arts. Rather we are thinking of those contributions in the philosophical sciences which the great thinkers of the world have left us in their works; we are thinking of the world's literature, where the story of man has been unfolded by the great writers in this field, and of the fine arts, where the products of the mind and hand of man are able to elevate us in the enjoyment of things beautiful, so often a reflection of the beauty that permeates the physical world about us when not spoiled by the ugly productions of man.

2. The Arts of Communication

These intellectual arts, of course, are exercised by students in all fields of study, but some of these studies bear more specifically on the arts of language since they are so essential, not only as the means for the communication of knowledge, but also as a means to aid students in their own thinking in any field. In the primary school it is common to call the arts of communication the "three R's"; but a little reflection reveals that they are multiple. Among the abilities to be developed here is the ability to read and write with the written symbols of letters and words integrated as sentences and paragraphs in composition. These are the ordinary means for man's communication of his own ideas to others as well as the means for receiving from others their ideas for his own enlightenment. With the development of the radio, the abilities to speak and listen have taken on more importance and are receiving more attention in the school today. Here the symbols are sounds. Finally we have the abilities to count and compute with figures and symbols, which are means of communication as well as are words and sounds. It is one thing for the child to learn how to count, but computation on the higher levels of mathematics is one of the severest disciplines the mind of man is ever subjected to, and training in this discipline is definitely appropriate throughout the higher levels of the secondary school as well as in the liberal college. For some it is an absolute prerequisite to carry on effective work in the upper biennium of the college and the graduate and professional schools of the university. But for all, fundamental training in this basic discipline is a necessary requirement if we are to expect that the product of the liberal education the college provides is to be a truly cultivated man or woman.

Figure 3. THE LIBERAL ARTS

The Arts =	The Ability to:	Products	Primary Subject Matter
Intellectual Arts (something to communicate)	observe carefully	percepts	natural sciences, fine arts
	think reflectively	concepts	humanistic and philosophical sciences
	imagine creatively	images	fine arts, literature, applied arts
	remember retentively	(all the above)	(all the above)
Arts of Communication (language arts)	read and write	communication	the trivium { grammar logic rhetoric
	speak and listen		
	count and compute	measurement	mathematics

It will be noticed that in Figure 3 we have unified the literary arts in the trivium. This is a form of integration urgently needed in our colleges today. As John Stuart Mill phrased it: "Consider for a moment what grammar is. It is the most elementary part of logic. It is the beginning of the analysis of the thinking process. The principles and rules of grammar are the means by which the forms of language are made to correspond with the universal forms of thought. . . . The structure of every sentence is a lesson in logic." Sentence analysis as a severe discipline in forms of thought, is an excellent introduction to abstract reasoning; even a child is capable of it in dealing with the materials of language, that is, the parts of speech. Since grammatical analysis is almost entirely neglected in elementary school and high school today, the college must teach it together with logic and rhetoric as a unitary discipline. We will discuss this procedure in some detail in chapter 6 when we consider "The Universal Discipline," and again in chapter 7 when we present suggestions for an integrated college curriculum. (See below, pp. 151 ff. and pp. 160 f.)

III. Proliferation of the Arts and Sciences

The most difficult problem the liberal college is confronting today is well indicated by the title of this section, "Proliferation of the Arts and Sciences." Knowledge has increased to such an extent and so many specific skills are called for in everyday life that it is evident that the school, on all levels dealing with general education, can do no more than introduce the student to the more important fields where some knowledge is necessary. We have striking illustrations of this increase in knowledge in the field of philosophy. In the United States less than a century ago it was common practice to use a textbook in secondary schools and colleges that bore the title *Natural Philosophy*. This contained the only training in science, particularly in physics, that the students of that day received. If any biological science was taught, the text had some such title as *Natural History*. In the same way, what we call the social sciences (economics, sociology, and politics) were treated in philosophy as social ethics, which established rights and duties in regard to private property, the family, and government. But the expansion and specialization of knowledge during the past century has imposed its demands on secondary education.

The first attempt of the American college to meet this problem of the growth of knowledge was the introduction of the elective system. Following this came departmentalization of college courses. The dissipating effect of the elective system on the mind of the student was soon evident to all, and restrictions were placed on it; one year's work in a laboratory science during the first two college years and the selection of major and minor fields in the last two were required, so that a student's advanced study would be confined to not more than two fields instead of being distributed according to his caprice among all the courses offered. The worst feature of the departmentalization movement was that as the great fields of knowledge disintegrated, the courses offered by the college within the various parts of a field came to be presented as if their sole purpose was to prepare students for graduate study on the university level instead of being organized and presented as integral parts of a general education that all students should have.

1. Present Attempts at Integration

The excessive departmentalization which followed the elective system was in turn followed by the introduction of "survey courses" in which a broad field of knowledge was covered by a survey without giving particular attention to any parts of the field or to any particular developments within it. This approach is now recognized as shortsighted, for students receive little benefit from a survey course that by its very nature is "usually superficial, insubstantial, thin, vapid." [2] Today the broad courses offered are called "general" or "integrated" courses. The problem remains, however, and no mere change of name meets the issue. There must be a selection and reorganization of the materials to be presented in any such course, and a new technique of presentation must be employed that will introduce the student to some of the

[2] Norman Foerster, *The Future of the Liberal College*, p. 70; used by permission of Appleton-Century-Crofts, Inc. (1938).

major problems within the field and furnish him the opportunity to practice the discipline that is characteristic of it and essential to success within it.

Credit must be given to Columbia University College for making the first definite attack on the integration problem by the introduction in 1919 of its now famous course in "Contemporary Civilization." In the *Announcement* for 1948–49 (p. 78) this course is described in these words: "The course in Contemporary Civilization is a two-year sequence organized and conducted on a collaborative basis by members of the Departments of Economics, Government, History, Philosophy and Sociology. The course is administered by an interdepartmental committee." Here the departmental organization is retained with a chairman as coordinator.

A different approach was taken at Chicago University. The college there is now organized with the last two years of high school and the first two of college functioning as a single institution; the time requirement has been dropped and the university departments no longer function as departments within the new college. In their place are four divisions: (1) humanities, (2) social science, (3) physical science, and (4) biological science. The academic credit is abolished, and the bachelor degree is awarded on the satisfactory passing of comprehensive examinations in these four fields and certain others, most of which vary with the student, depending on his intentions to do advanced work in one of the divisions or professional schools of the University. Here is an effective attack on the problem of reorganizing general education in this country. This combination of high school and college must not be considered, however, as making any great change in the length of time spent in university study for an advanced degree. A student, for example, wishing to qualify for a master's degree in chemistry will usually study as long at Chicago University as he would have studied at another institution if he took his bachelor's degree with a major in the last two years of college and studied an additional year for the master's degree. The main idea in the reorganization is to provide a better general education for college students and to give it to them in less time as an integrated experience through intensified study in the four fields listed above.[3]

The most extensive inquiry into the problem of integration undoubtedly has been what is familiarly spoken of as "The Harvard Report," which is entitled *General Education in a Free Society*.[4] The best part of the report is the first four chapters, which face the problem presented by the organization of American secondary education in high-school and college units, in contrast with European systems, where the secondary school is a single continuous institution lasting seven years or more, preparing the student for life and for entrance into the university. The fourth chapter, "General Education in Harvard College," presents one section on "Proposed Requirements in General Education." Here a threefold divisional organization is adopted: (1) the humanities, (2) social studies, and (3) science and mathematics. Sixteen courses are required for graduation, four each year, and a student must take at least one of the courses classified as "Elementary General Education" in each of the three fields, and three other courses which may be from these general courses but ordinarily will be from what are called "Second Group Courses," that is, advanced work in these fields. It would be a mistake to infer from this requirement that Harvard has discarded the elective idea. Far from it! In the first place it was a matter of choice whether the student followed the old or the new plan. In 1949, however, all freshmen were required to take at least one course in general education. In 1950 the requirement was increased to two courses, and in 1951 freshmen pursued elementary courses in all three

[3] *The Idea and Practice of General Education* (Chicago: University of Chicago Press, 1950), p. 333.
[4] Cambridge: Harvard University Press, 1945.

fields. According to a publicity release dated March 9, 1949, the "enthusiasm of both students and faculty for this experiment proved the usefulness of this approach." The new program of studies is organized as follows:

During his freshman and sophomore years, each student will take one introductory course in each of the three great fields of learning. Most students will select these three courses from the 12 or more elementary courses offered in general education. Students concentrating in a natural science or premedical students, however, may count three laboratory courses or two laboratory courses and a mathematics course as fulfilling the general education requirements in natural sciences.

During his four years of study, a student must take a total of six courses outside the department in which he is concentrating. Only the three elementary courses will be prescribed; the others may be selected from advanced courses offered by the Committee on General Education or from the courses given by the departments.[5]

That a great deal of election is still possible is evidenced by the fact that within each of the three fields of knowledge at least three "Elementary Courses" are offered, and in the "Second Group Courses," that is, those that are advanced, the 1948–49 Bulletin No. 10, *Courses in General Education*, lists eight courses in the social studies alone from which choice may be made.

2. The "Great Books" Curriculum

The attempt to meet the integration problem that has received the greatest publicity is undoubtedly the "Great Books" curriculum at St. John's College, Annapolis, Maryland. Great books, of course, have always been the basis of the curriculum in literature courses, both English and Amer-

[5] "General Education Course at Harvard University" in *School and Society*, May 7, 1949, p. 332.

ican and those in foreign languages. This plan uses them also as the basis for courses in mathematics and natural science for all four years. The chronological order is followed. Beginning with Euclid's *Geometry* and the scientific experiments of the Greeks, the curriculum follows the development of mathematics and science from that time, repeating the great experiments that have brought science to its present stage of development. Undoubtedly a general grasp of the more important scientific postulates is an integral part of a good general education, but as Howard Mumford Jones puts it, "That a method so cumbersome and inefficient as the historical repetition of experiments which have long since outlived their first usefulness is the only way or the best way to secure this end is an astonishing assumption." [6] His criticism of the unification that is to be effected in the student's mind by reading the great books is even more severe:

If the list approaches unity, that unity must lie in the majority of its titles, and the majority of its titles seems to indicate that the intellectual tradition of western Europe is, to a surprising degree, a tradition of scepticism, authoritarianism and despair of ordinary humanity. It is difficult to see how such a tradition can help education. If the list does not represent unity I do not see that it really cures the confusion of the present curriculum. For, if these texts are to be intensively studied in order to develop some sort of coherent whole, confusion is increased by the necessity of finding a common denominator between Lucian, the Greek sceptic, and St. Bonaventure, the medieval Catholic; between Sophocles, who held that man is a noble being, and Swift, who held that he is not; between Rousseau, who trusted in altruism, and Malthus, who trusted in selfishness. [7]

I believe that the real contribution of St. John's college to the solution of the problem of general education is the

[6] *Education and World Tragedy* (Cambridge: Harvard University Press, 1946), pp. 59 f.
[7] *Ibid.*, p. 61.

technique there introduced whereby instructors and students read and discuss the great books together in seminars. In these small discussion groups the student is challenged to active participation in the learning and teaching process. The principle operative here is that all learning comes through self-activity and all education, therefore, is self-education, the student using the teacher as counselor and guide in his efforts to grow in knowledge and skill in the liberal arts and sciences and to develop the attitudes and ideals of a true liberal education.

3. Experimental Programs in Catholic Colleges

New college curriculums based on the reading of the great books are now being offered by two Catholic colleges; in both instances the program is experimental in nature. In September, 1950, the College of Arts and Letters of the University of Notre Dame offered a "masterworks" curriculum to a group of about 50 students out of 1,200 entering the freshman class. The hope is, however, that it will prove its worth as a program in liberal or general education in college, and, as financial resources permit, will eventually be extended. The Manhattan College program, the conclusions of a faculty committee working on the problem since 1945, was required of all students entering the freshmen class in 1949. It is not announced as "experimental," but some changes have already been made and others will undoubtedly follow as experience suggests. The Notre Dame *Bulletin* announcing the new program for 1950 makes no reference to the great books, but uses instead the label, "Masterworks." The Manhattan program, on the other hand, differs from that of St. John's College in that it does not exclude the use of textbooks. Its announcement states that "competent professors will make actual class use of the relevant classical works of the period under study, . . . often in translation, but not necessarily to the exclusion of a comprehensive textbook, if such be advisable." [8] The curriculum is constructed for integration by being "built solidly on the foundation of history . . . as marking out and highlighting a single theme for the whole four years, . . . the Heritage of Western Civilization. . . . Variation of the theme is achieved in the following historical break-down of the program":

Freshman: —Greece and Rome to 180 A.D.

Sophomore:—Christian Antiquity and the Early Middle Ages, from Christ to 1200 A.D.

Junior: —The Urban Middle Ages and the Formation of the Modern World, 1200 to 1770.

Senior: —The Modern and Contemporary World, 1770 to the present.[9]

The question immediately arises: Will this program of "theme courses" in history, literature, fine arts, philosophy and religion, and music be anything more than a prolonged series of survey courses extending over ancient, medieval, and modern history of the West (but no reference to the Orient) with the reading of the great books thrown in for good measure?

The Notre Dame program, in contrast with this, uses the cycle system covering the whole of the "Western Christian Tradition" by studying the easier masterworks during the first two years and then repeating the process with the more difficult works during the last two years. It is of some interest, from the point of view of Catholic authorship, to compare the St. John's "List of Great Books" with the Notre Dame "Basic Reading List." If we interpret the word "Catholic" to mean everything from the Bible to Galilei, the St.

[8] *The New Liberal Arts Program* (New York: Manhattan College, 1949), pp. 8 f.

[9] *Ibid.*, pp. 5–8.

John's list contains nineteen Catholic books, and the Notre Dame list, from St. Cyprian and the Roman Missal to Jacques Maritain and Pope Pius XII, contains just twice as many.

In the Notre Dame curriculum, as in St. John's, three different teaching "instruments" are used, the seminar, the tutorial, and the lecture. The seminar consists of the rapid reading of the masterworks and a discussion of their principal ideas. The function of the tutorials is to train and guide the student to some understanding and proficiency in the principles, problems, and skills appropriate to the "basic subject matters." The lectures will be given by authorities in the various fields drawn from other faculties at Notre Dame and from other universities. This is the freshman program:

Seminar in Masterworks of Western Christian Civilization
   I. From the Greeks to the end of the Middle Ages   4 hrs.

Tutorials:
   1. Language and Literature   5 hrs.
   2. Mathematics and Science
      I. Ancient Mathematics   3 hrs.
   3. Philosophy
      I. Philosophy of Nature   2 hrs.
   4. Theology   2 hrs.
Lecture Series in Historical Backgrounds   1 hr.
                              17 hrs.

The students, of course, will not meet together seventeen times a week since the seminars and some of the tutorials will be double periods or longer. In the sophomore year the historical period covered in the seminar and the tutorial in language and literature will be: "II. From the Renaissance to the Moderns," which, with that of the freshman year, will be repeated during the junior and senior years. The tutorials in mathematics and science will be: II. Modern Mathematics;

III. Physical Science; IV. Biological Science. The Philosophy tutorials will be: II. Metaphysics; III. Ethics; IV. Philosophy of Politics. No specifications have yet been published for the tutorials in theology.

The outstanding weakness of the three great-book programs described above is their limitation of the college student's study to the European tradition. As Jones states it, "If ever there was a time when we should learn what values, hopes and ambitions are *cherished in the vast* areas of Russia, the rest of Asia, Africa, South America and the islands of the sea, now, if ever, is the time." [10]

Those advocating the programs at Notre Dame and Manhattan College point out the advantage of the integration effected through the theology and philosophy which all conducting the programs hold in common. I once heard Dr. Buchanan (then dean at St. John's) emphasize before a Catholic group this weakness in the program at St. John's College, where various philosophies and theologies animated those conducting that program. He added further that if Catholics thought that any of the great books on his list were teaching only error and should not be studied even for purposes of refutation, there were plenty of great books from which the Catholics could easily make up their own list. I must admit, however, that I have never come across a convincing statement by any Catholic educator how this integration "so devoutly to be wished" is brought about through the formal teaching of theology and philosophy. The best descriptive statement I have seen concerning this matter is that contained in the three and a half pages of the Manhattan College *Bulletin* under the paragraph titles, "Philosophy" and "Religion." [11] When one looks at the curriculum, however (pp. 16–17), one cannot help but wonder how freshman students carrying ten subjects, most of which run

[10] Howard Mumford Jones, *op. cit.*, p. 73.

[11] Supplement, 1950–51, *The New Liberal Arts Program*, pp. 8–12.

throughout the year, can integrate the many fields of knowledge they have been studying. In the description of the courses for the four years the word "survey" is used several times, and we have already made sufficient comment on this approach. The integration we are concerned with must be in the mind of the student. The danger is that the integration within the curriculum or in the mind of the professor, assuming that it is there, will pass from the lecture notes of the professor to the notebook of the student without passing through the mind of either.

I believe that the most effective force for integration is not the curriculum, however devised, but rather the life within the institution, or as we commonly say, the "college atmosphere." This seems to have been John Stuart Mill's idea when he spoke about the "pervasive tone" of an institution.

4. Criticism of Catholic Educational Theory

Some people seem to think that since we Catholics are in agreement on the ultimate goals of education, Christian perfection in this life and life with God hereafter, therefore for us the ways and means of arriving at the many proximate goals which life in a changing society presents to us, are all determined for us by ecclesiastical authority. This seems to be the opinion of John Childs in his recent book, *Education and Morals*. The two Catholic college experimental programs just presented hardly indicate this assumption.

Childs puts the question, where do the "critics of the social interpretations of education" get their "method for the determination of the purposes and the content of the program of the school." He lists four groups as chief among these critics: Supernaturalists, Essentialists, Classicists (great books), and Life Scientists. Concerning the first of these (ourselves) he says, " 'Supernaturalists' believe that this superior source is to be had in the declarations of revealed religion as authoritatively interpreted by the leaders of the Church."[12] We understand how Childs could be led to make such a statement in the light of the cloudy thinking which only too often characterizes the pronouncements of Catholics on the intricate problems of education. To listen to some of these one might think that we Catholics believe that we have the solutions to all the problems of determining "the purposes and the content of the program of the school" or college made known to us through revelation. Any supernaturalist that believes anything like this is due for a rude awakening if he remains in school work very long.

When Dr. George Johnson, at that time the head of the Department of Education at the Catholic University in Washington, was conducting the parochial school of a neighboring parish as a demonstration school, he called it a "progressive school." This he did in spite of the disrepute that name carried as a result of the lunatic fringe among the group which is always attracted to any movement characterized by novelty. Father O'Connell, in his book *Are Catholic Schools Progressive?* lists four practices of progressive education which he recommends to Catholic teachers.[13]

In a changing civilization such as we are now immersed in, a solution that seems to work today may be a positive hindrance tomorrow. Belief in the revealed truth that the purpose of man's life on earth is the glorification of God by a Christian life, has saved us from the blunder of the state-supported system in the United States, which has yielded to the secularizing influences of the day in turning away from the practice of all early American schools, in which religion was an integral part of the cultural inheritance to be passed on to each oncoming generation by the school as the agency of formal education. But this is not the difficult

---

[12] John S. Childs, *Education and Morals,* p. 41; used by permission of Appleton-Century-Crofts, Inc., New York (1950).
[13] St. Louis: Herder Book Co., 1946; cf. pp. 154 f.

phase of the problem. Religion has been retained in the curriculum of the state-supported systems of Holland, Great Britain, and other countries that have not succumbed to the academic dictators of pseudoscientific positivism and secularism or to the political dictators in Russia and the Soviet satellites. The difficult problem is how to make religion as the core of the curriculum the dominating influence in the lives of pupils and students, not merely in school but particularly in their later lives when school days are over.

It is one thing to teach young people to know their religion. The school can do this easily by formal instruction. But it is quite another thing to lead them to love it and to live it. How often are we Catholics embarrassed by the lives of public men and women who, products of our own schools but forgetting the lessons of their fathers, become involved in corrupt politics, or who in their personal lives, through divorce and remarriage, become a scandal to their fellow Catholics and a disgrace to the Church in which they were reared? Divine grace itself, that is, help from on high, is no guarantee that man will not give in to the impulses of his lower nature. God respects man's freedom, and the business of liberal education is to enlarge that freedom by giving him control of his animal nature while developing his rational nature.

Another example of the misunderstanding of the Catholic theory of education is found in Howard Jones's book already referred to. He makes a series of quotations from Father Geoffrey O'Connell's address on the occasion of the semicentennial celebration of the Catholic University of America, published in the volume entitled *Vital Problems of Catholic Education in the United States*. These citations rightly interpreted make no extravagant claims that Catholics have all the answers to all the problems in education. Nevertheless, Jones makes the statement that "it does not seem likely Americans not of Catholic faith will agree that the only proper study of Shakespeare and conic sections is one conditioned by infallible dogma." [14] Catholics as well as others know that exaggeration is the chief note of American humor, and luckily most Catholics have a sense of humor and can smile at a statement like that. They also know that revelation gives us the answer only to the ultimate goals of education, and not to what we have called the seven "mediate goals" or to the three "immediate goals" in Figure 1 (p. 30). This was stated almost explicitly by the Holy Father himself in his radio address to the Catholic Inter-American Education Confederation assembled in congress at La Paz, Bolivia, October, 1949: "The Christian ideal of education is identified with the latest findings of psycho-pedagogical science, surrounding it with a light which perfects it and facilitates the educative process with the complete and fruitful development of the individual personality." [15]

Since Jones and Childs reject revelation as a source of knowledge, we understand how they differ from us in the ultimate goals of education, but they can hardly be unmindful of the fact that we have another source of guidance which is our greatest asset, the teaching Church and the centuries of tradition that it carries forward to meet the problems of the day. We have quoted in the Introduction (p. 4) Robert Maynard Hutchins' appeal to us not to be unmindful of that intellectual tradition in education, and most Catholic educators would agree that when we have blundered, as did so many Catholic institutions in going over bag and baggage to the elective system, it was because we were unmindful of what that tradition should have taught us. We must strike a balance between tradition and new ideas, evaluating the latter in terms of the former, guided by the two principles which we will formulate in chapter 11, the principle of permanence and the principle of change (pp. 242–46).

[14] *Op. cit.*, p. 55.
[15] N.C.W.C. News Service, October 14, 1949, "Radio Address," p. 3.

IV. The Academic Lockstep

We turn now to another problem that is peculiar to democracy as we in this country understand it. In the totalitarian regimes man is a creature of the state. As Alfredo Rocco states it in *The Political Doctrine of Fascism:* "For Fascism society is the end, the individual the means, and its whole life consists in using individuals for its social ends. . . . Our concept of liberty is this that the individual be allowed to develop his personality in behalf of the state."[16] This is anything but the concept of the state in the American interpretation of democracy. From the time those ten famous words were enunciated in the Declaration of Independence, "all men are endowed by their Creator with unalienable rights," until today we have traditionally held that among those rights are "life, liberty and the pursuit of happiness," and "that to secure these rights, Governments are instituted among men." In this interpretation the state is a means to the end, and the end, in the words of the preamble to the Constitution, is "to promote the general welfare."

In a democracy the school is one of the necessary means to secure this end. So widespread has this view been that with the secularization of tax-supported schools, education has almost become our national religion. We seem to think that it can accomplish everything for the "general welfare," altogether oblivious of the fact that Germany, with illiteracy completely abolished, was the most highly educated country in the world; and yet we know what happened in Germany. When the depression was at its worst in our country in the early 1930's and the young people graduating from high school had to be kept out of the labor market since there were not enough jobs for adults, what was to be done with them?

[16] Quoted by Joseph Leighton in *Social Philosophies in Conflict*, p. 15; used by permission of Appleton-Century (1937).

The C.C.C. Camps took care of some, but not of many thousands in the large cities. Hutchins told the people of Chicago that there were only three choices for these youths: (1) they could be allowed to walk the streets, which for many would mean the pool halls and tough dives; (2) they could be put in penal institutions; or (3) they could be kept in school. The only intelligent solution was the establishment of junior colleges offering two years of schooling beyond high school. Now we have the President's Report of 1947 concerning the community college. The prediction for 1960 is that there will be 4,600,000 students in schools beyond the high-school level. This means mass education in colleges. The inevitable tendency of this situation is to gear the pace of the college to the preponderant number of medium students. This pace is too slow for the quick learners and too fast for the slow. The latter group is provided for in some sections by institutions like the General College at Minnesota University and other institutions which offer a two-year terminal program for the lower 25%, geared to their abilities and planned to meet their needs. But what are we doing for the upper 25%?

This undoubtedly is one of the most pressing problems in college education today. We seem to be victims of a theory that may well be called egalitarian democracy: that all persons are equal in ability and industry as well as in rights and duties. The testimony of all measurements in educational psychology is just the contrary. The fact of individual differences is questioned by no one and is seen on all school levels. Here is a statement from the authors of a recent text on secondary education for high-school teachers: "Students most academically gifted are now most severely handicapped." [17] In May, 1940, Dr. Frank Aydelotte, past

[17] Thomas Briggs, Jr., Paul Leonard, and Joseph Justman, *Secondary Education* (New York: Macmillan Co., 1950), p. 455.

president of Swarthmore College and at the time director of the Institute for Advanced Study at Princeton, was quoted in the press as follows:

Actuated by the most democratic motive, we have geared our educational system to the capacity of the average and in so doing we are unjust to the best. We can never build up an educational system which will meet the needs of the modern world until we break this academic lockstep and provide for the best and most ambitious the freedom and the stimulus which will lead them to attempt and succeed in tasks impossible for the average. Socially what happens to the best is far more important than what happens to the poorest.

The worst feature of this situation is the effect it has upon the gifted students unless they spend their surplus energy and ability as leaders of student clubs and other school activities. On the principle that all students should be kept working at their capacity, in the above situation the gifted students develop habits of sloth and laziness, if not worse, and lose all ambition to compete with their peers since it is so easy to excel over the average student. Another appeal to do something about this matter has now been reported by the Associated Press, June 4, 1950. This is from a subcommittee of the American Association of School Administrators, which fifteen years ago set up the Educational Policies Commission. The Commission urges that:

1. All gifted youth (the top 10 per cent in intellectual ability) be educated with the expectation that they will go to college.
2. All highly gifted youth (the top 1 per cent in intellectual ability) be educated with the expectation that they will continue higher education beyond graduation from college.
3. More money be devoted to research in the psychology and education of the gifted.
4. More scholarship funds be made available to needy gifted

youth to enable them to complete high-school and college training.

The chairman of the committee told a news conference that less than half the talents of gifted Americans are now being used because many of them fail to finish high school or college. The report condemns what it termed the "tendency to idealize the average man and belittle the exceptional man." It throws new light on the dilemma of democratic education, which is thus commonly stated: if we educate our youth in a dual system as is done in Europe (one system for the leaders and one for the led), we make social solidarity impossible; if we educate them in a single system as our own today, we fail to provide for the individual development of those who hold the greatest promise as leaders in a democracy. The Commission warned that the American ideal of a casteless society is endangered by current social and educational practices which tend to recruit leaders in business and the professions from so-called upperclass families. This system, the Commission said, restricts the vocational opportunities of youth from the low economic classes without regard to individual ability.

The first attempt to capitalize the abilities of this upper group was inaugurated by Swarthmore College in 1922 by setting up an Honors Group at the end of the sophomore year. If later graduates have continued their education as did those reported in the first study, in which more than forty percent entered graduate and professional schools, a real beginning to meet this problem has been made. [18] Other institutions use some such title as Independent Study Plan (Stanford University). This seems to be a better label since it indicates the chief characteristic, which is release from class attendance, thus putting the student on his own re-

[18] Robert C. Brooks, *Reading for Honors at Swarthmore* (New York: Oxford University Press, 1927), p. 92.

sponsibility with directed reading and small group seminars followed by comprehensive examinations as the final test.

It is interesting to note that none of the institutions mentioned earlier in this chapter, which have new plans for the integration of studies, announce their plans as being for a picked group of better students. This is true of those using the great books as well as all the others. The claim is made that the great books were written for the person of average intelligence, and the American college student is considered at least that. They must realize, however, that since students select the college, the selective factor cannot be eliminated completely. All these plans call for more work than does the ordinary college program, and not many students are willing to work harder than they must to get a degree. In the second place, selection by the student means a certain spirit of adventure which young people constantly display in sports but seldom in the intellectual adventure of reading the "classics." Those who do are well above the average in mental ability and power of application.

To the contention that setting off the better students by themselves in a special group is undemocratic, perhaps the best reply is that of Dr. Buttrick: "To the extent that the colleges level down they injure and frustrate democracy." [19] This was Wilson's point of view when, as president of Princeton, he set up the Preceptorial System. As he phrased it, any other treatment of the product of the American high school meant making democracy synonymous with mediocrity.

Undoubtedly the greatest obstacle preventing the extension of these provisions for gifted students is the expense. A high teacher-student ratio means more money expended as well as more work for both teachers and students. A thousand students in a lecture hall with good acoustics is an inspiration for both teacher and student; but two or more

[19] *Ibid.*, p. 65.

instructors directing the reading of a handful of students and receiving written and oral reports thereon in seminars and tutorials, is another matter. For our Catholic colleges with limited financial resources, this problem seems almost insurmountable. Very few have as yet introduced anything in the way of independent study plans, and those that have are university colleges. But the superior students should be our special concern. Submerged as they now are in the great mass of students (in which the tempo of the discipline of study is inevitably geared down to the pace of the average), the students of superior ability have no incentive or opportunity to develop their God-given powers in a way that will bring them to full fruition. Here, then, is an opportunity for the Catholic liberal college to do something distinctive for the Catholic life of the nation and make a special contribution to the apostolate of the laity. Results might not show for a generation, but if we believe that there is such a thing as a Catholic tradition in liberal education, and if we hand this tradition on to a carefully selected group of students under the competent guidance of a carefully selected group of instructors, we can rest assured that time will prove the wisdom of our decision and God will bless the work.

Following this brief review of the problem created by the proliferation of the arts and sciences in all fields, we are ready now to inquire whether in the Catholic view there are certain fields of knowledge which must form the core of any general education that is to be truly liberal. Then we must inquire what other fields should be included within the experience of the student so that his education will be characterized by balance and symmetry. And finally we must inquire into the advantages of his selecting one field, a part of one field, or even a program carrying him into several fields in intensive study of one particular problem. We make these three inquiries in the chapter that follows.

Chapter 5

THE LIBERAL STUDIES IN THE WHEEL ANALOGY

With the analysis in the preceding chapter of the social inheritance that is to be passed on to the student by the school through a process of social transmission, thereby bringing about his individual development, we are one step closer to designing a curriculum for the liberal college. In the case of the Catholic, for whom theology and philosophy constitute the area of the philosophical sciences, these two are central in any education that is truly liberal. For us there is only one controversy that arises here with regard to the content of general or liberal education, namely, the applied arts. Do they have any part to play in the curriculum of the liberal college? We will discuss this question briefly in section III of this chapter (pp. 121 ff.).

To emphasize the necessity of integrating the college student's program of study, we use the analogy of the wheel. The wheel, with its application of the law of the lever, is perhaps the most universal mechanism in the development of current technology. As such it is rich in suggestions for building the mechanism of the school, which is the curriculum. The parts of the wheel (hub, spokes, and rim) suggest the three groups of studies into which we are now going to divide the college student's program of study. The parts of the wheel must be integrated to form a whole. Otherwise as a mechanism it is useless. The same is true of the college curriculum. In our grouping of the liberal studies, these parts must be integrated if the curriculum is to do its work of carrying the student forward in his efforts to assimilate the social inheritance and develop his powers of thought and expression.

I. The Hub or Core Studies (Base)

The most important part of the wheel is the hub. This must be well built so that it holds firmly in place the spokes, which must hold the rim secure. So too with the curriculum. Its hub, or what is commonly spoken of today as the "core," is its most important part. But when secondary-school educators speak of the "core curriculum," they mean those subjects that are carried by all students. This is not our meaning of the term, for in our terminology this is true also of the other two groups of studies corresponding in our analogy to the spokes and rim; they, too, are carried by all students. When we have in view all of the great fields of knowledge that constitute the spiritual inheritance of man, the first question is this: Is there any group of studies which merits special attention on account of their inherent worth and the integrating function they perform relative to all other studies? Our answer to this question is a very definite affirmative. These studies form the "core," in the dictionary definition of the term, in which it is the "essential part" of anything. Shakespeare gives us this meaning in the words of Hamlet:

> Give me that man
> That is not passion's slave, and I will wear him
> In my heart's core, ay, in my heart of heart
> As I do thee.[1]

Our use of the word "core" carries this deeper meaning. The core studies are not only common to all students, but they

[1] Act III, scene 2, lines 76–79.

permeate at least in spirit all other subjects and in effect integrate them to form a whole if they exercise their proper function. What are these subjects? In our analysis of Catholic liberal education there are four that fall within this category: language, theology, philosophy, and history. These form the base upon which all other subjects rest. A word concerning the vitalizing and integrating function of each of these four subjects is now in order.

1. Language

Philosophers may debate and decide that thought comes first and the word symbol for the expression of the thought follows. We have all felt somewhat like this in our own experience when we say that we have a thought but cannot exactly put it in words. In everyday experience, however, it is probably true that we think with language symbols, i.e., with words. This is certainly true in building a vocabulary and attaining a clear knowledge of the various shadings of nearly exact synonyms. By no mere chance, nor because of the ease of the subject, is English a required study on every school level in the United States.

2. Theology

In the Catholic college theology is the second part of the hub, or core of the curriculum. Advisedly, "theology" is used in this presentation rather than "religion," a word so commonly employed in discussions of the liberal arts. The term religion is a broad one and, if it implies something more than a vague emotionalism, it refers often to a relationship between man and his Creator that is moral and aesthetic rather than rational and intellectual. In this section, accordingly, the designation "theology" refers primarily to what is professionally called dogmatic and moral theology. The fundamental reason for the inclusion of this study in the core studies of all Catholic colleges is that theology, like philosophy, rationalizes the relationship between the First Cause and all other causes. We place this subject second in the list of important fields of liberal studies, not because it is less important than language, but because the language arts must be acquired before they can be used as the means of communication for transmitting to the student the best thought of man in any field of knowledge.

Although God has revealed himself to man, man's knowledge of that revelation must still be scrutinized to discover its objective value. Philosophy can at least appraise theology inasmuch as one of its fruitful applications is to point out that there is no contradiction in the deepest mysteries of faith. But theology opens to the finite mind of man the world of infinite reality. There is infinite beauty of thought as well as incalculable inspiration of the will in such truths as those of the Trinity, the hypostatic union, the indwelling of the Holy Spirit, and the concept of the mystical body. It would be folly indeed for the designers of the curriculum in Catholic colleges to be satisfied with what, in the light of the supernatural, can be called only the husks of true and complete living, and not to be deeply concerned with a fruitful study of God and His attributes.

More than once the charge has been made that in too many Catholic colleges the study of religion has not always been maintained at the college level. We do not depreciate the aesthetic value of the study of religion. The splendor of revealed truth is infinite. The beauty of the Church's liturgy, imposingly performed according to the rubrics, can vivify even the most indolent of human hearts and human minds. We are concerned, however, with theology as a part of the core studies, and it cannot be worthily pursued except by an intense application of the highest rational powers of man. Too often the word "theology" has been avoided in college curricula since what is studied is the history of religion, the romanticism of religion in individual lives, and even the poetry of religion in its appeal to the heart of man. In such instances there may be very little, if any, intellectual progress beyond the study of religion as given in the lower schools. Because of its subject matter, however, theology demands an intense application of the powers of the intellect. When offered as a field of concentration in a college of liberal arts, theology, while not necessarily taught as in the professional seminary, should be at least the equal of seminary courses in difficulty of content and in its demand on the student's reasoning powers.

3. Philosophy

The case for philosophy has been so well put by writers on liberal education as to need no extended explanation. It is clear from an analysis of its aim and objective that philosophy tests, evaluates, and synthesizes. For its own accurate appraisal every department of learning leans heavily on philosophy. All reality is the object of philosophy's scrutiny. All the manifold manifestations of man's powers, of man himself, his essence and attributes, all the marvels of nature and her secrets yet to be explored, even God Himself, lie within the field of philosophy's operation. Particularly does philosophy study the diversity in the unity of all being and arrange that diversity in a rational, harmonious, and beautiful pattern. In this alone might rest the whole case for the inclusion of philosophy among the core studies.

Yet there is something more to be said for philosophy, especially if we wish to make explicit what is contained implicitly in the statements of the preceding paragraph. Philosophy is the test tube of the mind itself. Our everyday experience in Catholic colleges witnesses the fact that young men and women with thought processes slow, uncertain, and fumbling, remain mentally callow and immature until they begin formal training in philosophy, particularly in metaphysics. Then suddenly, granting, of course, real college aptitude, their minds begin to function briskly, their mental processes increase in sureness as they themselves decrease in cocksureness; the student becomes intellectually self-reliant, and if unvarying accuracy is not immediately attained, at least the percentage of faulty conclusions is satisfactorily reduced. No one can deny that something of the same effect is produced by intensive training in any one of the other fields of learning. Yet other studies discipline the mind indirectly, whereas philosophy directly invigorates the mental functions and gives to the human intellect a sharpness of vision, a balance of judgment, and a tolerance in disagreement which remain as permanent characteristics of the individual's intellectual life.

4. History

The initial reason for placing history among the core studies of liberal education may be put in one brief phrase: vicarious experience. The individual student can have only a very restricted personal experience; through the study of history he is acquainted with the experience of all men. Of even greater importance, however, is the fact that history, at least when it is informed by philosophy, provides a second type of thought processes as it traces through the ages a sequence of cause and effect in the religious beliefs, the loves and hates, the greed for wealth, and the lust for power of all mankind. Modern life cannot be understood fully without this knowledge of the past. More than one perplexing situation that appears modern, whether it is in government, in economics, or in social life, is really an old difficulty, and in many cases it has been solved partially or wholly in the past, although in the present we may have forgotten the solution. Both the unsuccessful and the successful attempts of the past to solve these questions should guide us helpfully in our efforts to cope intelligently with the problems of the present and the possible complications of the future. There are always so many current problems crying for solution that it is a waste of time and energy to ignore the experience of the past and repeat the same experiments from generation to generation. The study of history, too, will serve to diminish that insularity which results in inexperience. Youth always takes a modern or contemporary view of life. We must all be contemporary, but being modern implies a regard for the present in the light of the past while looking forward to the future.

Not only life, but every activity of life has its past and present and will have its future. Thus chemistry, economics, and literature have their past that we can know, their present we are occasionally aware of, and their future we can partially foresee. History records all this. Therefore, by its very nature history, like philosophy, is a subject with universal incidence. Philosophy evaluates all human phenomena, but it must have something to evaluate before its proper function can begin, and that something is the record of human phenomena made available to the student by the liberal science of history.

Summary

From the study of theology, philosophy, and history the student should learn to think easily and precisely. Thought may be true and yet not sharply focused, as the daydreamer has often discovered to his chagrin. The development of facility in precise thought is one of the principal aims of liberal education. Yet precise thought is deprived of much of its value unless the thought is expressed in language equally exact. Language, as the art of communication, makes available to men all the treasures of thought contained in every field of learning. Like history, it is a study of universal incidence, which is basic inasmuch as it makes available in everyday life the light and shadow of every thought the mind of man can possibly conceive.

II. THE SPOKES OR SPHERAL STUDIES (BREADTH)

In our analogy of the wheel, the number of spokes gives the balance that every wheel must have, and their length gives the breadth indicating the work it can do. Applying these ideas to the curriculum, what we are calling the "spheral studies" are those liberal studies not included in the hub. The dictionary defines "spheral" as that which gives "symmetry" to the whole.[2] It includes, therefore, all branches of knowledge forming an integral part of liberal education not included in the core studies. The curriculum we propose is designed to give the student a broad yet comprehensive acquaintance with all of these. Our position is that to a greater or less degree the fields enumerated in the preceding section of this chapter and in this section should form the study content of the curriculum in every Catholic college of liberal arts and sciences. Briefly to study the anticipated effects of each may be helpful and suggestive. Such a summary consideration, however much it may disappoint specialists in any one of the fields we discuss, may nevertheless help us to understand how, in combination with the core, the spheral studies develop in the student qualities of mind and heart we associate only with the wise and self-controlled man or woman.

1. Literature

Down through the ages literature has concerned itself with the noblest thoughts and highest aspirations of the human race. It stands higher than mathematics and the natural sciences, at least for its humane values. It is beauty of thought set to the music of expression. In some measure it can console the weary and dissipate a loneliness all human hearts occasionally feel. Literature not only has appeal for the intellect; through the presentation of inspiring personalities for our admiration and imitation, it strengthens the

[2] *Webster's Secondary School Dictionary.*

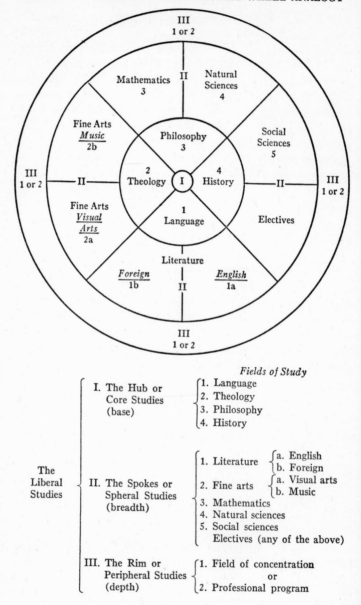

Figure 4. THE LIBERAL STUDIES IN THE WHEEL ANALOGY

Fields of Study

The Liberal Studies

I. The Hub or Core Studies (base)
- 1. Language
- 2. Theology
- 3. Philosophy
- 4. History

II. The Spokes or Spheral Studies (breadth)
- 1. Literature
  - a. English
  - b. Foreign
- 2. Fine arts
  - a. Visual arts
  - b. Music
- 3. Mathematics
- 4. Natural sciences
- 5. Social sciences
- Electives (any of the above)

III. The Rim or Peripheral Studies (depth)
- 1. Field of concentration

  or
- 2. Professional program

will. In the natural order literature does for the heart of man, especially of a cultured man, what religion does for his soul. Improperly taught, however, it becomes not the weal but the woe of liberal education. Properly taught, its impression on the human soul is, next to that of theology, probably the deepest of all the arts and sciences. Literature is the means by which the finest and most deeply inspiring thoughts of all time are made available for man today. The liberal college therefore has always demanded that the student be at least introduced to one of the world's great literatures other than that of his own language. This is the minimum; but the student who selects a foreign literature as his field of primary interest and develops sufficient skill to think in the language he is reading, achieves the real values available in this area.

2. Fine Arts

The fine arts constitute a discipline which has been slighted in colleges of liberal education, at least in colleges for men. By awakening the imagination and developing a taste for the beautiful in thought and expression, literature leads insensibly to a study of the fine arts. Music, painting, sculpture, and architecture are all forms of expression, the expression of the beautiful in sound and color and form. In her liturgy and in her worthy edifices, notably the great cathedrals, the Catholic Church has given an official stamp of approval to the cultivation and appreciation of the beautiful. It ill befits a Catholic college, then, to omit from its program courses which teach at least the principles of all this beauty, a beauty that contributes greatly to the education of the whole man.

Visual Arts

The fine arts are largely taught indirectly in the classroom. Plato affirms that the most effective way to teach the young to love the beautiful is to surround them with it, and the Greeks of Plato's time certainly followed this principle. Catholic education is now well out of the immigrant stage. There is no longer any excuse, as there may have been a century or even a half century ago, for grimy corridors and drab lecture halls, and a campus of bare earth sprinkled with pebbles and hedged by ugly brick walls. A little land-scaping, much soap and water and paint, new lighting fix-tures, lighter color schemes, and tasteful pictures on the walls will do more to develop an appreciation of art and a love for the beautiful than well-conducted tours of metropolitan museums of art.

Music

Music is the one of the fine arts which offers the best ex-ample for bringing out clearly the obligation of the liberal college to deepen the education of the general student in this field. Here it is easy to distinguish levels of artistry. At the top is the creative artist, that is, the composer. Few students, even within a select student body, have sufficient talent to concern themselves profitably for any appreciable time with this skill even on an amateur basis; the profes-sional school of music has this as its special concern. The second level is that of the performer, that is, the virtuoso. Here the group is much larger and every liberal college should be staffed to give training in this field, not for the same purpose as does a professional school, but for developing talented students for the enrichment of their own lives and the lives of those to whom they will bring enjoyment. The third level is that of the listener. On this level every student should be an artist, and the college that does not include within its educational program opportunity for all students to enjoy good music is failing in its task as an agency for the liberal education of American youth.

We must add a word here with regard to the means that

should be taken by every college for elevating the taste of its students in the field of fine arts. On the general principle that we learn only through our own activities, we point out that in this field, as in every other, the learning experiences should be threefold in nature: (1) thinking about it, the intellectual phase, (2) doing something about it, the operational phase, and (3) enjoying it, the emotional phase. It is the second, the operational phase, that presents the greatest difficulty in trying to reach all students. A rich extra-curricular program, however, can be a great help. Art clubs and music clubs will reach many students and put vitality into the courses in appreciation, which without this activity will be almost valueless for many students. In music the phonograph and radio can be of service, of course, but the active participation of students in choral clubs, orchestra, and band, if skillfully conducted, can be the best possible experience for students in this field.

3. Mathematics

Since mathematics is a system of the most abstract reasoning and is not necessarily associated with any sensory perception, it might be included in the core curriculum; many programs of study, if they provide for a core, would so include it. In this study we place mathematics outside the core because its peculiar type of abstraction seems by experience foreign to the genius of many students. Mathematics is an indispensable tool for the pursuit, at the higher level, of all scientific study, natural and social. Indeed there are mathematicians who assert that mathematics is the tool of all studies, or that all studies are only mathematics under varying forms. Thus mathematics, they say, constitutes the most transcendent poetry. Whatever one may think of this assertion, no one will deny that mathematics is a necessary tool for the study of the sciences, and that as the most abstract of the sciences it disciplines the mind rigorously in precision and logical sequence and coherence of all thought processes. Practically all colleges today require one unit in algebra and one in geometry for entrance, but pursued on the higher levels by students capable of profiting by it on these levels, mathematics is one of the most valuable disciplines the college student can undergo.

4. Natural Science

With discoveries being made daily by thousands of research workers, the field of natural science has grown enormously. While much of this discovery is of interest only to technicians, every educated man should be acquainted with an explanation of the major natural phenomena surrounding him, and if not with all its significance in modern life, at least with the general principles on which its modern applications are based. The important reason for including in the curriculum courses in science, however, is not so much the information as the specific training by inductive reasoning that such subjects afford the intellect. It is true that science alone may not lead to a development of the full powers of the intellect; the inept conclusions to which many men of great scientific attainments occasionally commit themselves are proof of this. But within its own field of sense perception, the study of science, whether physical or biological, should develop accuracy of observation, mental honesty in tracing effects to causes, patience in the pursuit of elusive data, and balance of judgment between apparently conflicting facts. Scientific laboratory experiments afford excellent training in objectivity and precision which a student of the liberal arts can well apply to other problems in life.

5. Social Science

Perhaps in no other field of learning has the liberally educated man or woman as great an opportunity to serve

the community as in that of social science. We do not mean
a professionally paid service. This general field has yet to
develop its distinct sciences. Its laboratory is the community
itself, and men and women whose intellects have been sharpened and wills strengthened in sharing the privileges and
responsibilities of community life, can contribute notably to
a solution of contemporary problems in political science,
economics, and sociology. The obligation on the part of all
college students to prepare themselves to do just that was
impressively stated at the close of the war years by President
Isaiah Bowman in an address to the freshmen of Johns
Hopkins University.

You are not here, we hope, merely to gain the smartness required to beat other men. You don't need to go to college for that.
In fact, you can learn that better outside college where the real
specialists in acquisition are to be found. . . . We hope that
you will think of your growing knowledge and skill always in
relation to your duty to the community. It would be terribly
lonesome business to know how to do something well only for
the purpose of advancing a personal interest, to get ahead of
someone else. . . .
You see peace on this campus and perhaps incline to think
that war is something far off. Let me assure you that no place is
far off today. All are near each other. Danger for one is danger
for all. . . . What can you do about it?
Soon, very soon, you may be required to do something about
it. You may have to fight about it. Surely the issue should be
clear to you if your life is at stake. The difficulties in the international field are not about votes in the Security Council or the
disposition of Trieste or any of the things you see so frequently
in the headlines. It is rather a choice between two systems, one
democratic, the other totalitarian; one depending on the secret
ballot; the other on secret police. Let no sophistry, no errors of

government in our free society blind you to this distinction. Look at the whole balance sheet of America, not just a single detail, before you begin to disparage America.[3]

This is an excellent statement of the Catholic point of view if we interpret the concept "citizenship" as including citizenship in the kingdom of heaven, our ultimate goal, which we gain by the proper performance of all our duties as citizens of the nation to which we owe allegiance. Study of the social sciences should make a notable contribution here. Most of the sciences making up this field are in their infancy, but by studying and perhaps by occasional writing and speaking, men of judgment can do much to bring them to maturity. That such a mission is important must be inferred from the place that political science, sociology, economics, psychology, and education have in the scheme of world reconversion to peace.

Summary

Since we are treating electives in the section that follows, we conclude this section with some general statements on breadth in the curriculum. To secure proper breadth, the student should be introduced to the fields of cultural inheritance treated above with the purpose, not of assimilating every detail, but of becoming acquainted with the most important aspects of these arts and sciences and of understanding the principles on which each discipline is based. Attention must also be given to the integration of each branch of learning with the totality of human knowledge. The student's introduction to each field ought not to be so superficial as to prevent him, if later he has occasion to do so, from taking up the detailed study of any general area of knowledge or of a particular aspect or part of that area. If the period of his general education is really successful, it will leave the

[3] *Time,* October 21, 1946, pp. 94 f.

student with a distinct feeling that his education has only
begun and that it should continue under his own guidance
throughout his life.

III. The Rim or Peripheral Studies (Depth)

To continue our analogy of the wheel, with its application
of the law of the lever, as a figure of the curriculum, which
carries the student forward in his assimilation of the social
inheritance and the development of his powers of thought
and expression, the third group of studies constitutes the
rim, which completes the wheel and is the culmination of
general or liberal education. We will call these the "Peripheral Studies." The term etymologically considered (to carry
around) refers to the surface of a sphere, thus suggesting an
extensive treatment of a subject. It is used in this treatise
to carry forward the analogy of the wheel, in which the rim
completes and perfects the wheel, suggesting intensive as well
as extensive study. There is justification for this in the dictionary definitions. In zoology an illustration of "peripheral
organs" is "the wings of an insect." [4]

The field of primary interest constitutes the peripheral
studies taking up more than half of the student's time during
the last two years of the curriculum we are recommending
(Figure 6 and 7, pp. 166 and 167). Besides, during these last
two years the core studies are retained in the study of philosophy, and the spheral studies are made optional. Ordinarily
the choice of a professional program as the field of primary
interest does not permit such a deep awakening in the mind
of the student as he would experience through the continued
study of one of the liberal arts or sciences; yet much can be
said in favor of this provision. For real professional preparation the student must first master the elementary knowledge
and skills in the profession of his choice, and if these are
presented liberally, as befits the liberal college, he will see

[4] *Century Dictionary*, V, 4401.

their bearing on the other fields of knowledge and he may reap in breadth what he has lost in depth.

1. Concentration, Not Specialization

There must be some compromise between breadth and depth in the entire curriculum, since each has its advantages and disadvantages. The tendency of modern educators is usually in one of two directions. Either they encourage a student to devote himself to a specialty to the exclusion of all other branches of learning, or they rush the freshman through pretentious surveys of fields of knowledge so that he knows nothing well. The shortcomings of each plan are obvious. We have seen some of the advantages of breadth; but why should students of the liberal college give their attention to depth in a field of study or in a part of that field?

We are emphasizing that a field of concentration in the liberal arts or sciences is an integral part of a student's general education. This is not specialization in the university meaning of the term. Rather it is concentration in one field or in some problem that may cut across departmental lines but nevertheless forms an integrated whole, which the student will study as thoroughly as possible in the time available during the last two years of college. What value will this have for the student who never has had such an experience during his previous school career? It is refreshing to find an answer to this question in an educational classic of the seventeenth century, Locke's essay, *The Conduct of the Understanding*. In section 44, entitled "Bottoming," Locke says:

Another thing in the conduct of the understanding that is not less necessary is to accustom ourselves in any question proposed, to examine and find out upon what it bottoms. Most of the difficulties that come in our way, when well considered and traced, lead us to some proposition which, known to be true, clears the doubt and gives an easy solution; coming to the bottom of the question, the only place of rest and stability for an inquisitive mind whose tendency is only to knowledge and "truth."

This is the specific function of the provision for concentration, that the student may have the experience of "bottoming" one field of knowledge, not with the purpose of producing the erudite scholar, but rather with the purpose of putting the student through a severe intellectual discipline in one field of knowledge with confidence that such an experience is the best possible preparation for thinking through to the bottom the many problems with which life in a changing world will inevitably confront him. Writers on general education have pointed out that only by thorough investigation will a student be led to realize the possibilities of one field and infer the advantages of thorough investigation in other fields. Perhaps the infallibility of youth can be corrected more surely in no other way than by putting a student to the thorough investigation of a problem in one of the fields of knowledge. Students thereby develop understanding and respect for intellectual humility and acquire an appreciation of thoroughness and of perseverance under difficulties and of that measured self-reliance which independent work, even under the direction of an adviser, is bound to produce; all of which will help tremendously to produce the liberally educated man.

One of the books that helped greatly to extend this interpretation of the field of concentration as something different from university specialization with its emphasis on producing narrow specialists, was Richardson's report to the president of Dartmouth College, *A Study of the Liberal College*. This is the point of view presented in this book:

The student should devote at least half his attention in the last two years to this field, and in the senior year it might profitably be more. . . . We should reject the idea of building the provision for concentration by adding together separate courses;

. . . it should be carefully planned as a coherent whole. The student should be put upon his own resources more than he is now; he should be placed in the attitude of one who must master a wide field, the material being before him, largely by his own initiative. . . . No pretentious spirit of research should invade the course; it is to be planned, not for the professional scholar, but for the intelligent man of the world.[5]

It is gratifying that the Report of the President's Commission makes a strong protest against specialization in the undergraduate college. It says that when the "major" was introduced "to make sure that every student's college experience would include a measure of intellectual discipline," the emphasis went too far and "today in many undergraduate colleges, particularly in the large universities, concentration has proceeded so far that it has almost destroyed the historic values of liberal education." Then it follows with illustrations of this over-emphasis, one of which is that of an undergraduate college in which "majors in the physical sciences took on the average 95 hours in that field—more than half of the number of hours required for a bachelor degree." [6] Such a procedure for a liberal-arts college, the report goes on to say, means that "it gives up its liberal birthright and becomes in fact a professional school." In bold print the report makes this statement:

The imposition of the narrow specialization of the graduate school on undergraduate education is unfortunate because the purpose of the senior college is basically different. Specialization at the graduate level is organized to train a few highly selected persons for careers in research and scholarship. Programs of concentration in the senior college, however, need to be built around

[5] Leon B. Richardson, *A Study of the Liberal College* (Hanover: Dartmouth College Press, 1924), pp. 176 f.

[6] Report of the President's Commission, vol. I, *Establishing the Goals*, pp. 71 f.

a much wider range of intellectual and occupational objectives to serve a much larger and less selected body of students.[7]

This section of the report continues by calling attention to the fact that not all college students will become specialists and therefore should not be educated as such, and concludes with this: "The specialist himself will be more effective if he can see how the smaller problem of his special concern is related to larger issues and values." [8]

Educators are agreed that the full effect of a liberal curriculum cannot be secured unless one field is studied and grasped thoroughly both in its principles and in the application of such principles. Such an opportunity the field of concentration is designed to afford. The designation "peripheral" as applied here to the liberal arts and sciences, accordingly refers not to a subject matter differing from any of the other fields, but rather to the manner in which one small segment of a wide area of knowledge is handled.

A brief résumé of the relationship between core, spheral, and peripheral studies may now be helpful. The core, required of all students, is a group of basic subjects in which the time element is sufficiently ample to provide for some depth as well as breadth. The spheral studies are also required of all students and cover the other fields not embraced in the core. They are sufficiently comprehensive to provide for breadth. The peripheral program in one of the fields chosen by the student on the advice of his counselor, is one in which the student's work is intensive. Thus, it seems to us, breadth of view and depth of attention are adequately provided for throughout the entire four years.

If core, spheral, and peripheral study programs are adopted, only the larger Catholic colleges and universities will be able to offer courses in the entire peripheral program.

[7] *Ibid.*, p. 72.
[8] *Ibid.*, p. 73.

No item of this program should be offered unless the college possesses adequate equipment and facilities for student use. Thus it would be a mistake for a college to offer a field of concentration in physics unless the physics laboratory is much better equipped than are the physics laboratories of most Catholic colleges. It is easy to criticize, though the criticism may be nonetheless true for the facility with which it is made; but some Catholic colleges have been too ambitious for their resources. If a college is not honest in assessing its own capabilities, how can it expect students to pursue, with any greater conviction of honest appraisal, the truth as embodied in the liberal arts and sciences?

Place for the Peripheral Studies

We must consider briefly when these peripheral courses should be pursued. Evidently there is no place in the first two years of college for concentration, since freshmen and sophomores are not prepared for this type of work. We believe, therefore, that the peripheral program should be taken in the last two years of college. By that time the student has derived full benefit from his almost completed general education. If the core studies are basic, they should be completed before the junior year, philosophy excepted. By tradition the study of philosophy has been assigned to the junior and senior years because of the belief that its fruitful study requires an intellectual maturity which is presumed only in college juniors and seniors. Another reason for such placement is the belief that, as it evaluates the data of all other branches of learning, philosophy should come only after these subjects have been studied. Traditionalists have continually affirmed that philosophy is the crown of all the studies in liberal education, and since we agree with them on this point, we place it in the crown position of the entire four-year course. For two reasons, therefore, our study places the peripheral program in the last two years. First, a general knowledge of all fields will serve as a proper preparation for the intensively pursued study of one field or division of one field, at which concentration aims. Second, with an intellect matured by the basic disciplines, a student can accomplish much more within a given time during these last two years.

We have registered above a protest against advanced specialization as an extension of graduate study into the undergraduate field, since our contention is that undergraduate education should remain essentially general or liberal education and concentration is merely the completion of that experience. If circumstances compel the student to forego some part of his general education in order to prepare himself to earn a living, let the part omitted be the field of concentration in one of the liberal studies. If professional courses are taught liberally and the liberal spirit of philosophy permeates such professional work, in a real sense, although not to an equal degree, a professional discipline studied intensively may secure a part of the advantages the student would otherwise obtain from an intensive study of one of the liberal disciplines.

2. Culturalists versus Vocationalists

This reference to professional programs introduces us to a controversy that it now raging among advocates of liberal education in the undergraduate college. The controversy, culturalists versus vocationalists, may best be stated, we believe, by pointing out the extreme positions of two men writing on this problem today, Robert Maynard Hutchins and Howard Mumford Jones. In a Rectorial Address, "The Outlook for Education," delivered at the University of Dubuque in 1944, Hutchins said, "The thing to do with vocational training is to forget it." In contrast with this statement Jones declares: "The amalgamation of the work of departments giving professional or vocational training with this general education should begin in the freshman year and be continuous throughout college, . . . a problem of administration that will require great tact and skill." [9] And this from a professor of literature at Harvard! In contrast, an eloquent proponent of the separation of liberal and vocational education in the college, Henry Wriston, now president of Brown University, writes: "It has become a commonplace now to say that the American liberal arts college was originally founded for a vocational purpose—namely, the preparation of men for the ministry of the church." [10] To bolster this point of view the vocationalists often use Harvard as an example and quote the famous tract, *New England's First Fruits*, published in 1643. After stating how they had built their houses, reared their churches and "settled the Civill Government," the tract continues: "One of the next things we longed for, and looked after was to advance *Learning*, and perpetuate it to Posterity; dreading to leave an illiterate Ministry to the Churches, when our present Ministers shall lie in the Dust." This is President Wriston's comment on this quotation:

But if one observes what that passage says, it does not at all indicate that Harvard was to be a theological school with courses of a professional character preparing the graduates for the ministry. Quite the reverse. Its emphasis is wholly upon learning, upon the necessity for ministers who were broadly educated, who were scholars. The early curriculum of Harvard did not include courses in exegesis, the construction of sermons, pastoral relations or any other field associated with a theological school. It was the classical curriculum descended from the Middle Ages and designed to produce a "learned" (not merely professionally trained) as well as godly ministry.[11]

[9] *Education and World Tragedy*, p. 152.
[10] *The Nature of the Liberal College*, p. 165.
[11] *Ibid.*, pp. 165 f.

The other side of the controversy is presented by another author in this statement:

The assumption that the cultural and the vocational are mutually exclusive is absurd. If they cannot coexist in education, how can they coexist in life itself, of which education, after all, is but a part. The real antagonism is between a culture remote from life, which despises work, and a vocational training which has no time for culture. Culture, like every other phase of direct preparation for life, should at each stage of education parallel specialization and be paralleled by it.[12]

All would agree, we believe, that the Catholic tradition has leaned heavily to the side of separation, that is, the completion of general or liberal education before specialization is begun. The distinction in practice between minor and major seminaries is a case in point. But even here the matter is not quite so simple as these two separate institutions seem to suggest. Does philosophy belong in the minor or major seminary? For long it has commonly been the first two years of the six-year course in the major seminary, and through this union with theology has taken on a certain professional emphasis. Now, however, with the necessity of seminaries in this country playing a part in preparing priests as teachers and administrators of schools, we consider philosophy as the culmination of liberal education, that is, the "major" or field of concentration in the undergraduate college leading to the bachelor degree. But in most instances the degree must be received from an accredited college if the holder is to qualify for a teacher's certificate. Hence the tendency now is to treat philosophy as part of the curriculum of an undergraduate college, thus putting the emphasis on its liberalizing influence rather than its professional aspect, though it still retains its propaedeutic function for theology.

It is of some interest that two Catholic writers of books

[12] A. D. Yocum, *Culture, Discipline and Democracy*, p. 143.

on education, one a philosopher, the other a college president, defend the position that the two types of education must go on together. Thus Jacques Maritain, the philosopher, when formulating his third fundamental rule, "the whole work of education and teaching must tend to unify," writes as follows:

> This means that from the very start, and, as far as possible, all through the years of youth, hands and mind should be at work together. This point has been made particularly clear by modern pedagogy as regards childhood. It is also valid for youth. The importance of manual work accompanying the education of the mind during the high school and college training is more and more recognized. There is no place closer to man than a workshop, and the intelligence of a man is not only in his head, but in his fingers too. . . . Youth might cooperate in many kinds of labor, harvesting, for instance, needed for the common welfare. But as a rule, and from the educational point of view, it is craftsman's labor—and also, for the sake of our mechanical age, mechanical and constructive dexterity—that should constitute the manual training of which I am speaking. I should like to add that this emphasis on manual work in education seems to me to correspond to a general characteristic of the world of tomorrow, where the dignity of work will probably be more clearly recognized, and the social cleavage between *homo faber* and *homo sapiens* done away with.[13]

Edward Fitzpatrick, president of Mount Mary College, Milwaukee, uses even sharper terms with his "dichotomy."

> The dichotomy between liberal and vocational education is too absolute, the interrelations are too many, both liberal and vocational education lose by their isolation. There is individual and social need for both in relation to each other. The reaches of vocational education are greater if they are integrated with a liberal

[13] *Education at the Crossroads,* pp. 45 f.

education. Liberal education is added for the vocation offers liberal education the opportunity to descend from its heights and to become incarnated in the social milieu for a richer environment to be utilized in the formation of men by their self-activity, or else it is condemned to a Narcissian complex of self-admiration, vain, futile, demoralizing.[14]

I firmly believe that perhaps the best presentation of this controversy is that given in a monograph by a professor of philosophy, Henry Waldgrave Stuart, which appeared over thirty years ago under the title *Liberal and Vocational Studies in the College.* The emphasis throughout, as in Jones' book above, is on the necessity of furnishing better motivation for the student of the liberal arts by linking his liberal studies with the vocation he is planning as his life career. Hence Stuart advocates strongly what in 1918 was a departure, namely, that colleges accept the first year in a law school or medical school as the fourth year of the college course qualifying the student for the Bachelor of Arts degree. Then he continues:

As for the later stages of more special work in the professional curricula, it is desirable that after four years of associated professional and non-professional work in the college, the mind of the student should be left free for three years to grapple with the purely technical elements and divisions of his subject. Concentration upon exclusively professional work at the age of twenty-three is vastly different in its effect upon a man's whole intellectual and moral attitude from a like step taken at nineteen at the end of the high school course.[15]

The first thing to be said about this statement is that no longer is it true that the average age for graduation from

---

[14] *How to Educate Human Beings,* p. 95.

[15] Reprinted from: *Liberal and Vocational Studies in the College,* Leland Stanford Jr. University Publications, University Series, by Henry Waldgrave Stuart, with the permission of the author and of the publishers, Stanford University Press, p. 35.

high school is nineteen years with graduation from college at twenty-three. Rather, before the veterans came into the college the average age for graduation from high school was about seventeen and a half years. Undoubtedly it will return to that age or lower by the time the college students who spent several years in the armed services have graduated. Then the average age of college students will be still lower than it was before the war. Motivation is certainly a reality in the so-called "premedic programs," but if this is what is meant by linking liberal and professional studies, the controversy no longer exists, since any intelligent proponent of the liberal studies sees that the sciences demanded for entrance by the medical schools can be easily provided for as an integral part of general education in any well-planned curriculum of a liberal college. That these programs have been overdone in many colleges, particularly in university colleges, is evident from the illustration given above (p. 118) from the Report of the President's Commission of Higher Education. A more recent protest by the dean of the Faculty of Medicine at Columbia University uses very strong language:

Medicine is becoming a social as well as a biological science. We would rather have a student with intellect . . . and a rounded capacity for life than one whose only view of humanity was gained as he passed from one laboratory to another.

Socalled "premedical" education should be abolished in the colleges. . . . There is no such thing as "premedical" education, nor should students in colleges who plan to enter professional schools be regarded as premedical or predental students.

College education is not "pre" anything, but should be devoted to the objective of providing as broad a cultural education as the institutions can provide. It should be a preparation not for medicine or dentistry or public health, but for life.[16]

[16] *Time*, August 7, 1950, p. 44.

For anyone sympathetic with a statement like this, the controversy has been settled in favor of the culturalists. This writer believes, however, that the experience derived from working is one of the most educative influences in life, and this is one of the great advantages of our long summer vacation. Many a college student has received great profit from employment during this period over and above the financial returns. Those of us who passed our boyhood in the nineties know how hard we had to work after school and on Saturdays even though we were not reared on a farm. The experience of chores and odd jobs has now practically disappeared for most young people in this urbanized industrial age. Recreational programs like the Boy Scouts and Girl Scouts are doing something to provide a substitute, but the question persists: cannot the school do something to bring this experience of work to the young, for whom it holds such valuable opportunities for learning one of life's fundamental lessons, that of personal responsibility for a job well done? In college the staging of a carnival for foreign student relief is an example of an extra-curricular activity in which many students spend hours of labor, building and decorating booths, for a worthy cause. Working one's way through college certainly has many disadvantages, particularly for the average student; but there are compensations. I heard an experienced college professor state that many of his former student secretaries later told him that they learned more working for him than they did in any class they ever took in college.

The small independent college (and this is particularly true of the Catholic women's colleges, since they are not part of a university) has only one choice in this matter, and that is to offer both liberal and professional studies and as far as possible have each vitalize the other. The university college is commonly set off from the professional schools, but they should work closely together. I once heard a dean of a liberal-arts college explode in anger at the suggestion that the faculty of the law school might profitably draw up for him a recommended three-year college curriculum for those students planning to enter law school, in a six-year program leading to two degrees, one in arts and the other in law.

The ideal is, of course, that even the teacher of crafts will develop a technique of liberal teaching. This is the art of teaching men, and not merely of transmitting knowledge and developing specific skills. As Robert Ulick states the problem in his essay, "The Meaning of Liberal Education," the question is: "How can the liberal quality of education, which means at the same time the inspirational and comprehensive, be preserved side by side with the specific concentration necessary in our pre-professional and professional training?" [17] His answer is that when speaking "to the typical modern scholar, particularly one who works in the natural sciences," about this inspirational quality of teaching, this does not mean inviting him

to cut out five minutes of each class for some kind of semireligious sermonizing loosely connected with the content of the course.

Nothing would be more ridiculous from any possible point of view. On the other hand, it is not easy to explain what is meant. Perhaps it can be done by relating the statement of the German philosopher-statesman, Walter Rathenau, that there is no point on the surface of life from which one cannot travel into its center. To give practical examples, one can teach the history of the great revolutions merely as a strife of parties, a sequence of political and economic conflicts, and a displacement and replacement of forms of governments. But one can also teach it in such a way that the student feels himself as one of the actors on the

[17] Robert Ulich, "The Meaning of Liberal Education" in *The Teaching of Religion in Higher Education*, edited by Christian Gauss (New York: Ronald Press, 1951), p. 53.

battleground between great ideas and stiff realities, progress and conservatism, success and failure in man's attempts to meet the challenge of change. One can include in the discussion the problem of relation between leaders and their followers, and of the strange mixture of greatness and baseness which is the very characteristic of periods of crisis.[18]

This truly is liberal teaching. This is teaching which we like to think reflects the American culture in which both teacher and taught are living, and which holds promise that it will broaden and deepen the student's understanding of the current problems of that culture and inspire him to resolve to do his part in working towards their solution. This is the very function of the liberal college, to turn out young men and women with a philosophy of life that is characterized by a deep sense of social responsibility which they will carry with them and make operative in whatever cultural situation they may find themselves after graduation from college.

In the Catholic theory of divine providence everyone is called by God to a particular vocation in which he is to serve God to the best of his ability by serving his fellow man and particularly those dependent on him. The concept of the mystical body of Christ, in which we are all members one of another, stresses this idea. Priest or plumber, surgeon or carpenter, should carry on his work animated by the same idea. This is a mandate of Christian living. But whether this means that in school the preparation for both living and earning a living is best provided for by carrying on the two activities at the same time in the same institution, is another matter. The evidence at hand tells us that there are advantages in each procedure often determined by circumstances. Prudence dictates that each individual and every institution should weigh these advantages one against the other, and make their decision in terms of the situation in which they find themselves.

[18] *Ibid.*, pp. 53 f.

Chapter 6

THE LIBERAL DISCIPLINES

Following the analysis in the preceding chapter of the liberal studies which the college should build into an integrated curriculum to bring a liberal education to its students, we turn now to the question of values with particular attention to the disciplinary values which these studies hold for those who apply themselves to them with energy and perseverance. Before doing this, however, we must call attention to a limitation that characterizes any well-planned educational program. This is the fact that it is utterly impossible to transmit through any curriculum or any combination of sequential curricula in elementary school, high school, and college, the totality of human knowledge. Comenius thought this could be done in his day, and we speak of his curriculum as pansophic. This is the great weakness of survey courses; erudition seems to be the aim. But the compilers of these courses in their efforts to pour into the minds of students great bodies of knowledge, leave the student little opportunity to have any real experience in applying the methods characteristic of a field of study, which the liberal college must do. It must face the fact that it can only introduce the student to the great fields of knowledge. But if it does this in the major areas, whether it be language and literature, the fine arts, the natural, social, and philosophical sciences, it will have conferred upon him a habit of study which there is every reason to believe will continue to function as he carries on his self-education when college days are over. Such a mind will be liberally educated in the true sense of the word. It not only will be free from ignorance of those fields with which it has come in contact; but better than that, if a student has made his own the mode of thought of any field, he will be free from the limitation of undeveloped capacities, and when faced with the necessity of assimilating further knowledge in that field, he will be prepared to dig deeply therein even though he has had no more than an introduction to it.

The Values of a School Activity

This question of values is perhaps the most important question that can be asked in planning any program of studies. The reason for this question is that the answer given to it determines not only what we put into the program, but also how we attempt to put over what we put in. Thus content and method are both involved. We lay down the principle that no subject merits a place in the curriculum unless it holds value for the student. What are the possible values that a study may hold for the college student? These may be classified as utilitarian, cultural, and disciplinary. This leads to the statement of a second principle, namely: any subject meriting a place in the curriculum will make some contribution in all three of these values. For example, Latin, selected for the foreign language to be studied, has certain utilitarian values for everyone. The vast majority of polysyllabic words that give beauty and ornamentation to English, are Latin in origin (e.g., "mansion"); whereas the monosyllabic words, for the most part symbols of the simple things of life (e.g., "house," "hound"), are Teutonic in origin. Through the use of the dictionary the vocabulary can be enriched by the addition of these polysyllabic words with an understanding of the original meaning, e.g., "manufacture," from the Latin words meaning "made by hand." Similarly cultural values may be achieved if the study of Latin is correlated with the history of the Roman Empire. In the third place a real disciplinary value can be acquired if special attention is given to the syntax of the language, comparing it with the English term expressing the same thought.

The importance of these distinctions in values is that teaching should be planned in terms of whichever value is primary. Thus, for example, one teacher of a class of slow learners in a high school that offered only Latin as a foreign language, planned her attack on the problem with one objective in mind, namely, that the pupils after two years of Latin would be able to use the missal intelligently while hearing Mass. There was no reading of Caesar's *Gallic Wars* in the second year of that class. Use was the specific objective, and this was achieved by studying the missal in class for its use at daily Mass. The earning of two units for college entrance had little interest for most of the students in this class, since in all probability they would not go to college. In addition to this, the cultural and disciplinary values were undoubtedly achieved to a greater degree than ever would have been possible if these slow learners had been taught by the traditional method with the traditional content of Latin I and Latin II.

The recent war has done much to re-establish the idea of discipline as an integral part of any process of education worthy of the name. The principle is easy to state: self-development comes through self-discipline. This has always been a characteristic emphasis in Catholic life. In the physical sphere, athletics, we call it training. In the moral sphere we call it asceticism, that is, self-imposed self-denial. This is the purpose of the seasons of penance, Advent and Lent, and of the practice of abstinence from meat on Fridays. The word "asceticism" comes from the Greek word meaning exercise, and a dictionary definition is, "spiritual exercises in the pursuit of virtue," that is, the moral virtues. Since the mind of man is a spiritual reality with no divisions, it would be strange indeed if this strengthening of the will through the practice of asceticism did not suggest a strengthening of the intellect by a similar process. In our use of the term, therefore, mental discipline as a process means mental exercises in pursuit of the intellectual virtues, or mental power. The experience of mankind throughout the ages has confirmed this interpretation. Nevertheless, in the words of Nicholas Murray Butler:

As a result of a few hopelessly superficial and irrelevant experiments, it was one day announced from various psychological laboratories that there was no such thing as general discipline and general capacity, but that all disciplines were particular and that all capacities were specific. The errant nonsense of this and the flat contradiction given to it by human observation and human experience went for nothing, and this new notion spread abroad among the homes and schools of the United States to the undoing of the effectiveness of our American education.[1]

There is a certain irony in the fact that the leader of this attack on general intellectual discipline as one of the most important phases of the educative process, was an educational psychologist from Butler's own institution, Professor Thorndike of Teachers College, Columbia University. His theory of identical elements in any learning process, and his thesis that all learning was specific, resulted in a proliferation of courses in all subjects, not only in the high school and college, but in the professional schools as well. It was the *Gestalt* psychologists who first underminded the supposedly scientific foundation of this theory and showed that transfer of training was a real outcome of learning if the learning processes were properly arranged and directed. For a Catho-

[1] *The Faith of a Liberal* (New York: Charles Scribner's Sons, 1924), pp. 110 f.

lic it is most refreshing to read a statement of this reversal in educational theory in one of the recent books on general education in which a purely secular philosophy of education is the dominant theme.

It has been shown by Tylor and others that where this capacity for generalization is made an objective of instruction, material so learned is retained longer than specific information they [the students] had learned in courses previously taken. The generalization or laws which they had learned, however, were retained nearly completely, and the student was able to apply them in the solution of problems with which he had no previous experience.[2]

The same book, however, when it discusses the organization and presentation of course materials in the curriculum of a college that is to give general education, draws a sharp distinction between the so called "functionalists" and "anti-functionalists." The former group is made up of those who contend that nothing should be taught that does not carry over and "function" in life activities; while the latter group is supposed to support the idea that knowledge for its own sake should be the only concern in the classroom. This writer is convinced that this is a false dichotomy. No two such groups ever existed. We contend that among intelligent educators no one ever held any theory that could properly be labeled "anti-functionalism." There is a difference of emphasis, of course, but the moderates of both groups have the same aim, to teach materials that will play an important part in the intellectual formation of students and carry over into their lives when school days are over.

When we attempt a descriptive definition of mental discipline, we must distinguish between process and product.

[2] *Cooperation in General Education, Final Report of the Executive Committee of the Cooperative Study in General Education* (Washington, D.C.: American Council on Education, 1947), p. 20.

Mental discipine as a process means a series of mental activities (exercises, operations) under competent guidance (the teacher), the carrying on of which results in facility, skill, and power in the performance of these activities or operations. Mental discipline as a product is the power, attitude, aptitude, or habit so generated. When applied to certain fields, this outcome is sometimes spoken of as "training in the various methodologies of thought," [3] but President Wriston of Brown University gives a fuller statement of what is meant by discipline in this connection:

Discipline, as I define it, . . . is the essential mode of thought in a field of study, the inherently characteristic mental method of attacking that kind of problem. The discipline is a type of intellectual experience involved in a successful approach to a problem of knowledge. Note that the word does not imply merely the techniques of the subject; it refers not to the form only, but to fundamentals, to essential qualities without which the subject may not be successfully mastered. Those essential elements, those intellectual ultimates, are the disciplines.[4]

Categories of Disciplines

The first category in this analysis is what we may call the disciplines of thought. Here we are attempting to identify the primary fruits of learning in such fields as history, philosophy, mathematics, and natural science. In the latter field, will a student learn to think as a scientist thinks if he studies chemistry or biology for a year? Our answer to this question is a decided affirmative, but on two conditions. The first is that the student has the intellectual ability to do abstract thinking on a fairly high level and that he puts this ability to work during the course. The second condition is the teacher; in his lectures, his direction of the student's

[3] *Ibid.*, p. 203.
[4] *The Nature of the Liberal College* (Lawrence College Press, 1937), pp. 146 f.

reading, and his conduct of experimental procedures in the laboratory, he must give a real demonstration of how a scientist thinks. The question whether in an integrated course in the natural sciences, demonstrations can replace laboratory experience, is now being debated by the experts in this field; but the general opinion seems to be that the intricate details of the experimental process thought necessary for producing the incipient scientist, are nothing less than time wasted for the general student. Nevertheless, all educators admit that there must be some experience in the laboratory even for the student of general education if he is to learn to think as a scientist thinks; that is, if he is to reap the full fruits of the discipline.

When we turn to fields like literature and the fine arts, however, we have another kind of discipline. Here we are interested primarily in an emotional attitude, although we must recognize that every emotional experience has as its base an intellectual insight and calls for some understanding. There is a third type of discipline, however, which we may call the discipline of action. Here our primary concern is human behavior. This discipline is pre-eminent in the study of the social sciences, but acquaintance with human behavior in social life is not the chief aim of study in this field. Rather, the purpose of the social sciences for the general student is the remaking of his own social life both in school and in the world when college days are over. This requires his recognizing his own responsibility as a loyal citizen in preserving and improving the social life of the community and in adding his contribution to the democratic society in which he lives. Finally, there is a discipline that pervades all fields of study, and for this reason we call it the universal discipline. It is the discipline of language, which by its very nature is the medium of instruction in all fields. It is in terms of this analysis that we now attempt to identify the chief fruits of learning in each of the fields into which in the preceding chapter we have divided the liberal studies. What are the intellectual disciplines in the different fields for which the curriculum of the liberal college should make provision so that within the time limits imposed, its students will have an opportunity to make them their own? We begin with those fields in which the development of the thinking process is the primary fruit of learning for the student.

I. THE DISCIPLINES OF THOUGHT

1. Perspective—History

History is a study of universal incidence. It plays an interesting and important role in all six of the fields of knowledge into which we have divided the spiritual inheritance of mankind.[5] Many students will come to college with two units of high-school history besides the history studied in grade school, where the history of the United States is generally presented. Further, the historical approach is the most intelligent in all divisions (except psychology) of what I call the humanistic sciences, the story of human behavior and human relations within society. We include under this term, besides history and psychology, the social sciences: politics, economics, and sociology, and even anthropology and human geography if time allows. History must necessarily be included in any intelligent introduction to these fields. But it is the discipline of history that is our primary concern, the mode of thought characteristic of the true historian, and this can be conveyed to the student through historical presentation in any field if it is well done. If the student learns to look at the past record of man in true perspective and grows in his power to discern the origin of present events in the light of the past, he has achieved the discipline of history. The assimilation of historical knowledge is secondary to the possession of this mode of thought and can

[5] See above, Figure 2, p. 75.

easily and quickly be acquired when it is necessary in any field for the intelligent interpretation of present events when attempting to meet today's problems.

History must be taught as much more than a chronological recording of events. Rather, the events must be seen as the culmination of that great variety of forces—psychological, economic, social, political, geographical, scientific, cultural—which constitute human living in an imperfect world. Consequently, the teacher of history must be a philosopher of history. He can hardly be such if a stilted education has left him a stranger to the liberal culture and intellectual discipline that helps to make the true philosopher. Further, since many of the factors in the shaping of history contain elements of religion, the instructor will need a broad background of religious knowledge in order to present this subject properly. The aim is not to produce the finished historian, but to give a view of the interrelations of historic factors and at the same time acquaint the student with sources and procedures in historical studies with the hope that these will function in later life whenever occasion calls for historical investigation. This is a broad aim, but an important one. We believe that the best name for the mode of thought—that is, the discipline—that has for its fruit this kind of thinking is perspective.

2. Unification—Philosophy

Philosophy is the synoptic science. In the literal meaning of "synoptic," philosophy brings to the student a general view of the whole universe in which he lives, including, therefore, God, man in his individual and social life, and the physical universe. The studies of these three topics, theodicy, psychology, and cosmology, are departments of special metaphysics. Behind them lie ontology, the theory of being, and epistemology, the theory of knowledge, completing the realm of speculative philosophy. In the realm of practical philosophy we may assume that the principles of aesthetics will be covered in the courses in literature, fine arts, and ontology; and the principles of logic in the trivium; but ethics should be specifically provided for so that the student may know the fundamental principles of all three of the eternal verities, the good, the true, and the beautiful. Some may question whether this can be done in the time apportioned to this field in the curriculum suggested in the next chapter [6] unless a student chooses it as his field of concentration; but we must remember that the college can only introduce the student to any field of knowledge. In the field of philosophy, however, the important thing is that the student be introduced to it as a whole; he must begin at the beginning and go through the course to the end to have a complete view of reality.

The teacher of formal philosophy in the Catholic college should be a person of learning and conviction in the philosophy of scholasticism, with an understanding of erroneous systems of thought and a broad cultural acquaintance with all the liberal arts where philosophical truth and error come into flower and fruit. Only with such broad knowledge will the teacher be able to cultivate in his students a grasp of philosophical truth that will ensure them against staggering and falling when they come into contact with the thinking in a world rife with naturalism and materialism. In Matthew Arnold's fine phrase, philosophy should train the student to "see life steadily and see it *whole*." The appropriate name, therefore, for this discipline, that is, the mode of thought that should be the fruit of study in this field, is unification.

3. Precision—Mathematics

In the field of mathematics, election of courses must be a prominent characteristic. Many students, even in a college with a selected student body, will receive little if any

[6] See below, Figure 6, p. 166.

profit from continuing the type of mathematics they studied in high school. But a course in general mathematics, beginning with arithmetic if a placement test indicates the need, will have great value for them, particularly if part of the course is devoted to the practical problems that are continually confronting everyone in the world today. Leave college algebra, trigonometry, analytical geometry, and calculus for those students who have the type of mind that can profit from the kind of abstract thinking demanded by them. Both groups, however, should to a certain extent achieve the discipline characteristic of this field.

The chief function of mathematics in the life of man today is measurement, and precision is its characteristic. When the child has learned that two plus two equals four and that they can never add up to anything else, he has had an experience that is in sharp contrast to that which he will have in those fields of knowledge where opinion is pre-eminent. An integrated course in the physical sciences will make more mathematical demands on the student than a similar course in the biological sciences, but mathematics will be used in the latter also. More important, however, than the general cultural or utilitarian values a student may reap from the study of mathematics on the college level, is the passion for precision which, when well taught, it will generate within him. Here there is only one appropriate label for the mode of thought that characterizes this study, and that is precision.

4. Objectivity—Natural Sciences

We can well imagine the storm of protest which the specialist in a natural science will raise against the proposed curriculum, since it makes no provision for his natural science in the freshman year.[7] The chemist, for example, will say, "Even if a student takes chemistry in the sophomore year, continues it for his field of concentration, and adds to

[7] See Figures 6 and 7, pp. 166 and 167.

that the twenty-four hours of electives allowed, he will have only a total of fifty-six hours of science; and we can never make a chemist out of him in that time." Our reply is: that is precisely what the liberal college should not aim to do. If a student wants to become a chemist, that is one of the functions of graduate study on the university level, but not of the liberal college. The aim of the college is to turn out young men and women with informed, cultured, and disciplined minds, not uneducated specialists. To achieve this aim in the field of science, a student's high-school experience must be viewed as part of the whole, and an intelligent selection of his courses in science should be made on that basis. One prescription can be laid down, however; namely, that at least one year of his work must be devoted to a natural science with some laboratory experience to bring the student into intimate contact with the discipline characteristic of this field.

What is the best name for this discipline? Induction has been suggested; but the philosopher, as well as the scientist, must use both induction and deduction in his thinking processes. The difference between them lies in the fact that the scientist performs his experiments in the laboratory, the clinic, or the observatory, under controlled conditions, whereas the laboratory of the philosopher is life itself. This fact suggests the name "experimentation"; but we could hardly say that this is the characteristic feature of sciences like astronomy and geology. What was it that characterized the thinking of Copernicus when he revolutionized our way of thinking about the material universe? We suggest that it was the relation of the mind to a thing as it is in itself, ignoring all predispositions. If a year's work in a natural science under a capable teacher can develop this attitude of objectivity in a student's mind, it has made a contribution to his liberal education that will free him from many a preconceived idea. We believe, therefore, that the best label for the mode of thought characterizing the natural sciences, that is, for the discipline in this field, is objectivity. The categories of the disciplines we are now presenting, along with the fields in which each is dominant, are given in Figure 5, p. 143.

II. The Discipline of Feeling and Emotion

Appreciation—Literature and the Fine Arts

For the general student the discipline characteristic of literature and the fine arts is the same. With poetry so often spoken of as the finest of the fine arts, we see how intimately these two fields are related, though working in different media. If a student does not increase his appreciation of the beautiful as a result of following a course in these fields, that course has failed. If a course in literature does not lift his leisure reading to a higher level, or a course in the fine arts does not elevate his taste so that he finds pleasure in contemplating the beautiful creations of the hand of man as well as the beauties of the natural world around him, it is time wasted.

The chief storehouse of our cultural inheritance is literature, both that which is factual and didactic and that which is imaginative and creative. In the latter is to be found the chief source of that phase of education which trains the emotions. The educated person will, therefore, require a familiarity with the great literary productions and an easy command of the language in which they are written. He will necessarily, then, study the literature of his own tongue while acquiring the ability himself to use it with precision, power, and elegance in both writing and speech.

With regard to content, the study of the great books has always been the approved approach in literature; but the point to be kept in mind is that it is better to read a few great books entirely than to sample many by reading selections, as is done in survey courses. A student's study of that litera-

Figure 5. THE LIBERAL DISCIPLINES

Categories	Disciplines	Fields of Study		
I. The Disciplines of Thought	1. Perspective 2. Unification 3. Precision 4. Objectivity	History Philosophy Mathematics Natural Sciences		
II. The Discipline of Emotion	Appreciation	Literature Fine arts	{ English { Foreign language { Visual arts { Music	
III. The Disciplines of Action	1. Responsible citizenship 2. Christian life ideals 3. Freedom 4. Intensification	Social sciences Theology { Electives { Field of primary interest { Field of concentration or Professional program	{ economic { political { sociological	
IV. The Universal Discipline	Expression	Language	{ The vernacular { Foreign languages	

ture closest to him must be more than a fleeting glimpse of all the great writers and their works. In terms of the modern college no one receives the discipline of this field by way of the customary survey course. He must study more thoroughly selected works that will deepen his understanding of his fellow men and arouse his sympathies for the tribulations they encounter and his admiration for their heroic qualities. Some teachers of literature will assert that in the liberal college no student should be allowed to graduate without a course in Shakespeare. In the two-semester course to be suggested, Master Works of World Literature, we believe it advisable to devote the first semester to the great prose writers and the second to the great poets, among whom Shakespeare would have a prominent place as the ranking genius of all the world's literatures.[8]

The Fine Arts

The educated man is one who appreciates the fine arts, not necessarily one who devotes his time to them. He will have become acquainted with them while pursuing his studies in literature, particularly in the course just outlined. Knowledge and appreciation thus gained should advisedly be expanded through concerts and visits to museums, and so forth. The fully educated man has fine taste, a cultivated sense of harmony both to the ear and to the eye, a recognition of the beauty of simplicity and restraint—all values inherent in the study of the fine arts. In the course to be suggested, one semester will be devoted to music, the other to the pictorial and plastic arts. But here again we must bear in mind that it is the discipline, in this case, the type of emotional response aroused, that is the primary concern. With appreciation developed in any section of this diversified field, we have every reason to believe that it will spread to others as life experience broadens an individual's interests and enriches his knowledge. There is only one appropriate label for the discipline that should be the fruit of study in these fields, and it is appreciation.

III. THE DISCIPLINES OF ACTION

1. Responsible Citizenship—Social Sciences

In the evolution of the social sciences, which has been going on now for many years and is still in process, they have left their original home, the house of philosophy, and set up housekeeping for themselves as separate sciences. The major

---

[8] This section on literature is based on an unpublished report made by Rt. Rev. Julius Haun before the N.C.E.A. Liberal Arts Committee.

developments were all taught as problems in social ethics until after the middle of the nineteenth century: politics, the problem of government; economics, the right of private property; and sociology, the problem of the family. For the Catholic these sciences, as they develop scientifically, will always remain ethical sciences with moral obligations pressing on every member of the community as major considerations in their presentation. No scientific technique has yet been developed common to all of them, though the statistical approach to their problems has become almost universal. But this approach never removes from the citizen the necessity of making moral judgments when planning or participating in social movements for the advancement of the community.

It is not easy to determine the best name for the intellectual discipline which characterizes study in the social sciences. President Wriston in one of his treatments of this topic uses "The Discipline of Hypothesis" as his paragraph title, but the opening sentence says the basic discipline here is that of "opinionation." [9] We have thought sometimes that a more appropriate name would be "suspended judgment." The natural sciences, of course, carry this discipline also; but it is of particular importance in the sciences dealing with man's social life. If we ask a German what were the causes of World War II, we will receive one answer. The same question put to a Frenchman will call forth another. These are opinions, as President Wriston calls them, but they rest on knowledge, although this knowledge lacks the precision characteristic of mathematics and the natural sciences. But no one should determine his opinion in any social problem until he has in his possession all the important facts bearing upon it. The recognition that much can be said on both sides of most of the problems arising within the field of human rela-

[9] Henry M. Wriston, "Nature, Scope and Essential Elements in General Education" in *General Education*, ed. by William S. Gray (Chicago: Chicago University Press, 1934), p. 11.

tions in a democratic society is most important; but that is not enough. Study of the social sciences should bring home to the student his responsibility in preserving the advantages of that society of which he is a member, and in eliminating the bad features that are all too common. This means social action of a contributing type. Since we learn what we live, if the student is not minded to make his living in those communities better than it would have been if he had not studied the social process by the scientific approach in so far as that has now been developed, it is a question whether he has gained any profit from the study. The fruit looked for in the mind of the student is the implanting of an attitude that will carry over into his worthy actions in the community.

We have already quoted the words of the past president of Johns Hopkins University, the famed geographer, Dr. Isaiah Bowman, addressing the first freshman class after World War II, when he pressed this point home to the entering students. The concluding paragraph of this address as quoted in the press bears so specifically upon the discipline which should be the fruit of studying the social sciences, that we give it here.

In time you will become scientists or engineers or humanists or economists or doctors. . . . What we can do for you is of no lasting importance if we have not taught you that citizenship comes first today in our crowded world. . . . No man can enjoy the privileges of education and thereafter with a clear conscience break his contract with society. To respect that contract is to be mature, to strengthen it is to be a good citizen, to do more than your share under it is to be noble.[10]

Social opportunity for advanced education means social obligation of a high order. It carries along with it a heavy responsibility. Responsibility here means that the student

[10] *Time,* October 21, 1946, pp. 94 f. See p. 113 for the preceding part of the address.

recognizes that he has a positive obligation to live his community life in a way that will "promote the general welfare," as the Preamble of the Constitution phrases it. Nothing less than developing in students this attitude of personal responsibility should be the aim of every teacher of the social sciences. For the teacher in the Catholic college and for the students, developing this attitude towards community living is the fulfillment of Christ's explicit commandment, "Love your neighbor as yourself." If this fruit is not achieved, knowledge gained by students in the social sciences may be a means for outwitting their fellows instead of serving them. We therefore identify the discipline of this field as responsible citizenship.

2. Christian Life Ideals—Theology

The English historian, Lecky, says, "The world is governed by its ideals." Whether this is true of the world might be disputed; but it is certainly true of individuals, and when individuals so governed are the dominant influence in a community, it is true of the community. If the ideals exerting this influence are Christian life ideals, then we have a Christian community. What do we mean by life ideals? Someone has defined ideals as "master ideas." They are master ideas because they are dynamic and move one to action. An ideal in this interpretation is an *idea* which is an intellectual insight into a life situation manifesting itself in conduct or behavior. What does the "l" stand for? We suggest that the "l" in this word stands for loyalty. Thus anyone who is animated in his everyday activities by the ideal of honesty is one who knows what honesty is and will be loyal to that idea even when such loyalty demands the sacrifice of what some would call his own best interests. Thus we have the intellectual, the emotional, and the volitional aspects of such behavior summarized in the one word, ideal.

T. S. Eliot makes this statement: "The need of the modern

world is the discipline and training of the emotions; which neither the intellectual training of philosophy or science, nor the wisdom of humanism, nor the negative instruction of psychology can give. . . . This I have found is only attainable through dogmatic religion." [11] We do not believe that implanting life ideals in the minds of the young in such a way that these ideals will become dominating influences in their everyday life is a matter of dogmatic religion alone. Dogmatic theology can give the ideas that people should live by, but developing an attitude of loyalty to these ideas is another matter. Here we are reminded of what the great English statesman, Edward Burke, said: "Example is the school of mankind; it will learn in no other." Teachers can teach the truths that men should live by, but their example is the potent influence in implanting these life ideals in the minds of students. If students come from homes where ideals of Christian life have been taught by practice as well as precept, and if the school continues this twofold teaching during these formative years of later adolescence, we have every reason to believe that these life ideals will become a part of the very being of the young who have been living under their influence.

Nor is this all that the college can do. With example as a great influence in forming the character of the young, the curriculum and outside reading can exert a powerful force through literature, by the stories of the great heroes of life, and through history, by biography and hagiography. I have described elsewhere the course in religion which I think is best for freshmen in those colleges that require religion during the first year.[12] This course uses the Bible as the text, following the liturgical year. During the first quarter the students study the historical books, where the Decalogue is

[11] "Religion without Humanism" in *Humanism and America,* ed. by Norman Foerster (New York: Farrar and Rinehart, 1930), p. 110.

[12] William F. Cunningham, C.S.C., *The Pivotal Problems of Education* (New York: Macmillan Co., 1940), pp. 254 f.

found twice, and then the moral books, where it is applied to life problems. In Advent they become familiar with the prophetical books, particularly those concerned with Christ's coming. After the Christmas holidays they cover the first part of the Synoptic Gospels, with Our Lord's temptation in the desert introducing Lent. Holy Week finds them at the Passion and Crucifixion. After Easter they consider the founding of the Church in the Acts of the Apostles, and the beginnings of the early Church in the Epistles. Thus they would become familiar, not only with the Bible and the liturgical year, but also with the life of Christ and its meaning in their lives today as members of His mystical body, the Church. The appropriate name for the fruit of such study, that is, for the discipline that should be its product, is Christian life ideals.

3. Freedom—Electives

At first sight it may seem that the suggested curriculum furnishes little opportunity for the student to experience freedom in choice of subjects; but it must be remembered that there is a certain amount of selection in all fields except philosophy. Even this field with all its required courses offers some selection, since it may be chosen as the field of concentration, and when this is done, the electives during the last two years are more than doubled. In other fields also a choice must be made. Which foreign language or which of the natural sciences shall be studied?

The most important choice of all is the field of primary interest. This may be either a field of concentration or a professional program. We are urging that, if possible, the student elect to concentrate in one of the arts or sciences to culminate his general education; but economic circumstances and the meager resources of our Catholic colleges for student aid will only too often compel a student to elect a professional program during the last two years of college. This is particularly true in the women's colleges where expenses are high and opportunities for student employment low. Here very definitely a choice of profession must be made. Is it to be teaching, nursing, library science, or secretarial service? Here we are confronted by the problem of guidance as one of the most important functions of the college. The student should be led to make intelligent choices in the light of his previous school experience, his present interests, and his probable future career. The choices he makes during these four years will hold great importance for him all the rest of his life, and making them wisely or foolishly will teach him much about the decisions he will have to make later as he takes his place in a democratic society, where freedom of choice is one of our most highly prized possessions. That is what we mean by the discipline of freedom.

4. Intensification—Field of Concentration or A Professional Program

In the peripheral curriculum, whether a field of concentration or a professional program is selected, an intensive study in one field is the chief characteristic which this choice imposes. We have advocated that concentration be made in one of the several fields of the core and spheral studies of our proposed course of liberal education; but we recognize that necessity may demand professional study. It is a common practice for universities to offer a six-year program in the liberal college and the law school leading to two bachelor degrees, one in arts and one in law. If the program is well administered, the freshman student of law will have the experience of intensive study in his law courses even though the only subject he may be carrying that has any close connection with the work of the seniors in the liberal college is ethics, and this will be legal ethics. But intensive study should be the chief characteristic of his work here, and this is commonly the case since now the student has vocational motivation for applying himself with vigor to the mastery of his profession. The name we suggest for this discipline is, therefore, intensification.

IV. THE UNIVERSAL DISCIPLINE

Expression—Language

When we come to identify the discipline that should be the fruit of the study of languages (both the vernacular and foreign languages), we set this off by itself and classify it as the universal discipline. The reason is that, as the medium of instruction in all other studies, training in the vernacular is common to all of them. This is true in the study of foreign languages even when taught by the direct method with the vernacular seldom used, since at first a student is thinking in his own language and only later develops the ability to think in a second language. The difficulties encountered when one attempts to express exactly in a foreign language an idea that is clear in the word symbols of the vernacular, constitute a particularly severe discipline in the use of language. So also when a student takes up a new study in science, whether natural, humanistic, or philosophical, his first job is to become familiar with the technical vocabulary proper to that science. Without such familiarity he can never make his own the methodology of that science. Likewise in literature, particularly in poetry, if his emotional reactions are going to be aroused to the degree that he can be said to have any appreciation of poetry, he must have a command of the language in which the poetry is written that carries him far beyond its everyday use in conversation or reading the newspaper. The most important consideration to be kept in mind in this connection is that language is the most effective tool of thought as well as of communication.

The arts of language are multiple, but basic to them all is grammar, the science of word symbols and their combinations. The science of grammar we are referring to is universal or general grammar, "the science concerned with the general principles which underlie the grammatical phenomena of all languages." [13] Teachers of freshman English and foreign languages will ordinarily spend considerable time reviewing the particular grammar of the language they are teaching, but this is their opportunity to introduce the student to the principles of universal grammar. Universal grammar is introductory logic. In the course on the trivium which we are recommending in chapter 7, universal grammar leads through logic to rhetoric. The course may be described in these words: The trivium, a unified discipline in which grammar is the science and art of the symbols of thought; logic, the science and art of the rules of correct thought; and rhetoric, the science and art of applying these rules in the use of these symbols in the effective communication of thought.

Foreign Language

We are reminded here of the situation that was in vogue before departmentalization invaded secondary schools, when one teacher taught all the subjects in each class division. Correlation was a reality then. Today an attempt is being made to train teachers of freshman English to include in their courses universal grammar with logic and rhetoric, but even this doesn't bring in the foreign-language element. I will never forget my introduction to foreign language, in my case, Latin. In the elementary school I had learned all the rules of English grammar and could repeat the definitions of all the parts of speech, but this knowledge was not functional until I began the study of foreign language. Then for the first time I really understood what a noun, a verb, etc., really were, and what part they play in language. Possibly this experience is more likely to come at the beginning of the study of a foreign language; but even when a foreign language begun

[13] *Oxford Universal Dictionary.*

in high school is continued in college (and this is preferable to beginning a different one, since in the latter case there is little likelihood that either will be learned well), college teachers in their review of the grammar of the language they are teaching should introduce the student to universal grammar before passing on to the study of literature. Here they can reinforce the emphasis of the trivium so that students will really have an understanding of the science of language and a real introduction to its artistic use. We must remember that we are dealing with a twofold ability, the ability to communicate one's own thought in clear and forceful language (writing and speaking) and the ability to comprehend the thought of others when so communicated (reading and listening). The best name for the discipline acquired with this twofold ability of expressing one's own thought effectively and of comprehending the expressed thought of others is the very word which must be used in stating this idea, namely, expression.

Liberation through the Disciplines

If the ideal fruits of study just described are achieved in any adequate degree, the student while undergoing these experiences has been undergoing a process of real liberation, the very aim of training in the liberal arts. In this case we have three freedoms. The first is freedom from ignorance, for the student has come in contact with all the great fields of knowledge, at least in their theoretical aspect, and is now ready to deepen his knowledge in these fields and work out applications as occasions may demand. In the second place he is freed from undeveloped capacities and has developed abilities that make him an educated person, the powers of thought and expression. And in the third place he is freed from the domination of animal impulses by motivation through human ideals or, as the Catholic would state it, Christian ideals. This surely is a goal high enough for any liberal college; but for a college that is truly Catholic, nothing less than this is acceptable.

We conclude this chapter with a warning to the reader that he should not interpret our attempt to identify the disciplines of the different fields of study as meaning that these disciplines can be achieved only in one field. Just the contrary is the case. To a certain extent all these mental disciplines are common to all fields. Thus precision, for example, perhaps the most limited of all, is certainly not restricted to mathematics. It is experienced also in the study of the grammar of any language, and it is dominant in logic; but since it is pre-eminent in the study of mathematics, we identify it as the chief discipline that all students during their period of general education should acquire through study in this field. So, too, with all the other disciplines. Appreciation of the mysteries of the physical universe surely should be a fruit of the study of the natural sciences, but such an emotional response is pre-eminent in the fields of literature and the fine arts.

CHAPTER 7

AN INTEGRATED LIBERAL-COLLEGE
CURRICULUM

AFTER reviewing the fields of knowledge, the liberal studies, and the liberal disciplines that play an integral part in any education meriting the name "liberal," we see the difficulty of the problem that confronts the college. How can all these elements be brought together into a unified whole? With four distinct fields in the core studies that form the base and should permeate the whole, and with five fields in the spheral studies that are to give breadth, balance, and symmetry to the whole, no one questions the fact that integration is the most pressing problem in general or liberal education today. The common solution at present is to group all these fields into three major areas: natural science, social science, and the humanities. In this grouping ordinarily the term "humanities" embraces three of the fields that were the fruit of our analysis: the philosophical sciences, the arts of communication, and the fine arts.[1] Only denominational colleges include religion or theology as one of the philosophical sciences; but it is interesting to note the attention that the Cooperative Study in General Education of the American Council on Education gave to the question of the student's philosophy of life. In chapter 4, "Major Projects in the Humanities," fifteen pages are devoted to this topic.[2] With reference to the fine

[1] See above, Figure 2, p. 75.
[2] *Cooperation in General Education* (Washington, D.C.: American Council on Education, 1947), pp. 83–90.

155

arts, our point of view is that this distinction between the arts and sciences is fundamental and should be preserved, although we realize, of course, that if integration is to take place, the distinction must not eventuate in separation. Knowledge and skill are so intimately connected in most fields that they must be sought together, as far as possible, without permitting the distinction between them to disappear. Before turning our attention to the specific problem of drawing up a curriculum with the aim of effecting integration in the student's college education, we lay down several principles to guide us in this difficult task.

I. PRINCIPLES OF OPERATION

In the proliferation of the arts and sciences with the introduction of the departmental and elective systems, we point out that, although the Catholic college has been much more conservative than the secular college, nevertheless our institutions followed the general trend of multiplying courses, with resulting confusion in the college student's experience. If we consider the unity that characterized the curriculum of the Renaissance secondary school as the Catholic tradition, we must recognize that to a certain extent this movement towards integration is a return to Catholic tradition. This means for us that we should be leaders in the movement and not mere followers. Our characteristic conservatism, however, has been holding us back. A review of the literature of the movement reveals that the great difficulty secular educators are laboring under is the fact that there is no philosophy of life (and, therefore, of education) on which they can agree. Here we have a great advantage. With the same theology and the same philosophy of life held by all, we ought to be able to proceed from this basis and work out a plan in education which in essentials, at least, will be common to all. With this in mind we lay stress on the following principles.

1. Concentration

The first principle, concentration, concerns the number of courses a student should carry in college. Here is a phase of the problem of integration in which we can learn much from secular educators. We are referring to the multiplication of courses within the college curriculum, where to the five courses meeting three times a week, commonly carried by the college student, Catholic colleges add a sixth course in theology. Little wonder that the students' energies are dissipated when distributed over so many fields! In contrast with this plan, university colleges like Harvard and Chicago, for example, limit the number of courses to four, so that a student can diligently apply himself to the fields he is studying. We contend that if integration is to be effected, this procedure of concentration should be followed. We can thus state this principle: The student's time should be distributed over four fields; that is, he should not carry more than four courses. In the upper biennium, concentration means that half or more than half of his time should be devoted to one field of study, his field of primary interest, commonly spoken of as his major.

2. Progressive Freedom

When a student passes from high school to college, it is assumed that, though still an adolescent, he is well on his way to maturity and therefore more self-dependent. Thus he should spend less time in class under the tutorial direction of the teacher and more time by himself as maturity advances. In high school he has been attending at least twenty classes per week, and in the Catholic high school two or more are usually added for classes in religion. It would seem sufficient, therefore, if a college student spent seventeen or eighteen hours a week in class during his freshman and sophomore years, and fifteen hours during the last two years, to be followed by a maximum of twelve hours if he continues in the graduate school. We may thus state our second principle: The student's time in class should be limited to seventeen or eighteen hours during the first two years, and to fifteen hours during the last two years. Common sense indicates this arrangement provides that the bachelor degree should be awarded for 128 hours as a minimum or 132 hours as a maximum.

3. Measured Achievement

The credit complex is the curse of the American high school and college. This system indicates the time spent in class rather than actual achievement. A more satisfactory measure would be comprehensive examinations in the liberal arts and sciences which constitute the content of liberal education. Most colleges will not dare to drop the credit system at once. The transition to this desideratum, however, can easily be made if the credit is made a requirement for admission to the comprehensive examinations in the major fields of learning, the satisfactory passing of which, not the amassing of credits, determines graduation. Once this principle has been operating effectively in any college for some time, the credit will be dropped as an encumbrance to effective study.

4. Variant Capacity

The students who attend college usually are a selected group, but even so, the great diversity of student ability and student attitude towards hard work is an outstanding characteristic of the student body in every college. The real problem is not the acceleration of the brighter students, but their present retardation by keeping pace with the average students. By every measure that has ever been made, the brighter students mature more rapidly than their fellows, not only physically and mentally, but also socially. Administrative

procedures should therefore be introduced to make it possible for them to cover more ground in less time than the
average student does, since they are the ones who most
frequently will go on to graduate and professional schools.
Some should complete college in three years or less; some
could save a semester, and others with a summer session or
two could complete the work of college in less than three
calendar years. But every student should work at his capacity.
This means that the lower quarter of the student body may
need more time to cover the curriculum than the average
student in the two middle quarters. If the upper quarter is
allowed to carry a fifth course, this principle is not in conflict with the first two principles we have formulated above,
since students in this group will not only do the same work
as the average student in less time, but, working at capacity,
they will do more and better work in less time than the
average student who needs four years to complete the requirements for a degree.

II. Lower Biennium Courses

We turn now to the problem of laying out an integrated
curriculum for a Catholic liberal college. We call attention
first of all to the fact that we present this as a "specimen" curriculum. By this we mean that we do not expect any college
to put this curriculum into operation without changes which
will make it more adaptable to the situation in which that
college finds itself. In reorganizing its curriculum every college must study its students, the staff available or to be acquired, and its facilities: library, laboratories, and so forth.
There is a general agreement, of course, with regard to the
ultimate aim of Catholic college education; but the proximate or specific aims will change to a certain extent according to the type of student body a college is serving. Hence it
is necessary to analyze these specific aims and to plan the
educational program, staff, and facilities accordingly. We

begin our analysis of the courses to be conducted during the first two years of college by distinguishing between what we will call tool courses and field courses.

1. Tool Courses

The most important of the tool courses is the study of the vernacular language, which for years has been demanded of all students as Freshman English. Here is the one instance in which the leadership in striving for integration has been held by Catholic colleges. It would be of some interest to know how the three disciplines of logic, grammar, and rhetoric became separated instead of being taught as a single discipline in the art of communication; but this is not our problem here. Rather, our concern is to unite them again. Logic is the science and art of correct thinking, that is, the rules of thought. Grammar (universal grammar) is the science and art of using the symbols of thought, which are words; and rhetoric is the science and art of following these rules in the use of these symbols for the effective communication of thought. The poet Milton thus emphasizes the unitary character of these disciplines in the preface to his *Art of Logic:*

The general matter of the general arts is either reason or speech. They are employed either in perfecting reason for the sake of proper thinking, as in logic, or in perfecting speech, and that either for the sake of the correct use of words, as in grammar, or in the effective use of words, as in rhetoric. Of all the arts the first and most general is logic, then grammar, and last of all rhetoric, since there can be much use of reason without speech, but no use of speech without reason. We give the second place to grammar because the correct speech can be unadorned; but it can hardly be adorned before it is correct.

For years Freshman English has been taught in Catholic colleges as a three-hour course for two semesters, with logic as a three-hour course for another semester. By uniting these subjects in a single course, time could be saved. What we are recommending in the curriculum, therefore, is a single course, the trivium, of four hours per week, in which logic, grammar, and rhetoric will be taught together for two semesters, giving eight credit hours instead of nine. (See Figures 6 and 7, pp. 166 and 167.) Here is a comment by a secondary-school teacher in an excellent article on this situation in high-school composition courses.

In a monograph on *Instruction in English* issued by the U.S. Office of Education (1933), under a grouping of 18 specific aims of written composition, the 15th is: "Think clearly and honestly, forming independent judgments." The numerical placement of that aim was indicative of the alarmingly small number of junior, senior, or four-year high school teachers that had even mentioned it amongst their objectives in teaching composition.[3]

It is unlikely that a student can be made capable of logical thought, straight-forward expression, and effective discourse without integrated training in the fundamentals of logic, grammar, and rhetoric. But the three should be taught together, and a text is now available for such a presentation.[4] This integrated course would cover the four closely related areas of the language arts, reading and writing, speaking and listening, and it would be a mistake to let it continue to be dominated by the literary tradition of the old course which came to us from England. One writer commenting on the traditional introductory course for freshmen, says, "It was designed to serve the student's needs in advanced literature rather than his general needs in all subjects and his extra-

[3] Sister Ann Gertrude, "Disciplining Reason Through the Teaching of English Composition" in the *N.C.E.A. Catholic High School Quarterly*, January, 1950, p. 31.
[4] Sister Miriam Joseph, *The Trivium in College Composition*, St. Mary's College, Notre Dame, Indiana (revised ed.).

school language needs." [5] But with the emphasis shifted to the arts of communication, there is still need for the student to be trained in clear thinking; hence, the importance of logic as an integral part of the course.

The second tool course is foreign language. We have already referred to the fact that foreign-language teachers have a wonderful opportunity for teaching general grammar (the science of language) when they are emphasizing important points in the grammar of the language they are teaching. This calls for close cooperation with the English teachers. When foreign-language courses are advanced enough to be dealing with the literature of the language, here again close cooperation with the teachers of the course to be referred to later, Master Works of World Literature, is an absolute necessity if integration is to be achieved. Students from the classes in a foreign literature should report in the class in World Literature on the great books they are reading in the original tongue. No one is fully educated who knows only his mother tongue. Since he obviously cannot master all tongues, he should concentrate on one foreign language; but this should be pursued until he can use it with ease, and that use should be applied to the study of the major classics of its literature. The beginning of a student's mastery of a foreign language belongs properly to precollege education; at the collegiate level he should be concerned with the literature itself, where the impact of thoughts and emotions may be experienced by minds approaching maturity. Since all Western literature is permeated by the literary arts and thought of classical antiquity, the best preparation for the full development of the literary values in an educated man will be training in the classics on the collegiate level.

With regard to a speaking knowledge of a foreign language, the American school is in a situation very different from the

[5] Kenneth Winetrout, "Communications," *The Journal of Higher Education,* February, 1950, p. 87.

European. There people speaking a foreign language are so close that any travel at all creates the necessity of speaking other languages. Therefore the motivation for study there is very different from that of the American student. The armed forces showed what could be done in learning to speak a foreign language in a very short time, but this required living the language all day and often into the night, which is impossible in college. Hence a reading knowledge seems to be the highest aim the American college can set for itself; but the test of this ability should be the satisfactory passing of an examination (not the mere accumulation of credits) as a requirement for entrance to the upper two years of college. Club activities can often aid in developing a speaking knowledge of the language if there are foreign students on the campus who are willing to cooperate in the project.

The third tool course is mathematics. This presents the most difficult problem of all. We do not believe it should be a requirement for all college students, for some seem to have reached the limit of intellectual activity in this field with the study of algebra and geometry in high school. In the integrated courses to be referred to below, the students will have to use what mathematics they have, and the use of this tool should be a valuable part of their general education, but it cannot be on a very high level. For those students who have the ability and who will have to use mathematics throughout their later years, there seems to be no choice but to let them take mathematics in their freshman year in place of a foreign language, making up this latter requirement in their sophomore year. (See below, Figure 6, p. 166.)

2. Field Courses

There has always been general agreement on the necessity of the tool courses, but we cannot say the same concerning the necessity of what we are here calling "field courses," that is, courses covering a wide area of knowledge. The common objection is that they inevitably become superficial because they attempt to cover too broad a field. The name "survey" made them susceptible to such attacks. If, however, they really become "integrated" courses, they will hold values for the student that no specialized course could possibly have. If the result for the student is seeing as a whole the area covered, and if he has delved deeply into certain parts of it so that he has some concept of its depth, this experience should be one of the most valuable phases of his general education. Hence, the procedure is not to survey, but to pick out certain highlights and go thoroughly enough into them to reveal the profundity that the field holds for the one who concentrates his study within it.

Many Catholic colleges, particularly the women's colleges, have now been presenting courses in the humanities for several years. They feel that they have passed the experimental period, having now well-organized syllabi available to students. St. Catherine's College in St. Paul, for example, was one of the cooperating colleges in the Cooperative Study in General Education already referred to.[6] The courses in the humanities for the most part lean heavily upon history, literature, and the fine arts. This blending of the social sciences and the arts we do not believe to be the best approach. Our recommendation will be that the arts be considered by themselves, although, of course, there will be cross currents of thought wherever integration is the aim. But so far as we know, none of these courses has attempted to make theology the core. This is what we are now proposing in the course called World Civilization and Christian Culture. (See below, Figure 6, p. 166.)

If we really believe, as we so frequently state, that religion or theology is the social science par excellence, then by its very nature it should be the heart of our teaching in this field. Can it be this if it is set off as a separate course? We

[6] See above, note 2.

realize that this suggestion that we discontinue teaching theology as a separate course during the first year of college and integrate it with history and the social sciences is a radical departure from the common practice; but we feel that the situation is such that this procedure merits careful consideration. The continual complaint of pastors that college graduates returning to the parish do not take an active part in parish activities gives us real evidence of a need here. Our college graduates should be the leaders. This is the way one Catholic educator describes the present situation:

We have failed miserably in presenting the Church's full social doctrine—and yet social doctrine is what men live by in their daily contacts with the world. Our people are not familiar with the papal encyclicals. They do not have an understanding and feeling for the Mystical Body of Christ. They do not grasp the rich historical-religious heritage that is theirs.

Secondly, there is a weakness in the way we teach. Ironically, we, who have the living truth, fail to teach dynamically. Labor problems, race problems, international problems, all these and many more refuse to come alive. If students get any of the principles concerning these things they get them as detached situations divorced from their daily lives.[7]

Or as Maritain expressed the same idea, "We are still in a pre-historical age in regard to the application of the principles of the Gospel to the Social Order." [8] Would integrating theology with the social sciences prove to be any help here? We will never know unless we try it. Could the dogmatic, sacramental, and moral aspects of our theology become more meaningful in the lives of students if their development was traced through the centuries as they affected the lives of the

[7] John A. Elliot, "The Challenge of Catholic Education," *N.C.E.A. Catholic High School Quarterly*, January, 1949, p. 4.

[8] Jacques Maritain, *The Natural Law and Human Rights* (Windsor, Ontario: Christian Culture Press, 1942), quoted in the Preface by J. Stanley.

Figure 6. AN INTEGRATED CURRICULUM FOR A LIBERAL COLLEGE

LOWER BIENNIUM
Freshman Year

	Semester Hours			Year's Total
	1st Sem.	*2nd Sem.*	*Total*	
World Civilization and Christian Culture (humanistic sciences with theology as the core)	5	5	10	
The Trivium (grammar, logic, rhetoric)	4	4	8	
Natural Sciences (physical or biological, or both)	4	4	8	
Foreign Language (continued from high school) or Mathematics	4	4	8	
	17	17	34	34

Sophomore Year

World Civilization and Christian Culture (continued)	5	5	10	
Master Works of World Literature	3	3	6	
Fine Arts (music or the visual arts, or both)	3	3	6	
Electives	6	6	12	
	17	17	34	34

Comprehensive Examinations
{
1. The arts of communication
2. Theology and humanistic sciences
3. Natural sciences
4. A foreign language (reading knowledge)
}

UPPER BIENNIUM
Junior Year

Philosophy	4	4	8	
Field of Concentration or Professional Program } Field of Primary Interest	8	8	16	
Electives	3	3	6	
	15	15	30	30

Senior Year

Philosophy	4	4	8	
Field of Primary Interest (continued)	8	8	16	
Electives	3	3	6	
	15	15	30	30
Total for four years				128

Comprehensive Examinations
{
1. Philosophy
2. Field of primary interest)
}

Figure 7. STRUCTURE AND FUNCTION
of the
COLLEGE CURRICULUM

1. Distribution—Lower Biennium

Freshman Year 34 hrs.	10 hrs. World Civilization and Christian Culture	Foreign Language or Mathematics 8 hrs.	The Trivium 8 hrs.	Natural Sciences 8 hrs.
Sophomore Year 34 hrs.	(Theology, the core) 10 hrs.	Fine Arts 6 hrs.	World Literature 6 hrs.	Electives 12 hrs.
	2. Concentration—Upper Biennium			
Junior Year 30 hrs.	Philosophy 8 hrs.	16 hrs. Field of Primary Interest 16 hrs.		Electives 6 hrs.
Senior Year 30 hrs.	Philosophy 8 hrs.			Electives 6 hrs.

Total, 128 hrs.   3. Integration—Both Bienniums

The Three Functions

1. Distribution: lower biennium, students' time distributed over the five fields of knowledge.
2. Concentration: upper biennium, more than one half of student's time concentrated through a sequence in one field (or problem integrating several fields) or in a professional program.
3. Integration: lower biennium, through theology; upper biennium, through philosophy.

Note: The field of primary interest in the upper biennium calls for 32 credit hours. This is more than half the class time of these two years. If a student selects the natural sciences or a particular science within the group as his field of concentration and is allowed to choose his electives within the same field with no distribution among the other fields of knowledge to broaden his general education, he would have 24 hours more, 12 hours of electives in the sophomore year and 12 in the upper biennium. To these must be added the 8 hours in science required of all students in the freshman year. Altogether he would have 64 hours of science, one half of the total class hours in college (128). Whether such a procedure would be persons living in those times? Again, we will never know unless we give the plan a trial. I am thinking particularly of colleges for men where for years students have been required to take during the first two years a two-hour course in theology and a three-hour course in history or the social sciences. We propose putting the two courses together in a five-hour course for four semesters.

Two books are now available describing in detail this movement to build an integrated course in the social sciences; one is the outcome of the Cooperative Study in General Education by the American Council on Education;[9] the other was made possible by a subvention from the Carnegie Corporation.[10] More than twenty institutions are included in each study. There is general agreement in the two studies that the problem is threefold: (1) determination of objectives, both ultimate and proximate, (2) organization of materials, and (3) methods of presentation. The ultimate objective that seems to be almost universally agreed upon is the development in students of responsible citizenship in a democratic society. This fits in with the Catholic philosophy of life except that for us citizenship in the kingdom of heaven is the ultimate goal, and responsible citizenship here and now is a mediate goal; that is, a means to the achievement of that final goal. Here we have the twofold commandment of the New Law: love God, the Father of all, and love your neighbor for the sake of God. The proximate goals commonly accepted are a knowledge and understanding of society as a whole and its more important problems today, and with this

---

wise is determined by the answer to this question: Is the purpose of the liberal college to produce an educated person who will function adequately as a citizen of a free society in any life career, or is it to turn out the uneducated specialist, an expert highly trained in one narrow field?

[9] Albert William Levi, *General Education in the Social Studies* (Washington, D.C.: American Council on Education, 1948).

[10] Earl J. McGrath, *Social Science in General Education* (Dubuque, Iowa: William C. Brown Co., 1948).

comes familiarity with the techniques now used by the social sciences in understanding these problems and in working towards their solution.

With regard to content and organization, McGrath, in the conclusion of his *Social Science in General Education,* lists six types roughly distinct from one another: survey, historical development, social problems, mixture of the latter two, values, and the case method.[11] He says that the first is "rapidly becoming an extinct species," whereas the second and third "enjoy about equal popularity." In his *General Education in the Social Studies,* Levi's listing is fourfold: the historical, the problem, and the systematic approach, and a "mixture of all three." [12] In any college the decision regarding the type of organization to be adopted must be left, of course, to the members of the staff preparing the syllabus; but I cannot help but feel that in an institution making theology the core of the course, the mixed type would be the most valuable. Looking through the descriptions in the two books mentioned above of the many courses now being offered, it is evident that to a certain extent almost all of them belong to this type. The study by the American Council on Education assigns the first two years of college as the period for general education, and in chapter 11, "Organization and Content," devotes seventy-two pages to descriptions and detailed outlines of a proposed two-year sequence. This is a great help for any institution wishing to establish a course of this type. As presented in McGrath's book, the two-year sequence at Columbia University is primarily historical, whereas at Florida University it is definitely of the mixed type.

There are two methods of presenting such a course: by a single teacher, or by a group of teachers from the different departments working under a director who shares the teach-

[11] *Ibid.,* pp. 276–83.
[12] *Op. cit.,* p. 226.

ing. There are evident advantages for each method. The difficulty with the single teacher is finding teachers who are qualified to teach in all the fields included in the course. The special training of teachers already employed is the only way to meet the difficulty for the present; but here is a challenge to our graduate schools which we will discuss at some length in our chapter on the education of the college teacher. (See below, pp. 199 ff.)

The two-year courses we are proposing would offer a great opportunity to stress the importance of the lay apostolate through Catholic Action and the concept of the mystical body, in which we are all "members of one another" within the Church founded by Christ to bring salvation to all. We have no final answer to these questions of content and method, but we can lay down certain conditions that have to be met if there is to be any hope that this arrangement will achieve the objective aimed at: the integration of theology and religion with the student's life in college and his life in the parish when college days are over. Here are the conditions we propose:

1. Students who could satisfactorily pass a Religious Placement Test. Those failing this test would have to receive special instruction on the fundamentals of their religion; but even these could profit by the course and with due application could pass the comprehensive examination required at the end of the two years, one section of which would be on theology and its influence in molding Christian civilization.

2. A staff to organize and conduct the course. This staff should be selected from among those who believe in the course and are willing to work "over and above what's in the bond" to make it a success. It would be composed of:

a. A director in general charge, who will supervise the course both years and also teach.

b. Other instructors for the different sections, meeting

the conditions stated above, who would prepare that part of the syllabus which they will use as the basis for their presentation in class, and who will work with the others to make the syllabus a coherent whole.

c. Among these instructors might well be a theologian, a teacher of political science, a historian, an economist, a sociologist, a psychologist, and one trained in the science of education. Other departments which could make a real contribution to this course are anthropology and geography. The geography needed is human geography rather than physical, though it is true that the two can hardly be separated. In the small colleges and sometimes in university colleges two or more of the functions listed would be performed by a single teacher.

3. A carefully organized syllabus. We recommend a "Catholic Curriculum Workshop" in the early summer, in which at least several colleges conducting such courses (or planning to do so) and other courses similar to them, would meet for exchange of experiences. St. Augustine states the ideal situation beautifully in these words: "Each one learning from the other and in turn teaching him." [13]

We feel that such a course would be in perfect harmony with these words of Pope Pius XI's encyclical, *Christian Education of Youth:*

[13] St. Augustine, *Confessions,* Book I, chap. 8. The Catholic University in Washington, D.C., conducted a workshop on the college curriculum in the summer of 1947, the proceedings of which are available under the title *Integration in the Catholic College.* (See the Selected Readings.) The topic for the 1950 workshop was "Discipline and Integration in the Catholic College." The announcement reads: "The morning lectures will deal with the general problem of discipline in a Catholic college. The seminars, in the afternoon, will take up the problems raised by the necessity for integrating the studies in each of the major departments of a Catholic college." The discipline treated in the morning lectures is moral discipline, not intellectual; but five of the afternoon seminars are concerned with the problem we are treating here, the integration of the curriculum by means of theology and philosophy.

For the mere fact that a school gives some religious instruction (often extremely stinted), does not bring it into accord with the rights of the Church and of the Christian family, or make it a fit place for Catholic students. To be this, it is necessary that all the teaching and the whole organization of the school, and its teachers, syllabus and textbooks in every branch, be regulated by the Christian spirit, . . . so that Religion may be in very truth the foundation and crown of the youth's entire training.[14]

Then follows a quotation from an encyclical by Pope Leo XIII, which contains this statement, "If this sacred atmosphere does not pervade and warm the hearts of masters and scholars alike, little good can be expected from any kind of learning, and considerable harm will often be the consequence." Our conviction is that a well-planned and well-taught two-year course in the social sciences with theology as core, and required of all Catholic students, would do more to create "this sacred atmosphere" in a college than any series of courses in theology alone that could be devised.

The years of work involved in planning such a course is indicated by the experience of Columbia University College. Beginning in 1919, the college later published a source book entitled *Introduction to Contemporary Civilization in the West,* in which the student is put in contact with the writings of great thinkers of the West. This was accompanied by a *Contemporary Civilization Manual.* Now the work is available in two volumes entitled *Chapters in Western Civilization.* One reviewer of these two volumes makes this comment:

If there is any point at which the program of the *Chapters* breaks down seriously, it is in the inadequate account of the Christian story and experience which are the starting points of Western civilization. It might be that we see here a consequence of the orientation toward the present which is emphasized in the

[14] Edition by The America Press (1936), p. 27.

Preface. More likely it is merely the persistence of an earlier secular and rationalist tradition which could chronicle but which could not understand Christianity.[15]

This criticism, with its reference to the "secular and rationalist tradition," brings out the importance of the course which we are suggesting should be introduced by our Catholic colleges, in which theology will be the core, and the influence of religion in the lives of people throughout the ages will receive major emphasis. If it is well planned and well conducted, we cannot conceive any experience of greater value for the college student of today who soon will be immersed in a world in which secularization of both thought and action is the outstanding characteristic.

Integrated Courses in the Natural Sciences

If we admit many possible methods of presenting an integrated course in the philosophical and humanistic sciences such as we have been describing, this same fact will soon become evident when we turn to the problem of integration in the natural sciences. For a long time the procedure here has been to train specialists for the scientific world of today, and the student, if he took any science at all, had to take an elementary course designed to lay the foundation for future specialization. Such courses for the most part failed to meet the needs of the general student. We have stressed the paramount need here as that of bringing to the student the discipline of science, objectivity, through which he learns to eliminate prejudice and predetermination and to suspend judgment until the facts are known. Can this be done without demanding that the student become familiar with the enormous mass of detail always found in the elementary courses of the special sciences? The answer is that it must be done,

[15] F. Edward Cranz, Connecticut College, "Primarily for Students" in *The Journal of Higher Education,* February, 1950, pp. 108 f.

and for the past quarter of a century many colleges have been experimenting with new courses the aim of which is to do this.

The Cooperative Study of the American Council on Education referred to above does not seem to have brought to a satisfactory conclusion any findings it may have made in this field. At least it has brought forth no volume dealing with the integration of the natural sciences like its volume entitled *General Education in the Social Studies*. There is, however, the result of another study conducted by Earl J. McGrath, then dean of the College of Liberal Arts of the State University of Iowa (later Commissioner of Education, Office of Education, Washington, D.C.), which has done a remarkable job in presenting a general picture of this movement in the natural sciences.[16] Between an introductory section, "Science Courses in General Education" (pp. 1–22), and a concluding section by McGrath himself, "Trends in Science in General Education" (pp. 381–400), are given the accounts of what is being done on this problem in more than twenty different institutions throughout the country.[17]

As an illustration of the helpfulness of this volume, we include the statement that McGrath makes describing "why" and "how" the shift from survey to integrated courses has taken place in this field:

Though there is considerable variation from institution to institution in the purposes, content and organization of these courses, certain common features are apparent. They are like

[16] *Science in General Education* (Dubuque, Iowa: William C. Brown Company, 1948).

[17] Unfortunately not a single Catholic institution is included in the group. A few Catholic colleges are attempting to work out a solution of this pressing problem in the college curriculum today. When they believe that they have met with some success in their undertaking, they should make their experiences known. Among Catholic colleges now offering integrated courses in the natural sciences are the following: Marymount College, Los Angeles; St. Joseph's College, Collegeville, Indiana; and St. Xavier's College, Chicago.

neither survey nor elementary courses. They do not cover a large body of material in all the various sciences, nor encompass all the details of one. These new courses for the non-specialist treat intensively a few selected topics, laws or problems in several sciences without supplying all the connecting tissue of detailed fact included in the earlier survey courses. In the physical sciences, for example, a course of this type customarily includes material from physics, chemistry and geology, and sometimes astronomy and mathematics. Since such courses, however, usually consist of only two or three lecture-demonstrations, a discussion section, and commonly, though not always, several hours of laboratory, the necessity for a discriminating selection of topics from the constituent sciences is obvious, if superficiality is to be avoided on the one hand and fractionation on the other. Makers of general science courses have tried to steer between the Scylla of shallowness and the Charybdis of fragmentation by treating a few topics intensively to assure thoroughness, while at the same time tying the topics together with the connecting thread of scientific method, or some other binding principle. To stress the cooperative character of the scientific enterprise and the unity of scientific thought, problems are selected to which several of the sciences have contributed.[18]

We can see from this statement how the problem is twofold, one of purposes and one of procedures. There seems to be a rather general agreement on the main purposes to be aimed at: an acquaintance with the scientific method, an introduction to the history and philosophy of science, and an understanding of the impact of science on modern life; but when it comes to procedures, these are as various as the institutions themselves. Since the movement is still in the experimental stage and must necessarily remain so for some time, we may expect variations in the methods employed. The first problem of the Catholic college is to determine if

[18] *Op. cit.,* p. 383.

possible what modifications should be made in the purposes of education in science in Catholic colleges if it is to be Christ-centered, as we all agree it should be, instead of being world-centered.

Masterworks of World Literature

We have suggested above that an introduction to the great masterpieces of the world's literature is such an integral part of liberal education that this cannot be adequately provided for in a course in the humanities concerned primarily with the philosophical and humanistic sciences. It is easy to determine the specific objective of such a course, which merits separate presentation. It must elevate the student's taste in his leisure reading both in college and after college days are over. If it does not achieve this end, the course has failed. Once this objective has been accepted, we see the futility of anything approaching a survey course since such a course, giving attention to so many separate works of the world's literature, makes it impossible for the student to read in their entirety a few of the truly great books. If emphasis is placed here, superficiality will be avoided. If a student can be led to see the greatness of a few works of the masters, he will not waste his time on trivialities. A teacher who succeeds in this effort has made a contribution to the liberal education of the student which is immeasurable. It is a difficult task, but certainly one that merits inclusion as a separate course in the curriculum of a liberal college.

The Visual Arts and Music

The aim of courses in the fine arts (the visual arts and music) is appreciation, a love for the beautiful; but here the mediums are different, the sense of sight and the sense of sound. For a long time these fields found no place in the college curriculum at all. Something was achieved indirectly, of course, if the college campus, the architecture, and the interior decorations were beautiful; but this matter is so important in the life of modern man that we believe specific instruction in the fine arts merits a place in the curriculum. We cannot hope to bring the student in close enough contact with all the fine arts that his enjoyment of them will be an outcome of his experience with all of them. We maintain that general mental discipline is a reality in the life of everyone and that it can be provided for by intelligent teaching. If real enjoyment of the beautiful in one field is developed in a student, we believe that it will inevitably pass over to other fields of art, since all are so intimately connected. The extracurricular activities, of course, can be of great help, particularly in music. With the phonograph and the radio today it should be possible to develop in all students an appreciation of good music. But colleges for men have been particularly remiss here. We hold that the curriculum should make provision for acquainting the student with good music even though we recognize the great disparity in native ability and interest among students. The situation will always present the problem of making adjustments for individual and group differences that will challenge the patience and wisdom of the most capable dean.

3. Electives

Electives in the sophomore year have a special purpose, orientation. They should help the students find themselves and direct them in the choice of their field of primary interest. The selections they make should also broaden and deepen their general education, but this is the specific purpose of electives in the last two years. During the sophomore year, however, the student should pursue some intellectual interest aroused as he became familiar with the great fields of knowledge, and commonly these electives should be outside his field of primary interest; but preference cannot be insisted upon. The requirements of the various departments, especially of the professional programs, are so time-consuming that careful planning will be required to keep them within bounds that will make it possible for the student to round out his general education by an intelligent choice of electives.

III. Upper Biennium Courses

Passing now to the second two college years in the suggested curriculum (Figures 6 and 7, pp. 166 and 167), we find that the student's work is distributed in three areas, philosophy, his field of primary interest, and electives. We have already considered the matter of electives. The course in philosophy is the one course that all the students of the upper division carry in common. It should function therefore as an integrating factor for all of them. Here at least they will be pursuing a common intellectual interest, and the fact that their fields of primary interest vary should enliven their study of philosophy since it has applications in all the fields they are studying. The important point is that all students should cover the field of philosophy as a whole, both in its speculative aspect (the metaphysical point of view) and its practical aspect (the normative point of view), with special emphasis on ethics. Such a course should aid them in formulating their own philosophy of life as Christians, using reason as the basis for the supernatural motivation that should guide their lives. We have already emphasized the discipline (unification) that should be the fruit of study in this field (chap. 6, pp. 138 f.). There is no need, therefore, to add anything further.

The field of primary interest offers two possibilities: a field of concentration in one of the liberal arts or sciences, and a professional program to prepare for their life work those students who cannot afford to continue their general education.

1. Fields of Concentration

In organizing its fields of study in the upper biennium, a college should consider carefully both the staff and facilities it has available, and the needs and interests of the students it is serving. We have emphasized that when a student decides on a field of concentration in the liberal arts or sciences, the thorough study of this field is an integral part of his general education. It may determine his life career, but this is not its primary function; for it is not specialization in the university meaning of the term. Rather, concentration in one field of study or in some problem that may be treated in several departments, should form an integrated course which the student will study as thoroughly as possible in the time available. This will prove an experience he has never had before in either high school or college, and he should have it now as the culmination of his liberal education.

The College of Arts and Sciences of the Catholic University of America has been working on this problem for several years with some success. We present as a stimulus to other Catholic colleges the result of their experiment, adapting it somewhat to make it more applicable to other institutions. The pattern of the courses taken in the lower division of the program is of first consideration. The dean's office is concerned with a program that will correct the false view of formal education that the mere passing of semester examinations gives the student. At the same time the program aims to develop in the student a genuine intellectual interest so that he may discover for himself the pleasure that comes from personally organized knowledge. With this in mind, the program is divided into a lower division and an upper division. The lower division is concerned primarily with breadth, giving students a knowledge of the tool subjects which they will need for work in the upper division. In this respect it is much like the program we have presented in section II of this chapter. The student ordinarily takes four courses which may meet three or occasionally even five times a week; but these courses do not include religion and physical education. A student may take a fifth course if his work during the previous semester warrants it; but very few students do this, for the four regular courses provide enough work.

Before the student enters the upper division he must give evidence by examination that he can do outside reading in at least one foreign language and that he can express himself well in English. In the upper division the program centers around two courses, the Reading List and the Coordinating Seminar. These courses may be combined into one if the department concerned desires it. It should be said also that in these courses the student is encouraged to address himself continuously to segments of his field larger than those presented in any one course. He is encouraged to train himself in the habit of seeking out interrelations between things and between ideas. Many students do much of their reading during vacation periods, especially during the summer between junior and senior years.

It should be pointed out that the director (or teacher) of these courses must be a person with a broad liberal education. At times a department is not permitted to offer a program of concentration because the department does not have on its teaching staff persons properly qualified to direct the courses. The training of the teacher is a very important matter since a person without a general training could easily make out of the Reading List and the Coordinating Seminar a narrow intellectual experience. It is vital to the program that quite the contrary be the case. The teachers of these courses must lead the student into the important ramifications suggested by the reading and the discussion of the readings in the Coordinating Seminar. Thus, even in the upper division the student will experience a development in breadth as well as in depth. Comprehensive examinations are an integral part of the program, but we will leave this phase to the last section of this chapter.

Many institutions have added to their traditional program of majors and minors some features of this program, for example, the comprehensive examination and a reading list. They even go so far as to use the same terms, but purposes and procedures are confused in the minds of those who are responsible for these hybrid programs. All too often the comprehensive examinations are mere matters of routine and not serious tests. The program is usually aimed at mastery of a field in order to become a specialist in it, rather than the completion of general education.

We mention a few of the difficulties of such a program. First of all, it is very expensive because it cannot be carried on successfully except in small groups; classes should never be conducted with more than fifteen students, especially in the Reading List and the Coordinating Seminar. It is also difficult to get teachers who by their training and native intelligence can appreciate the objectives of the program, to say nothing about conducting them. These are genuine difficulties and to the administrators of some large institutions they seem insurmountable. It should be noted, however, that in this program of concentration it is possible to take into consideration individual differences. For this reason all students, even the poorest, leave school with a much better general education than could possibly be given them under the traditional plan. It is no doubt true, however, that only a small percentage of students properly achieve the maximum benefits the program offers.

A Field of Concentration in Theology

Since the curriculum we have suggested requires no course in theology, we emphasize the importance of offering theology as a field of concentration if it is to be held in high esteem by the student body as one of the great fields of knowledge.

We realize that in the usual curriculum requiring religion (or theology) for either two, three, or four years, there is little possibility of any student selecting theology as his field of primary interest; but in the curriculum we are suggesting this condition would not exist. The influence of religion and theology in the course called World Civilization and Christian Culture would surely catch the interest of some students who would choose to go more deeply into it. The department of theology may think it advisable to require a course in theology as an elective to be carried by sophomores if they have any thought of choosing theology as their field of concentration; but with a comprehensive examination to be taken at the end of the sophomore year, it would seem that satisfactory performance on the section on theology, if it is at all reliable, would be qualification enough to ensure that those students selecting theology would be prepared to concentrate in this field, which need not be limited to courses in theology. Here is where integration again is necessary. Courses in philosophy and history suggest themselves immediately as fields of knowledge intimately connected with theology. In the case of philosophy, however, the course accepted as part of the field of theology should be in addition to the sixteen-hour course required of all students. Organized in this way, the field of concentration, even if limited to theology, would put no heavy burden on the department of theology. Using the cycle system, whereby the work of the two years would be taught in alternating years, only eight hours need be offered each semester; and even the small college with only two teachers in this department would be teaching only eleven hours of theology while offering electives in the sophomore year. In all probability, however, these instructors would have an important part in planning and even conducting the course in World Civilization and Christian Culture; and when this is the case, they should not be overburdened with work.

2. Professional Programs

When we turn to the professional programs to be offered by a liberal college, we must distinguish between the college which is a part of a large university and the independent college. The liberal college of a university will commonly feel no pressure to offer any professional programs at all since the university has its own professional schools which take care of this matter. The schools of engineering as now organized accept students directly from high school, but we look forward to the development when this training will be extended to five years, the first two of which will be devoted to general education on the college level, where mathematics and the basic sciences will be offered, while the last three years will be devoted to specialized training in the engineering school. The schools of business administration in Catholic universities may not yet feel able to conduct their programs solely on a graduate basis as Harvard has done from the beginning, but they certainly should plan to put the first two years within the liberal college, since general education as well as courses in accounting are important disciplines a student should have for the world of business. If a student elects accounting as his field of concentration in either the university or independent college, there is little doubt that he will experience the discipline of intensification in this field since it is nothing other than applied mathematics.

Our women's colleges call for special concern. There are many of them; and on the principle that women have a part to play in a world that is distinctly their own and that they should be educated for it, the women's colleges have made up their minds that they are not going to be mere imitations of similar institutions for men. This applies to the liberal education that should be planned for women as women, as well as to the professional programs that are particularly

proper to them. First of all we think of the training of
nurses. In many institutions this requires a fifth year, as in
the case of engineers; but in some institutions this fifth year
will be made up of three twelve-week summer quarters (the
equivalent of a full school year) since hospitals must function
all the year round. Secretarial science is now offering unusual
opportunities to young women who, in addition to specific
training in office skills, have received a sound liberal education. If the graduates of one of the larger women's colleges
in the middlewest live up to the reputation which has been
reported to the writer, they are superior in both specific skills
and general education to the graduates of those few secretarial schools which demand college graduation for entrance.
Dietetics, with its year of internship in hospitals or other
institutions, offers a good opportunity for combining the biological and physical sciences with a professional program.
Teaching is, of course, the profession that most women graduates prepare to enter, but the excessive requirements of
courses in education for certification make it almost impossible for colleges to give to these students during four years
a good liberal education without at least an additional summer term. Otherwise they must load their semester programs
with hours that make concentrated study almost impossible.

3. Comprehensive Examinations

Everyone realizes that the great incubus oppressing the
high school as well as the college is the credit complex. The
credit functions largely as a unit of time spent in class and
a license to forget rather than an indication of satisfactory
performance. As the Canadian humorist and professor of
political science, Stephen Leacock, phrased it some years ago:
"In the United States, education is being poured into a mold.
Everything that is learned is marked out into little units and
credits and added up like the cash register in a factory. If the
student can establish the fact that he has to his credit so

many hours of sitting on his beam ends with his ears open and then support it further with an intelligence test, he may then be promoted a general right away." A university or college with the prestige of the University of Chicago can abolish the credit system overnight, but no such procedure seems appropriate for most other institutions. Rather, it seems necessary to continue the credit system at least for some time yet; but we offer the suggestion that it should function only for admission to the comprehensive examinations, some of which should be held at the end of the first two years of college and others at the termination of the last two years (cf. Figure 6, p. 166). Designing and constructing adequate comprehensive examinations for a course like World Civilization and Christian Culture, is a very difficult and time-consuming task; but there is no way it can be avoided. In this course it probably would be best to prepare the examination in sections, one of the most important of which would be theology, and these sections may well be given at different periods. Further, it would seem appropriate to have these examinations made up of both objective-type and essay-type questions so that there would be a real test of the student's ability to organize and present ideas in connected discourse. Such an examination should be given for the natural sciences as well as for the philosophical and humanistic sciences. In the foreign language studied by the student, since he has read some of the classics of this language in the original, he should be able to demonstrate that he has attained a reading knowledge of that language. The comprehensive examination in the natural sciences should be taken when the course is completed, but those in the social sciences as well as that in a foreign language should be taken at the end of the second year of college, the latter to demonstrate that he has another tool ready for use.

In the program adopted at the Catholic University, the student takes a comprehensive examination at the end of his courses after all other requirements have been fulfilled in order to impress on him the importance of gaining knowledge for its own sake rather than for credit, and also to give him the experience of studying a large and broad field of knowledge. This examination is not given merely to determine whether the student has mastered particular courses, but is intended to determine whether the student has a background in his particular field and a way of using that background in handling unknown material or material not immediately familiar in his particular field. It commonly comprises three different parts which are given on three different days. Even if the student passes all his regular courses, if he fails to merit a good grade on this examination, he is not graduated at the scheduled time. When this happens the student is given a remedial program which may be, and usually is, another semester's work or another year's work at the University. This remedial work is usually private study rather than the taking of more courses. If he fails to pass the comprehensive examination the second time, he may no longer hope to earn a degree at that institution.

It is evident from the point of view presented in this chapter that no two institutions will fall into the same pattern. Nor should they attempt to do so. Each institution must study its student body, its staff and facilities, and build an educational program that will meet the needs of that student body so far as means are available for doing this. The paramount need of all students is a good liberal education in conformity with the tradition of Christian culture. Holding fast to this tradition does not mean refusal to introduce changes called for by an intelligent appraisal of the situation in which the college finds itself and the student body it is endeavoring to serve.

The liberal college that lives up to its name makes provision for the student's intellectual development. This can be accomplished by a curriculum which features: (1) distribution over the great fields of knowledge; (2) concentration in one field; and (3) integration of the knowledge assimilated through the unifying disciplines of theology and philosophy.[19] The outcome of such a program of studies should be a life ideal that is truly Christian. The key to the achievement of these outcomes is, of course, the teacher. Now we must consider this problem of training and aiding the teacher in his work of bringing a liberal education to the students he is serving.

[19] See the explanation of Figure 7, p. 167.

PART III

HOW AND WHERE TO TEACH—METHOD
AND ADMINISTRATION

CHAPTER 8

IMPORTANCE OF THE TEACHER

OUR DISCUSSION of the theory and the practice of the liberal arts, as effected through the courses offered, might have suggested a digression to consider a question connected with the college curriculum that is of such importance to the product of liberal education that it calls for special attention. We have considered the curriculum as the first means in education, the tool in the hands of the teacher. But the teacher is the most important means, for on him depends the success of all education. Even if the assigned curriculum is inferior, a group of good teachers with good students will arrange a good curriculum provided they have freedom to do what they see should be done. Having given attention to the tool, we now consider the qualifications, the preparation, and the work of the one who must use that tool. Most students of education hold that the teacher is second in importance only to the student himself among the factors leading to the final product, the liberally educated person.

I. LAY, CLERICAL, AND RELIGIOUS TEACHERS

Three general classes of teachers staff almost all Catholic colleges of liberal arts: members of a religious congregation, members of the diocesan clergy, and laymen. In selecting a lay candidate for a teaching position, college authorities scrutinize the applicant's qualifications with considerable care. The layman is interviewed, and if he or she appears to be in poor health or is lacking in a pleasing and attractive personality, the first interview is generally the last. Some excellently administered colleges not only interview candidates but insist that candidates interview the institution by meeting members of the teaching staff and by living for at least a few days on the campus. Are the physical and personal qualifications of priests and religious candidates for faculty appointments scrutinized with equal attention?

The lay applicant's scholastic record is carefully studied. Specifically, his graduate work is investigated and its excellence or mediocrity analyzed and evaluated. If the applicant has had previous teaching experience, administrators of the school or schools where the candidate has taught are consulted and precise and searching questions are asked. Was he a good teacher, or only a fair one; was he cooperative with administrators and teaching associates; respected by students; an advancing scholar, or one who gave every indication of having reached the terminus of his mental and professional development? On the supposition that all these questions are answered to the satisfaction of the engaging college, is the applicant immediately given tenure, or is he not accepted on trial so that he may be dismissed without prejudice if he does not prove satisfactory? Again we ask, are these same procedures followed when priests or religious are assigned to teaching positions on the college faculty?

1. Types of Teachers: Craftsman, Creator, Scholar

The term "teacher" should be understood broadly as comprising not only officers of formal instruction on all levels, but even nonprofessional educators and teachers who, in this period of crisis, may become even more important than professional teachers; above all, parents. Among academic teachers one may distinguish between: (a) the craftsman-teacher concerned mainly with the transmission of knowledge and training in intellectual skills in a conventional manner; (b) the creative teacher capable of inspiring new ideas in students and devising original methods of teaching; and (c) the scholar-teacher devoted not only to the transmission of knowledge and training in intellectual skills, but also to scholarly research. Mere conservation is not enough. Tradition must be a living tradition. Thus it must be aimed at the further organic development of new knowledge, insights, and understanding on the basis of past achievements. Although higher education will always have to be largely historical, this history points into the future as well as into the past. Yet the progress of knowledge and culture is necessarily a task for the few rather than for the many. While there are many other sources for the creation of new ideas and inventions (both material and social), such as learned societies and art institutes, in America today this function is largely left to scholars in the colleges and universities. Not all academic teachers need be scholars, and not all scholars need be teachers, though there exists a mutual stimulation of great value between the two activities which becomes indispensable on the level of the graduate and professional schools.

General education must always be eclectic to a certain degree, and thus necessarily arbitrary in the composition of its curriculum. We can only introduce the student to the great fields of knowledge. Hence the best curriculum of the liberal college must be one that gives guidance to the craftsman-teacher and at the same time freedom to the creative teacher and the scholar. Students, too, should have some freedom in the selection of their instructors.

2. Liberally Educated Instructors

Granting that teachers have been carefully selected and that they are distributed among the three types listed above, we wonder about their actual teaching. The preceding chapters in Part II of this study have considered in some detail what should be taught. Now we must consider how those courses should be taught. We maintain that the various courses of the liberal-arts curriculum, professional as well as purely liberal, should be taught liberally and not professionally. As might be inferred from the historical development of the arts and sciences, to teach liberally is to teach the inner relationships of the various courses and the integration of part with part and of one subject with another. To teach liberally means more than to teach the bare facts and to give their explanation. It is to teach the history of the fact, the philosophy of the fact, and the theology of the fact. It is to bring to one's teaching all the wealth of information contained in the several fields of liberal study which a liberally educated instructor may be presumed to possess. It is also clear that to teach liberally does not mean that every individual fact should be so expounded. To do so would be to smother the fact under a blanket of erudition, and thus to hide its real significance. The power of selection is something we expect in a liberally educated man or woman. A discriminating teacher does not pile one fact upon another as a bricklayer lays one standardized brick upon another. Rather he chooses individual facts and puts them in perspective before a student as an architect selects and adapts the elements of his various materials to the well-proportioned and functionally efficient structure of the complete edifice.

The liberally educated instructor, moreover, will be objective. He will have no thesis to expound except the thesis of truth. He will project no hobby, reiterate no phobia, nor see in every phenomenon of nature the expression of and justification for some subjective enthusiasm. Of such a teacher it can never be said, as it has been said all too often about one type of instructor, that no matter how his courses are described and numbered in the *College Bulletin,* he always teaches the very same course with slightly different embellishments. Experience shows that even a subject that is not fully matured is raised to the dignity of a liberal art or science if taught liberally. When well-synthesized and maturely developed arts and sciences are taught liberally, the response, granting student aptitude and application, will be immediate, profitable, and satisfying.

Accordingly, as a rule, the only teacher qualified to develop the fully educated man through the liberal arts is one who is himself grounded in the liberal arts. Such a professor may be a specialist within the field he expounds; but, because of his own liberal training, his teaching will also give liberal training. No man can give what he does not have. Only the fully educated man can produce a fully educated man. This principle implies in addition that only a teacher who is grounded in the traditional philosophy is fully prepared to be a teacher in a Catholic college of liberal education. From these considerations it is evident that the important thing about teaching is, as Barzum puts it:

that in using it you must recognize—if you are in your sober senses—that practical limits exist. You know by instinct that it is impossible to "teach" democracy, or citizenship or a happy married life. I do not say that these virtues and benefits are not somehow connected with good teaching. They are; but they occur as by-products. They come, not from a course, but from a teacher; not from a curriculum, but from a human soul.[1]

3. Counseling

The full benefit of these teacher qualifications will be secured in the work of academic counseling even to a greater degree than in the classroom. The importance of proper, sympathetic, and wise counseling arises from the growth of the liberal-arts college during the past half century. Some fifty years ago small classes were the rule, and the class teacher prevailed rather than the subject teacher (the departmental method). Thus the student was brought into a much closer

[1] Jacques Barzum, *Teacher in America* (Boston: Little, Brown and Co., 1945), p. 9.

relationship with his teacher in and out of the classroom than is the case today. Nowadays classes in most colleges are large and the subject teacher, lecturing perhaps to large groups of students, gets to know only a few of them. If in addition to his lecturing the teacher has department and committee work to do (and curiously enough, the best teachers seem most often charged with this sharing of administrative responsibility), he cannot give each student who needs it that academic help to which the student is entitled. Academic counseling has thus become part and parcel of actual teaching, and no college of liberal education can afford to neglect it either by failing to provide an adequate supply of counselors or by not diminishing teaching loads, if it wishes the teacher to use the program of studies to his best ability.

Proper counseling, which is nothing but an employment of the best features of the tutorial system, will also secure the advantage of a more thorough student response. Most students in Catholic colleges have not been developed to exercise their mental capacities to the limit. Some teachers have been so intent on lulling students into a complacent acceptance of everything Catholic as to wink at academic failings for fear the insistence on standards might discourage the student and occasion his leaving a Catholic college for a secular institution. A counselor can be guilty of the same social and pedagogical fault; but he will be less inclined to complacency in dealing with an indifferent student because his detection of student delinquency will be more swift and sure. The liberal disciplines are just that: disciplines; and no discipline is worthy of the name unless it involves hard striving. At least in the past the students in Catholic colleges have had too much work done for them by their teachers.

4. Teacher Participation in Administration

Finally, if the teacher has disciplined himself, he is prepared to exercise a function which to an increasing degree in these days of enlightenment is regarded as a part of a teacher's service to his college. That service is participation in the work of academic administration. As will be mentioned in the succeeding chapter, some administrators, far from sharing their burdens with members of the teaching staff, pointedly resent even an offer of such assistance. Executive totalitarianism is often a mask for inexperience or for meager talent. In most cases, perhaps, administrators in Catholic colleges have caught something of the spirit of the liberal arts and the American theory of government, in which not only the executive, legislative, and judicial functions are partly separate, but according to which a graduated degree of power and responsibility is conferred on a hierarchy of officials.

Today most colleges call upon their teachers to share the responsibilities of administration chiefly through committees and academic councils. In such committee and council meetings, the attitude of participants should be characterized by patience, moderation, fearlessness in expressing convictions, respect for the opinions of others, readiness to face any situation in which the college may find itself, and willingness to compromise in matters not involving moral or intellectual principles. Newman, in Discourse II of his great classic on liberal education, says: "Compromise, in a large sense of the word, is the first principle of combination." [2] If all or most members of a faculty committee possess these desirable administrative qualities, the success of teacher participation in administration will justify itself and may even convert those sturdy isolationist souls, who, with the best of motives, still advocate institutional absolutism.

The majority of Catholic college administrators in the United States are members of a religious order or congregation. Although the vow of poverty which such religious take is not an easy promise to make and keep, it has its compensa-

[2] *Idea of a University* (Chicago: Loyola University Press, 1927), p. 41.

tions. Chief among these is the release from one of the fears that besets many lay teachers, the fear of economic insecurity and displacement by some young religious just out of graduate school. In far too many instances administrators have had no clear concept or appreciation of this fear, almost constantly before many a lay teacher in a Catholic college where tenure is lightly regarded. The assertion has been made that lack of economic security, or lack of tenure, constitutes only one of several grievances felt by lay teachers in colleges conducted by religious congregations. Such laymen fail to realize that all their other complaints are complaints which religious teachers might themselves voice if religious principle or acquired timidity did not counsel silence. The lack of tenure is a fundamental objection against the administration of too many Catholic colleges where the turnover of religious officials is rather frequent and where, with each change, the lay teacher without tenure rights is exposed, perhaps at middle age, to the whims of some immature administrator and to the uncertainty of starting all over again in another institution, if indeed he is able to secure even an instructorship in another college. Pressure is now being brought to bear in this matter by the regional accrediting associations on all member institutions, and we look forward to a rapid improvement among our Catholic institutions. This matter merits continued attention by the College and University Department of our Catholic Association, and the same can be said for extending social security to all employees. The federal law has now been extended to include them.

II. The Failure of Graduate Training in Preparing College Teachers

Attention has often been called to the fact that college teaching is the only profession for which no professional training is required. There are many years of preparation, of course, but when these are continued in the graduate school, they are devoted almost entirely to specialization in one field, and the only specific training is in the techniques of research proper to that field. It is questionable whether either of these two aspects makes a real contribution to the training of those college teachers who are to be concerned with what we have been urging, namely, the general or integrated course not limited to one field but covering a large area of knowledge. The Report of the President's Commission on Higher Education is very severe on the graduate schools of the country for their failure to make adjustments in their offerings that will prepare the kind of teachers the colleges need.

It is in the preparation of college teachers that the graduate-school program is seriously inadequate. Its single-minded emphasis on the research tradition and its purpose of forcing all its students into the mold of a narrow specialism do not produce college teachers of the kind we urgently need.

The more alert and thinking among college administrators have for years been asking, usually in vain, for teachers with different training and different skills. They want teachers with less narrow interests and more intellectual curiosity and aliveness; teachers with more stimulating personalities and more experience of the world off the campus; teachers with more ability to communicate ideas and attitudes.

Without such teachers general education and liberal education of broadened scope are impossible. Without such teachers we shall not achieve the objectives and the programs recommended in this report. The graduate schools must provide the sort of educational experience that will produce such teachers. The present requirements for the doctor's degree will not do so.[3]

Then follows a discussion of some proposals for reform, one of which, the division of the graduate school into a re-

[3] President's Commission on Higher Education, *Higher Education for American Democracy,* vol. I, *Establishing the Goals,* p. 89.

search institute and a graduate college for the training of college teachers, we will discuss shortly. Another proposal is a new degree, doctor of arts, for those aiming at high general competence, reserving the degree of doctor of philosophy for those following a program of intense specialization and rigorous training in research. Whether or not any such changes are necessary or would be helpful is a question, but the Report emphasizes one aspect of this situation which merits attention. "Our conception of scholarship must be enlarged to include interpretive ability as well as research ability, skill in synthesis as well as in analysis, achievement in teaching as well as in investigation." [4]

1. A Program for the Education of College Teachers

What can the graduate schools do that would give any promise of helping its graduates prepare professionally for college teaching? We offer three suggestions here which we are convinced would go a long way towards meeting the difficulty if they were put into operation by a graduate school that has a fairly large group of students preparing for teaching in college. The first is one dealing with the college teacher's academic preparation. It is of special concern for those teachers who will be engaged in conducting what we are calling general or integrated courses. Since each of these covers a great area of knowledge, preparation for dealing with it adequately means study of the major phases of that area without being limited to any narrow field within it. With the dissertation continued as a requirement for the doctor's degree, there is no limit to the problems involved in evaluating the integrated courses now being offered and in planning and constructing others that would hold promise for the future. Research in problems such as these may well be research in the highest sense of the term; but it would also broaden a student's general education in a manner that per-

[4] *Ibid.*, p. 91.

haps could not be achieved by any other procedure that we could suggest.

Our second and third suggestions deal with the college teacher's professional training, the study of educational theory and a period of apprenticeship. The latter is easily disposed of. Teaching is like everything else; you learn it by doing it. But since the young teacher, like the young doctor, is dealing with human personalities and not the crude entities of the material world, he must be carefully prepared for the task he is undertaking and he should begin it under guidance. If it is to be a real apprenticeship, the beginning instructor must carry full responsibility for the course he is teaching, but under supervision, which for the most part will be personal conferences with an experienced instructor. Then if there is a series of conferences with an experienced professor in which the apprentice teachers would present the problems they have encountered, there is no doubt but that all could learn much from the experiences of their fellows as well as from their own experiences. We have suggested a series of conferences between the student teachers, which in no sense would be a course lasting a semester or a year. It would continue only as long as the student teachers found profit in it, whereas the conferences with their supervisor would continue until the completion of the course they were teaching and would include the construction of the examination.

The other phase of the professional training would be a regular course in educational theory which all students looking forward to college teaching would follow. It would be in the nature of a student-faculty seminar conducted by one of the professors of education with teaching experience in college, but in which instructors from other departments would take part as their fields had bearing on the educational theory being discussed. These meetings would begin with a discussion of objectives, the aims of both general and special education in the American system, and this would lead to a comparative study of the European educational system that has been dominant throughout the world and is so different from the American system in both secondary and higher education. Some time might then be devoted to what has been taking place in Russia during the past generation. Following this, attention would be given to the learning and teaching processes. Since organization of materials is the major part of method, here instructors from different fields would have to present their particular problems; but if the apprentice teachers of all fields attended these sessions as well as those dealing with their own fields, the contribution of this experience to their general education might be one of the most valuable results of the course.

In *Higher Education* [5] for February 15, 1950, there is an excellent report, by Fred J. Kelly, of a conference on this problem held in the spring of 1949. We are impressed by the importance given to the topic in the section entitled "Apprenticeship." A paragraph concludes with this statement: "Even in the most favorable situations there is probably not as complete integration as there should be of the academic subjects being studied, the professional courses pursued, and the apprenticeship experience. Nevertheless, apprenticeship is widely recognized as the *sine qua non* of the preparation for teaching." In the section entitled "Knowledge of Teaching Problems," however, this statement is made: "A program for making available to prospective college teachers the essential knowledge of teaching problems is still regarded primarily as a responsibility of the student's major department." [6] We are convinced that the allocation of the work of the course on educational theory, as we have suggested above, is the way out of this difficulty.

This reference to "the student's major department" recalls

[5] The semimonthly publication of the Higher Education Division of the U.S. Office of Education.

[6] "The Preparation of College Teachers" in *Higher Education*, pp. 144 f.

an attack on the departmental system, with its overemphasis on specialization, as one of the two great evils affecting American education today. It is found in a book already quoted, *Education and World Tragedy,* by Howard Mumford Jones. These are his words (p. 119): "Departments are by and large one of the two greatest evils in our academic education, the present conduct of graduate schools being the other." We will take up the problem of departments in the following chapter, on the administration of the college. Here we point out the failure of the graduate schools to make proper provision for preparing the kind of teachers the colleges must have if they are to fulfill their mission of completing the liberal education of the leaders of tomorrow so far as that can be done by formal schooling.

Jones' indictment of the graduate schools is perhaps the severest that has yet appeared in print. In section 3 of chapter 4, "Who Is As The Wise Man," he takes up this problem and continues it to the end of the book, a matter of fifty-three pages. In general his accusation is that college teachers are supposed to teach as philosophers and yet they are trained as specialists. He admits that the training for specialism is superb, but claims that there is no training for general education, and that this failure on the part of the graduate schools to inculcate philosophical breadth culminates in the lack of social responsibility. He reviews the history of the graduate schools as they grew out of the colleges of the American university, being staffed from the same source and having their budgets lost in the budgets of the more powerful departments. Finally he speaks of them as "curiously immunized against social currents and general ideas" (p. 136). The only possible way to remedy the situation, as he sees it, is to organize a graduate college for the training of college teachers and a research institute to continue their present activities in preparing technological experts for the competitive society that characterizes the American scene.

2. Howard Mumford Jones' Program

Jones' four-point program for preparing college teachers is substantially the same as the one we have sketched above, but it carries some specifications that are interesting. The first point is that the graduate college should be a place for the philosophical consideration of the problems of the fields of knowledge, with instruction kept as informal as possible in friendly discussion groups. The second point is that the college be free to send its students anywhere in the university or outside of it as their needs require, to assure a sufficient degree of specialized knowledge. The third and fourth points are the same as the second and third suggestions we have given above for the professional preparation of college teachers, except that in the fourth point Jones does not use the word "apprenticeship" when advocating student teaching; and his third point, emphasizing the discussion of the philosophy of education and the nature of culture as essential to the problem, is more general than our second suggestion above. He admits the possibility that a professor of the philosophy of education might be appointed to the staff since this faculty is to be representative; but he says that such an appointment is not a *sine qua non*. Rather, these philosophical questions should be the common concern of the entire faculty. To make this scheme operative, Jones says that the graduate college must be small but completely autonomous, with its own head, its own budget, its own faculty, its own curriculum, and its own quarters. Nothing less than this can ensure successful operation.

How can such a plan be carried out? His contention is that with the extreme conservatism characterizing the staffs of graduate schools today, nothing less than outside pressure can put his plan into execution. He lists four possible sources for this outside influence: schools of education, government, the great educational foundations, and the liberal-arts colleges themselves; but he holds that the fourth alone can really accomplish the task. The colleges have now come of age and they hold in their hands the future of liberal education and the right of training teachers in that area. If they would refuse to engage doctors of philosophy trained in the wrong way, and through their own organization, the Association of American Colleges, would make their demands in no uncertain terms, they could soon change the situation for the better.[7]

The situation with regard to the professional tendency of college teaching and its recognition as a worthy career for the top-ranking college graduate is not so dark as the foregoing remarks would seem to indicate. An article in *Higher Education* for January 15, 1950, entitled "Fellowships for Prospective College Teachers," relates how four universities changing the requirements for the doctor of philosophy degree, have set up courses in the science and art of college teaching and have improved the apprenticeship procedures. At Princeton there is a special faculty committee for the Woodrow Wilson Fellowships interested in the selection and development of good college teachers as well as scholars. The chairman of the committee and one other member have a lengthy interview with the candidates and follow the subsequent performances of each fellow to determine if he has the qualities that make a good college teacher. At the University of Chicago ten graduate teaching scholarships are awarded, and the names of the students selected appear in the spring announcement of fellowships, which dramatizes college teaching as an important career calling for special aptitudes and special preparation. The University of Oregon has established five fellowships for the preparation of college teachers in the social sciences. The changes in the requirements for the degree of doctor of philosophy emphasizes the University's interest in the professional preparation for college teaching.

[7] Jones, *op. cit.*, pp. 136–42.

The University of Syracuse, however, has gone the whole way. It has set up nine fellowships, three in each of the fields of humanities, social sciences, and natural sciences; and the graduate faculty has adopted a special curriculum for training in each of these three fields. The requirements in all of them are much broader than those traditional for departmental specialization.

The article by Fred J. Kelley quoted on page 202 concludes with the one resolution that was adopted by the conference he is reporting. This calls for the establishment by the American Council on Education, of a Commission on the Preparation of College Teachers to study this problem and work for its solution. If the Association of American Colleges and the American Council on Education can unite in this endeavor, we have reason to hope that the movement will make real progress, and we may look forward to the time when it will no longer be true that college teaching is the one profession for the practice of which no professional preparation is necessary.

CHAPTER 9

COLLEGE ADMINISTRATION IN AMERICA

THE ADMINISTRATION of even a small college is a complex function. There are funds to conserve and property to manage, teaching programs to set up and supervise, public relations to establish and maintain, the needs of customers (that is, students) to supply, members of the academic and corporative family to provide for, with varying and various institutional objectives to achieve. This is a study, however, of liberal education in a liberal college. In it, accordingly, emphasis is placed on and attention given to those processes which are directly concerned with the work of educating. Thus, while the maintenance of a college's economic existence is a necessary and interesting function, and while the repute of an institution depends in some measure on the failure or success of its public relations, the main features of administration requiring attention in a study such as this are academic. In them we discern two main elements, which we shall discuss here: we shall be concerned with administration as it affects the teacher's teaching and the activity of the one taught. Administration and faculty relations have been treated in some detail in the previous chapter and need not be repeated here. To understand a striking difference between most secular and Catholic college administrations in the United States, however, a short historical study of the development of administration in American colleges is necessary.

I. Development of College Administration
in America

The administration of the original colonial college, Harvard, was modeled on the government at Cambridge, England, from which most of the founding fathers of Harvard had graduated. Even though Elizabeth and James I had deprived the ancient English universities of many of their privileges and a good deal of their local self-government, in important matters, at least, the old forms were preserved and Cambridge, for two or three decades before the founding of Harvard College, appeared to be more democratic than it really was. We are not surprised, then, to find that when Harvard was planned in 1636, considerable power of self-government was conferred on the teachers, who were at the time Fellows, or members of the corporation. By an accident all this was changed. Soon after Harvard began operating, several teachers who were leaders in the Congregational Church and at the same time Fellows of the corporation, began to resign from the teaching faculty and to accept appointment to pastorates in the rapidly growing Congregational Church of the Massachusetts Bay Colony.

While resigning their professorships, however, the Harvard teachers retained their fellowships. In this way internal control became lodged in the hands of the externs. In later days, not only in the colonial foundations but also in Eastern and Midwestern schools during the first half of the nineteenth century, a return to democratic practices was hastened by the influence of our American form of government. That influence showed itself in a tendency to separate more carefully the three chief powers of administration: executive, legislative, and judicial. In keeping with the forms of democracy, college boards of trustees have increasingly conferred on the teaching faculty powers of administration over a wide aca-

demic area. Thus a greater degree of local self-government
has been granted to or appropriated by the teaching faculty.

II. Catholic College Administration

The origins of Catholic college administration were quite
different. We mention here three points of difference that
have been a real handicap for the Catholic college. In the first
place its origins were:

1. **European, not American.** Most of the mechanics of
government in Catholic colleges in the United States follow
European rather than American procedures. To say it another
way, they are monarchial, and the tendency has always been
toward the extension of absolutism rather than its limitation.
Most of the Catholic colleges of the first half of the nineteenth
century were inaugurated by religious congregations founded
in Europe and only recently introduced into America. In some
instances decades elapsed before members of the group became imbued with American ideals. Even religious orders
have linguistic, racial, and cultural backgrounds which, while
not necessarily of this world, are in it. As a result we can
truthfully say that until 1900, the corporative spirit of a
majority of the religious congregations operating in the
United States was only partially American. One consequence
of this condition was that American traditions in government
failed to make an effective impression on some of the religious
congregations conducting colleges, and thus administration
of such colleges remained monarchial, that is, European,
rather than American.

2. **Monastic, not Scholastic.** One immediate result of the
monastic influence in the development of the Catholic college
seems to have done it serious harm. Life in a religious congregation is, so to speak, family life; and family life is a private
life. Life in a publicly chartered institution, as that in a college, is institutional life and, in a very real sense, public

life. Yet because the religious type of government has been transferred to the administration of a college controlled by religious, most Catholic colleges shrink from publicity. They may have nothing to hide except debt, but they avoid publicity and resent inquiry because they regard too many details of college administration as family matters with which the public is not concerned and into which the public should not pry. The text of college charters, though they are on file in the offices of various state secretaries, are jealously guarded; constitutions and by-laws of college government, if they exist at all, are carefully kept from circulation; annual reports, if made, are striking examples of understatement and vagueness; relations between administrators and teachers are looked upon as relations between parents and children. Often there may be reason for this attitude. The American questionnaire can be and frequently is more objectionably inquisitorial than most of the inquisitions of history. But a considerable element in this attitude of secrecy on the part of Catholic colleges seems to arise from the institutional origins of the college itself. It may not spring from any desire to conceal any real or humiliating skeleton.

At least in matters directly affecting teaching, a considerable amount of local self-government has worked well in Protestant and secular colleges and universities, and this fact ought to suggest to Catholic administrators that they might profitably redesign the pattern of government in the institutions over which they preside. Certainly scholastic or, to use the word more common when speaking of the college, academic self-government may create difficulties; but these are of minor importance when balanced against the desirable results of greater interest and more effective teaching which normally are found when teachers have some self-determination in their work as well as the duties and responsibilities with which they are always burdened.

3. **Autocratic, not Democratic.** This condition persists

today and is one of the characteristics that sets Catholic colleges apart from other collegiate institutions in the United States. True enough, there are non-Catholic colleges where administrative absolutism exists, and there are some Catholic colleges in which a considerable degree of academic power as well as responsibility is placed in the hands of the teaching faculty. By and large, however, that type of administration best suited to the internal government of a religious congregation is still mistakenly thought eminently proper for an educational institution at the college and university level. Fr. Keller quotes a passage from Lester D. and Alice Crow's *Introduction to Education* that has bearing on this subject and is worth presenting here.

ADMINISTRATORS

The Autocratic	The Democratic
1. Thinks he can sit by himself and see all angles of a problem.	1. Realizes the potential power in thirty or fifty brains.
2. Does not know how to use the experience of others.	2. Knows how to utilize that power.
3. Cannot bear to let any of the strings of management slip from his fingers.	3. Knows how to delegate duties.
4. Is so tied to routine details that he seldom tackles his larger job.	4. Frees himself from routine details in order to turn his energy to creative leadership.
5. Is jealous of ideas . . . when someone else makes a proposal.	5. Is quick to recognize and praise an idea that comes from someone else.
6. Makes decisions that should have been made by the group.	6. Refers to the group all matters that concern the group.
7. Adopts a paternalistic atti-	7. Maintains the position of

tude toward the group: "I know best."

8. Expects hero-worship, giggles of delights at his attempts at humor, and so forth.

9. Does not admit even to himself that he is autocratic.

10. Sacrifices everything—teachers, students, progress—to the end of a smooth-running system.

11. Is greedy for publicity.

12. Gives to others as few opportunities for leadership as possible. Makes committee assignments, then outlines all duties and performs many of them himself.

friendly helpful adviser both on personal and professional matters.

8. Wishes to be respected as a fair and just individual, as he respects others.

9. Consciously practices democratic techniques.

10. Is more concerned with the growth of individuals involved than with freedom from annoyances.

11. Pushes others into the foreground so that they may taste success.

12. Believes that as many individuals as possible should have opportunities to take responsibility and exercise leadership.[1]

For an administrator really desirous of converting the administration of his college into one that is truly democratic, there are many helpful hints in these twenty-four points.

Administration and the Student

With regard to students, our opinion is that all men and women in a democracy should enjoy a liberal education if they wish it, even at the expense of the state. The word

[1] James Keller, *Careers that Change Your World* (Garden City: Doubleday, 1950), pp. 162 f.

"all," however, must be qualified by two important reserva-
tions concerning the selection of students. First, students
must possess those intellectual aptitudes which the liberal
disciplines demand, and entering students should be tested
rigorously to discover whether or not they possess these aptitudes. Second, entering freshmen should have been prepared
for liberal education at the college level by an effective type
of secondary education leading directly to further development in the arts and sciences in the college. It does not appear to be within the province of this study to discuss the
kind and quality of education given to students in secondary
schools, since the principles enunciated here are operative on
all levels of education. Nevertheless, it may be observed that
many Catholic high schools have at least as much room for
improvement in this matter as there is need for improvement
in Catholic colleges. The extent to which this criticism is valid
needs no attention in this investigation.

It is fairly obvious that the college student can do better
work in literature, for instance, if adequate high school
preparation in the mechanics of language is possessed by in-
coming freshmen. Moreover, while language is basic to the
entire liberal curriculum, a great deal of preliminary work
in language should have been done in high school or even at
the lower educational level. To some extent similar preparation at the elementary and secondary levels will notably
advance college work in every other field of the liberal arts.
Consequently it appears to be a pedagogically sound principle for a college to base student selection not merely on such
widely varying and distressingly fluctuating standards as an
upper percentage of high-school senior classes, but also on
the student's ability to pass an examination or to produce
satisfactory evidence of accomplishment in the major fields
of liberal study. If not thus prepared, the applicant should
be advised to enter schools offering occupational training or
to secure further preparation in required fields before being

admitted to matriculation. Some students of the history of higher education think that the failure of liberal education in some Catholic colleges is partly due to indiscriminate student selection, and partly to the low student response which too many Catholic colleges (and high schools) tolerate.

III. Design for Administering a Liberal College in a Democracy

Following this theoretical exposition of college administration as it has been operating in our Catholic institutions, we pass on to the practical problem of converting what we have called the European "monastic" type of administration into one that follows the American democratic type now in evolution in this country. Administrators brought up throughout their school days in the monastic tradition have had little or no contact with the democratic way of handling men engaged in a common enterprise. When, therefore, they undertake the administration of a college or university, they often unthinkibly apply this traditional way of managing affairs to the problems confronting them. The fact that the enterprise they are charged with is operating in a modern setting, not in a medieval one, seldom seems to impress them. No longer, however, can this indifference to the changed situation in the modern world be continued. New problems are confronting us, and we must devise new ways of working towards the solutions of these problems. What are the major problems confronting the American college president?

1. The Three Problems of College Administration

The simplest way to answer this question is to analyze the administrative process and to determine as specifically as possible the distinct functions of the different divisions into which any large educational institution must be broken down for effective management. The main divisions are three.

Studies

There is first of all the problem which brought the school into being, the task of educating the oncoming generation, which is the specific aim of the school on all levels: primary, secondary, and higher education. This is the problem of studies. What studies should the student be engaged in so that he may develop his intellectual powers in the assimilation of the spiritual inheritance of the race? This reference to the two-fold aspect of all education emphasizes the fact that it is a single enterprise. The two processes involved, social transmission on the one hand and individual development on the other, are complementary, not conflicting. One cannot go on without the other. This is the problem of the curriculum and method: what to teach and how to teach.

Guidance

The second problem of administration is a phase of the educative enterprise which is going on all the time even though we are not aware of it. This is the problem of guidance, which also comprises two major aspects. The first is that of the extracurricular activities which play a great part in the educational program of any college, as they occupy the free time of the student under the guidance of faculty counselors. The second aspect of this problem is that to which the term "guidance" is now more commonly applied. This involves all the newer techniques now developed for intelligently counseling students, as the use of cumulative school records, measurement of native and acquired abilities and aptitudes, and records of out-of-school experiences, all of which are helpful in discovering a personal interest in and aptitude for certain life callings. The aim here is intelligent counseling to help students make wise decisions in all those problems continually confronting them in their personal as well as their academic lives.

Public Relations

The third administrative problem is primarily one of finance, but the best label to bring out its all-inclusive character is public relations. The one in charge here is dealing with the parents of students, the alumni of the college, who in many cases are the parents of the students of tomorrow if not of today, and the public in general, that is, the clientele to which the college is making its appeal. Most important of all is the raising of sufficient financial resources so that the college can continue to operate and improve its educational program.

Now it is of interest to note that anyone attending educational conferences soon becomes aware of the fact that in American college administration today these three problems are all recognized as distinct. Further, there has taken place a change in the titles of the executive officers who carry responsibility for them. Today at the gatherings of the various educational associations concerned with college administration, it is common to hear of the "academic vice-president" and the "financial vice-president." The "student personnel vice-president" is not so common, but this title is also coming into use. Here is the president's cabinet, more commonly called his council, since these officers are his counselors in the management of the institution's affairs and his assistants in keeping everything under control for the achievement of the institution's aims and objectives.

The academic vice-president is in charge of studies. The personnel vice-president handles all the problems arising among the students apart from studies: health and housing, the religious life on the campus, and the extracurricular activities in their varied forms of class organizations, campus clubs, intramural athletics, and so forth. The financial vice-president handles all public relations, with special attention to the problem of finance. Each of these three main offices

COLLEGE ADMINISTRATION

college or university. At times there may be overlapping of
authority, but the purpose of the council is to reconcile these
difficulties. Since the office of the president as it has developed
in this country is now primarily an off-campus job (repre-
senting the institution at educational conferences, addressing
audiences throughout the country, and serving on regional
and national committees, governmental or otherwise), he cannot carry on his duties without capable assistants at home
giving their entire attention to the details of these three problems as they arise on every campus. The extent of the democracy prevailing in each of these divisions will be indicated
by the extent to which each of the executive officers in turn
enlists capable assistants from the faculty and staff to help
him arrive at wise decisions in all the details that continually
call for action and cannot wait for recommendation from
committees, no matter how efficiently they may function.[2]

[2] An interesting illustration of the complexity of college administration
when the college is part of a university organization is that presented
by the changes inaugurated at the University of Notre Dame in 1949.
Strictly speaking this was not a reorganization, since the offices concerned were all functioning before the new titles were given to those in
charge of them. The University now has five vice-presidents, three of
which are included in Figure 8. They bear these titles: Vice-President in
Charge of Academic Affairs, Vice-President in Charge of Student Welfare, and Vice-President in Charge of Business Affairs. The distinction
in function between the last named and the Vice-President in Charge of
Public Relations is clear when it is known that the primary responsibility
of the latter is the Notre Dame Foundation, which is an organization
for raising funds for capital expenditures (e.g., the new Science Building)
and the increase of endowment. The Vice-President in Charge of Business
Affairs was formerly the Business Manager. One collects funds; the other,
operating through the budget, spends them along with the income from
the students. The fifth vice-president is the Executive Vice-President, who
is the president's first assistant with general supervision of all the other
offices. He substitutes for the president when the latter cannot fulfill
an assignment either on or off the campus.

In contrast with this we give the organization of Purdue University, a
neighboring institution with a student enrollment more than twice as
large. Purdue has only two vice-presidents, one of whom carries the

2. Mechanics versus Personnel

Before turning our attention to the two columns in Figure 8(p. 219) in which the divisions and subdivisions of the three major problems in college administration are presented, we must give a warning concerning the analysis of the administrative problem we have made in the preceding pages. The analysis presented in the diagram is purely mechanical. But mechanics alone never solves any problem dealing with human personalities. The key to the situation is the selection and training of personnel. With regard to the college faculty we have emphasized this fact in the preceding chapter. The school fortunate to have a staff of good teachers will give its students a good education for the simple reason that even if the curriculum has been poorly organized, these teachers will replan it and build a good curriculum unless prevented from doing so by the narrow-mindedness of the administrators.

The most difficult task the president is always confronted with is the selection of adequate personnel. From this situation arises the fact that the administrative organization in any two institutions will never be identical. In the college the major problems are always the same, but the personnel available for dealing with these problems is never the same. We have illustrated this fact in the above footnote giving the different organizations of Purdue University and the University of Notre Dame in the case of the several vice-presidents. But well-planned machinery, well lubricated by

---

title Vice-President and Executive Dean. All academic administrative offices are under his general supervision as well as those dealing with student personnel problems. This latter division is handled by the Director of the Office of Student Affairs and the Dean of Women. The financial problem is handled by the Vice-President and Controller. At the opening of the 1949 school year, however, another administrative officer was brought into the president's office with the title "Assistant."

Figure 8. THE ADMINISTRATION OF A LIBERAL COLLEGE

The President's Cabinet	Executive Chairmen Divisions.	Subdivisions	Functions The Development of:
I Academic Vice-President (Dean of studies)	1. Mathematics and Natural Sciences 2. History and Social Sciences 3. Theology and Philosophy 4. Language and Literature 5. Music and Visual Arts	The heads of the departments in each division	The Intellectual virtues
	6. Applied Arts (If professional programs are offered)	Home Economics, Nursing, Library Science, Business Administration, etc.	Professional knowledge and technical skills
	Guidance Program (Director)	Educational, Vocational, and Personal (All staff members dealing directly with students)	A Life Plan
II Personnel Vice-President (Director)	Health Program (College Physician)	College Infirmary (Nurses, etc.)	Physical health and vigor
	Department of Physical Education (Director)	Intramural Athletics (Coaches)	
	Student Council (Faculty Counselor)	Class Organizations (Faculty Counselors)	
		Student Clubs (Faculty Counselors)	The Moral Virtues
	Dormitories etc.	Dormitory Divisions etc.	
	Dining Hall etc.	Dining Rooms etc.	
	Department of Religion (Chaplain)	Student Religious Organizations (Asst. Chaplains)	The Theological Virtues
III Financial Vice-President (Controller or Treasurer)	Public Relations (Alumni Director) Publicity Bureau Athletic Board of Control (Intercollegiate)		Good Public Relations

the oil of human kindness and consideration, helps any mechanism function better.

Acknowledging the necessity of doing the best with the personnel available, we continue our analysis of the administrative problem, pointing out one of the phases of college administration that is causing particular concern at this time and one which merits special consideration if the American college is to be successful in its efforts to bring about real integration in the curriculum. We refer to the problem of setting up a divisional organization in place of the departmental organization that has long been traditional in the American college.

3. Administration through Divisions

We have had occasion in the previous chapters to describe in some detail what has been taking place in institutions determined to bring about a better integration. Apparently the College of Chicago University and St. John's College are the only two that have abolished departments.[3] Most of the institutions that have adopted a divisional organization of courses, such as Harvard College, retain departments; but their powers are restricted in the undergraduate college. A typical example of this arrangement is West Virginia University. The *University Catalogue,* in the section dealing with "The College of Arts and Sciences," presents an "Interdepartmental Program of Integrated Studies." [4] These "Integrated Studies" are given under the same divisional titles as at Chicago University: Humanities, Social Sciences, Biological Sciences, and Physical Sciences.[5] Under each heading an "Introductory General Course" is announced, running through two semesters. Integrated courses are offered by all four divisions, and these may be elected by students (of all

[3] See above, pp. 82 and 84 ff.
[4] *West Virginia University Catalogue,* 1948–1949 Session, p. 131.
[5] *Ibid.,* pp. 147–149.

four years). The introductory courses do not seem to be required, but they are strongly recommended as "providing (a) a general knowledge of subjects not covered by the student's field of major interest, and (b) perspective for later concentration in certain fields." [6]

A different approach to the problem of integration was made at Michigan State College. A separate administrative unit was set up with its own dean, teaching staff, and allotment in the budget. The same is true of the Notre Dame experimental program. The new unit is within the College of Arts and Letters, but it has its own director and teaching staff.

In our analysis in Figure 8, we have retained the sixfold division of the great fields of knowledge presented in chapter 4, "A Philosophical Approach to the College Curriculum," and applied to the curriculum in chapter 7. If, however, the college does not offer any professional programs, there will be no need for the sixth division, Applied Arts. The aim is to keep the number of divisions down to a minimum; but we cannot recommend that they be restricted to three, the natural sciences, social sciences, and the humanities, which is the common procedure now, since we believe that this curtailment does not provide for an adequate treatment of all the liberal arts and sciences.

In conclusion we emphasize again that a smoothly working system is helpful; but it is not the secret of good administration. More important is the spirit that animates the administrative staff and those teaching under it. If the members of these staffs believe that integration is the crying need of the American college today, and if all have had a part to play in arranging as well as conducting the educational program that is to effect integration, it is almost sure of success. But without this spirit of cooperation and enthusiasm for sharing in this common enterprise, no plan can be successful.

[6] *Ibid.*, p. 147.

CHAPTER 10

THE STUDENT COMMUNITY

SINCE the proximate objective of Catholic colleges and universities is the intellectual development of students, Catholic colleges have been founded and continue to function only because of the student. Too often administrators lose sight of this obvious fact, and their failure to bear it in mind can be detected in many a superficially worthy motive which administrators may propose to themselves. In this section of our study we must expressly admit the *raison d'être* of the college and be ready to implement it before we can carry our discussion further. All previous statements directly or indirectly depend on an assumption of the truth that schools exist only for their students. Two conclusions immediately follow. First, the college should be organized and should function for the spiritual and intellectual development of its students. Second, the college must prepare its students for their responsibilities as members of human society. Every proposal made in this section is designed to meet one or the other or both of these imperatives.

I. STUDENT ADMISSION AND STUDENT AID

Our first consideration of the student as an educable person is his admission into college, that is, student selection. This question is at least as important as the selection of the teacher. Catholic colleges do not go out into the highways to compel teachers to join their faculties. Why, then, should they indulge in indiscriminate canvassing for students? In perhaps the majority of cases the canvassing of students is discriminate; but there is something essentially ignoble in enticing outstanding students from one Catholic college to another by the offer of a more valuable scholarship. With regard to student selection, all that this study can do is assert that a Catholic college should have standards, that these standards should be reasonably high, and that they should be maintained rigorously and applied impartially to the selection of freshman candidates. Since every Catholic college of the liberal arts has its own peculiar spirit, no universal measurement for student selection can be offered to all colleges.

Accordingly, every college should formulate its own criteria for the admission of students, and preferably these criteria will include a personal interview. Through personal contact the admitting officer can become acquainted with the personality and, to a degree, with the character of the matriculant. Many applicants will be found unprepared for liberal studies in the college, either by defect of schooling or lack of talent. Such students should be advised to go elsewhere and refused if they continue to seek admission. This and supplementary admission practices will assist counselors from the very beginning to advise properly all freshmen who are eventually admitted to matriculation.

All this supposes treatment of the student as an individual, not as a mere unit in an entire class. The same supposition should determine the means by which the college teaches the pursuit of truth. Adequate teaching includes not only socialized or group instruction, but individual instruction, or what is generally referred to as tutoring. Most of our Catholic colleges are not sufficiently staffed to conduct tutoring on any large scale, and perhaps in our American atmosphere a system of exclusive tutoring on any large scale might tend to lessen the social and democratic ideas of the future citizen. Some tutoring, however, can always be done. The more individual attention given, the higher will be the achievement of the individuals in almost any group. Tutoring should not be given only to students who are slower to profit by class instruction or to those who can work efficiently only when given the stimulus of individual attention. Brighter students in any class stand in far greater need of tutoring than do the dull ones. The less talented may need individual attention so that they may at least pass; but the more talented, that in and after college they may excel. It is perhaps in its failure to spur more brilliant students that the average Catholic college most frequently fails to justify the reason for its existence. Hence the necessity of Honors Courses or Independent Study Plans in the later years when students have demonstrated their superior ability and industry.

Student assistance is an ever-pressing problem for the Catholic college. In aiding economically straitened but talented students, Catholic administrators have generally shown themselves so generous as sometimes seriously to impoverish their colleges and inhibit institutional growth. May not much of the assistance be mistakenly bestowed? The most intelligent assistance to a needy student is that which helps him to help himself. Gratuitous favors are often slightly appreciated and even more slenderly utilized. The grant of a partial or of a complete scholarship is often necessary if a student is to continue in college at all. In many cases opportunities for a student to work his way through school are immensely more valuable. These make it possible not only for a student to develop himself as an intelligent being, but also to prepare himself directly for an equally important task, which is that of readying himself as a member of society for the role in which he will spend the rest of his life after graduation. Abundant opportunity for student service is offered by our contemporary passion for records and measurement. Today almost every instructor in a progressive college needs the

help of at least a part-time secretary. By such assistance
many needy students can now remain in college when all
manual jobs are taken, and many of these students have
openly declared that working as secretary for a professor
was one of their most valuable experiences of learning.

II. TRAINING IN THE VIRTUES

Robert Maynard Hutchins, past Chancellor of Chicago
University, has frequently made the statement that no one
who has ever read Plato's dialogue, the *Memo,* can believe
that virtues can be taught. Since Hutchins is always insisting
that the aim of the college and the university is to teach the
intellectual virtues, it is evident that he is speaking here of
the moral virtues. The statement that it is impossible to teach
the moral virtues is so contrary to human experience, there
must be some explanation of his use of the term "teach." We
state here the general principle: anything that can be learned
can be taught, and in the teaching of it much time and effort
is saved and many blunders avoided. The real question with
regard to the moral virtues is not whether they can be taught,
but how they are taught. It is easily understandable that
their teaching may call for a technique different from that
ordinarily employed in developing the intellectual virtues.
The moral virtues are qualities of the will rather than of the
intellect, though, of course, knowledge and understanding are
basic to them as they are in every life activity. What Hutchins
meant, we are convinced, is that the moral virtues cannot be
taught by any form of direct instruction in the classroom. One
can teach something about the virtues, but the only result of
that teaching is knowledge and understanding; and that is
not what we commonly mean by virtue. How the moral virtues are to be taught has been suggested by the often quoted
statement of Edmund Burke, "Example is the school of mankind; it can learn in no other." Through the power of inspiring example virtue is taught every hour of the day by parents

and other members of the family in the home, by companions in neighborhood groups, and by administrators, teachers, and fellow students in the school. Of course, vice is taught in the same way and by the same groups if the example given is the opposite of virtue. But even here there is a negative influence that is conducive to a life of virtue if what happens to the malefactors giving the bad example is of such a nature (as it will be in any well-organized society) that the perpetrators of evil receive a just retribution for their evil deeds.

Every virtue and every vice is a habit. Habit generates the power of doing something with facility and skill. Thus there are habits of intellect and habits of will (or activity); in other words intellectual virtues and moral virtues.[1] The intellectual virtues imply the habit or facility of knowing what to do; the moral virtues, of doing it. Once this distinction is clearly grasped, we see the meaning of the statement that the school is concerned primarily with the development of the intellectual virtues. As Father McGucken, S.J., states it, "The Catholic secondary school has the specific function of training for the intellectual virtues."[2] The teaching situa-

[1] The classification of the intellectual virtues by Aristotle was adopted by St. Thomas. They fall into two groups: the speculative and the practical. The speculative virtues are three: (1) understanding, the power to grasp certain fundamental, self-evident truths, both theoretical and practical (for example, no effect without a cause); (2) science or knowledge, the ability to demonstrate universal and necessary truths and arrive at new and certain conclusions in the various branches of investigation; (3) wisdom, the power to put things together and coordinate the data of understanding and science so as to attain the ultimate explanation of all things and see everything in human life in relation to our last end. The two virtues of the practical intellect are art and prudence, which are distinguished by the expressive Latin phrases: *recta ratio factibilium* and *recta ordo agibilium;* that is, art is knowing how to do a thing, prudence, knowing what to do.

In contrast with these are the moral virtues, commonly called the cardinal virtues: prudence, justice, temperance, and fortitude. Thus prudence is both an intellectual and a moral virtue.

[2] "Intelligence and Character" in *The National Catholic Educational Association Bulletin,* XXXVI (May, 1940), p. 11.

tions within the school—the classroom, the lecture hall, the library and laboratory—offer little if any opportunity for the practice of the moral virtues. Yet virtue is a habit and as such it develops only through continued voluntary practice under guidance. College studies afford opportunities for practicing only intellectual habits, that is, the intellectual virtues; this brings out the meaning of the statement, "Character is caught; it cannot be taught." The power of inspiring example and for the most part the activities which go on outside the classroom, library, and laboratory, are those which result in the development of the moral virtues. These are the activities which characterize the student community. (See Figure 9, p. 229.)

The Moral Virtues and the Student Community

Certainly the college has an obligation to develop the moral virtues; but this obligation, using the words quoted below, is "secondary" and "auxiliary" to the development of the intellectual virtues, its primary obligation. One of the best statements of this function of the school is from the writings of Mortimer Adler, who, though not a member of our faith, is an ardent disciple of Aristotle and St. Thomas.

Because he knows the distinction between the moral and the intellectual virtues, . . . the philosopher knows that educational institutions cannot be primarily responsible for moral education. Institutionally, the primary responsibility for moral education lies in the home and the church and in the law-making and law-enforcing functions of the political community. Non-institutionally, moral education depends upon the ministrations of elders, [of parents and those] other than parents, and of friends. So far as educational institutions go, moral education is accomplished by them secondarily and only insofar as (1) they are communities which, as such, can by rule-making and rule-enforcement, regulate the conduct of their members; (2) the professional educators who compose the personnel of such institutions are elders who can advise and direct conduct, or otherwise stimulate the growth of moral habits; (3) strictly intellectual education (especially liberal and speculative), which is the primary work of educational institutions as places of teaching, is auxiliary to the formation of moral virtues.[3]

On the general principle that a student learns through his own activities, we must now analyze those activities of the student community which are of special value in developing the moral virtues. We may call these activities "cocurricular," meaning thereby that they are activities which, though not a part of the curriculum or program of studies, supplement the curriculum and, as part of the educational program, have a real contribution to make in the education of students. In some colleges these activities are taking up so much time and attention that they have overshadowed the program of studies. This, of course, is a situation that should be kept under control in every college, since the primary obligation of any school of general education is the development of the intellectual virtues, which is done primarily through the curriculum. But when we use the phrase "educational program" in the broader sense of the term, we must include therein these activities that accompany the curriculum. I refer specifically to student clubs, athletic, dramatic, and musical organizations, outdoor activities, and organizations for the promotion of Catholic Action and other forms of religious activity. These activities are excellent opportunities for the development of the moral virtues. For example, what better occasion is offered the student for the development of fortitude or courage than athletics and the participation in games of all kinds?

[3] Mortimer Adler, in *Philosophies of Education* (Forty-first Yearbook of the National Society for the Study of Education, Part I, 1942), p. 220; quoted by permission of the Society.

Figure 9. DEVELOPMENT OF THE VIRTUES IN THE
LIBERAL COLLEGE

Administrative Divisions	Purposes	The Virtues		Learning Activities
Division of Studies	Instruction—Intellectual Virtues (Educational guidance)	Speculative	1. Understanding 2. Science 3. Wisdom	Study
		Practical	1. Art 2. Prudence	
Division of Student Personnel	Discipline—Moral Virtues (Personal guidance)		1. Prudence 2. Justice 3. Temperance 4. Fortitude (courage)	Asceticism
	Counseling—Theological Virtues		1. Faith 2. Hope 3. Charity	Worship

Anyone who has ever taken part in athletics knows the nervous strain that every participant undergoes immediately before the game and at crucial periods during it. Facing the situation with determination and the resolve to go through with it to the end is perhaps the best preparation that youth can have for facing similar situations which will call for nerve and courage in his adult life. Dr. Robert Brown, the "golden boy" of 1946 who was paid a $50,000 bonus to sign with the New York Yankees, told ballplayers gathered at a banquet: "Professors in medical school can give a guy a bad time. Their oral examinations break many a medical student who can't take it. Big-league baseball conditioned me to hold up. I could look those profs in the eye and say: 'Brother, you can't scare me. I've been at the plate in Yankee Stadium with 80,000 fans screaming.'"[4] In dramatics and forensics

[4] *Time,* February, 5, 1951, p. 64.

we encounter the problem of stage-fright. Fear in this situation can be overcome in no other way than by appearing upon the platform and going through the ordeal that develops the courage and skill that will be required to face public audiences later in life.

In both athletics and debate there is wonderful opportunity for the development of the virtue of prudence. In athletics the decisions that have to be made in the fraction of a second and will determine whether a game is won or lost, are wonderful opportunities for training the student in practical judgment. Often he will make blunders, and the game is lost as a result of his mistakes; but these very mistakes may be a valuable experience for him in that he learns the importance of forming right judgments.

Perhaps the only occasion that the curricular activities offer for the development of justice is during examinations, when there is a positive obligation upon the student not to copy from his fellows. But in the community life of the student the opportunities for practicing justice are ever present, and if within the student community the attitude can be created which condemns the least infraction of this virtue through pilfering or dishonesty of any kind, it is one of the most severe disciplines for implanting in the hearts of the young the virtue of honesty, one phase of the virtue of justice.

In the virtue of temperance there is a special obligation when dealing with older adolescents, since college students are seventeen years of age and older, and temptations to intemperance are especially active at this age. Here again if within the student community the attitude can be developed which condemns infractions and indiscretions in this regard, it will be one of the most wholesome influences in forming those habits which characterize the man in later life who is truly Christian. Experience in dealing with young men in an institution where hundreds or even several thousands of them are living together in the same community, dictates that here the regulations must be very specific. In the case of drunkenness for example, commonly one infraction is allowed with only suspension for the remainder of the semester as a penalty; but the second offense means expulsion. All students must know that there is no possibility of getting around this rule, and when the occasion demands, it must be enforced with severity so that it will seldom have to be resorted to. Thus a wholesome attitude will be developed in the student body condemning indiscretions of this kind.

III. Citizens in the College Community

If the student is a rational and educable creature, he is not less a social being and as such a necessary subject of social training. It will not avail us to say that our ancestors did not make use of such psychological terms, for they erred in failing to recognize this obligation. Every educator who is even vaguely alert to life's reality, has learned to his regret what pitfalls await the student whose social training has been neglected. It is our belief that we are not justifying our function as teachers or administrators unless we plan this training of the undergraduate, not merely from the negative point of view, but through a constructive and positive program. If the faculty is to be made liberal minded, so too must the student. We are convinced that the Catholic college is here offered a great opportunity of developing the student as a citizen of the college community. If, because of traditionalism, or cowardice, or any other nameless fear, we here relinquish this challenge to leadership, it may well be that we shall not receive this opportunity again, at least in our day. Every effort should be made to develop within the college a community characterized by cooperation as well as competition, the two qualities that characterize American democracy.

There can be no cavil about the fact that our colleges in general, Catholic and otherwise, do little towards implanting the theories of democracy which we teach. It is a fact that we cast our graduates upon an uncharted sea so far as social responsibility is concerned. All this is the result, not of a pedagogic pattern, but of the lack of one. Our methods in college are barely advanced beyond those of the elementary school in this regard. We still make the rules and see that they are kept. We still impose authority from above while we teach that governments derive their authority from the consent of the governed. No one suggests that we subject a college or its faculty to the whims of a group of adolescents. No one proposes to divest the administration of its rights; but to say that we teach students to live in a democratic society by impelling our own discipline upon them without their cooperation in making the rules, is rather ridiculous. Whatever may have been the proper form in another day in another clime and country,—even though such a system may have operated effectively in the Holy Roman Empire, Jacobean England, or in Spain of the Aragons—it is reasonably certain that it should have to undergo some major changes before it can be attuned to the American scene.

1. Student Government

Specifically, we are content to believe that the independent college which is not a division of a large university and which fails to make the student an integral part of its government, is missing a wonderful opportunity. We are not here referring to student government as it is publicized. We mean exactly what the words denote. We stand for the largest measure of undergraduate responsibility commensurate with the genius of the individual institution. We do not advise that this plan be adopted *in toto* at once, but sincerity requires that it be honestly inaugurated where there has been little pretense at student control in the past. Such a plan supposes much more education on the part of the students, much greater effort on the part of the teachers, and subjects administrators to greater hazards than the present "safe" approach.

This is the hard way to teach but, as usual, the best. It supposes that we are prepared to relinquish some of the pseudodignity that we have always cherished. By making our students our partners, it places both of us in proper relation. It may seem revolutionary at first glance, but reflection will make us wonder that we have so long failed to see its utter necessity. Since the student is something more than a mere robot in the educative process, since he is in reality the other term, he cannot be considered as merely receptive or inert. He must be permitted, as far as is practicable, to live the things we teach. Our great deficiency in methodology has been that we have acted as though teaching was for our satisfaction. Too often we have used the undergraduate as a pawn where he has not been a victim. We have lost our vision and too often our dream because we did not know, or at least we did not seem to know, that the student is the end for which the teacher labors.

We maintain that the student should be given the widest latitude in rights and responsibilities consistent with his potentiality. We know that he is not equipped to dictate policies of curriculum, but he should be able to conduct, under guidance, most of the extracurricular activities. We think that the corporate body of students should be given a constitution setting up the rights and duties of that body, and that it should be permitted to retain those rights and duties as long as it upholds its part of the contract. The privileges can be extended as the student body shows itself fit. The college must decide for itself and by experimentation what rights it will cede. In a decent democracy and with proper inspiration, the students should be able to conduct most of their own business, and it is not visionary to say that the problem of discipline ought to be reduced to a very minimum.

There is no area of student activity that is foreign to this ideal or beyond the reality.

Naturally, all of the ordinary activities, such as dramatics, glee club, intramural athletics, study groups, and publications, should be included within the sphere of student control. We do not believe, either, that the faculty counselor, if he exists at all, should have the power of veto, which is sheer hypocrisy. We cannot retain supervision if we have divested ourselves of control. We must be brave enough to go the whole way, trusting enough to surrender all, assured that those in whom we confide will not betray us. Youth, now as always, careless, frivolous, irresponsible, is still fundamentally noble, basically sound, and essentially decent. If we expect the graduate to take his part in the democratic way of life the day after commencement, we must gradually prepare him for his responsibility. If we hope to make him a self-reliant man, we cannot treat him as a suspect. Confidence begets trust; suspicion engenders only rebellion. The faculty should always reserve the right to intervene when the common good is at issue; but such a prerogative should be exercised only when the need is genuine and extreme. To give the final decision in all matters concerning faculty-student relations, a superior judiciary court composed of faculty members should be set up.

Control by the students supposes that they will have complete supervision of their own finances, which are safeguarded by the requirement that an accredited member of the faculty countersign checks. Student control also means that all general disciplinary regulations should come from those who are to keep them. This plan also provides for the religious life of the student, where the chaplain is relied upon to provide the necessary spiritual challenge. Here, as elsewhere, the student must learn to become a part of the mystical body by actual living and by full participation. Whether or not the individual college is prepared to submit the administering of examinations to the students is a matter of individual judgment. We are not considering here an honor system, since that is essentially unsound psychologically and, if it fails, it fails irremediably. We mean that responsibility and honesty are to become a part of everyday living and not merely a matter of sporadic occasions.

We have indicated the spirit of this idea, and we are convinced that the Catholic college should provide the natural environment for its development. We think it has possibilities yet unsounded, even undreamed. What we have here advocated may apply pertinently only to the smaller college of liberal arts. Larger colleges and university colleges may have quite different problems and may be able to apply these principles only as in a representative democracy.

2. Student Guidance

In Figure 8, "The Administration of a Liberal College" (p. 219), the "Guidance Program" is located between the Division of Studies and the Division of Student Personnel with overlapping brackets to indicate that in the American school system it occupies a prominent place in both divisions. In the social systems of the old world a child's destiny was largely decided at birth, and the school systems were planned to prepare him for that destiny. Not so in a democracy! Here, theoretically at least, equal opportunity for all, both in social life and in the school system, makes it possible for anyone with ability and industry to become one of the leaders of his generation. Hence the necessity of guidance in helping him to choose his place in life and prepare himself to fill it. So prominent has this movement become in some school systems that its adversaries label it the "cult of guidance," ridiculing the idea that anyone can choose for another the career in which he is going to find happiness in life when such happiness is so dependent upon fortuitous circumstances and the personal aims and emotional reactions of each individual, of which he alone can have intimate knowledge. Nevertheless here is an area in which the young can be helped to make wise choices through both educational and vocational guidance.

In these two fields, educational and vocational guidance, the movement toward measurement in education holds out the greatest hope. Although the movement is still in its infancy, great progress already has been achieved in making it possible to give the student information and knowledge of himself concerning his own abilities and aptitudes, which may furnish a real basis for planning intelligently his future career. Hence it is necessary for every college to have a guidance program with an expert in charge trained in testing and measurement, who in turn will work with the teaching staff to impress upon them the fact that upon them, through their intimate contact with students, rests the chief responsibility for success of the guidance program. The chief responsibility of the director is to help prepare the teachers to carry out the program effectively.

Guidance in meeting the personal problems of life, which so often are moral problems, is quite another matter. In the Catholic college this matter should be the concern of the one in charge of the religious program, the chaplain and his assistants. Instruction in religion (or better, theology) is another problem, and often in the large institutions these two problems are handled by separate administrative officers, who, however, must always work closely together so that a student's knowledge and understanding of his religion and his participation in common worship (reception of the sacraments, etc.) will result in a deeper love for God and carry over into everyday life in the practice of the moral virtues. But the aim of those in charge of the religious program is the development of the theological virtues of faith, hope, and charity. (See Figure 9, p. 229.) Here inspiration and guidance are supreme. Thus those in charge of the religious program must never be administrative officers of student discipline.

Rather they must be the refuge of those students who come in conflict with the disciplinary regulations of the institution. They must function as father confessors, and students must be free to lay the whole situation before them, receiving sacramental absolution if the circumstances warrant it. We see here the difference between the office of the chaplain and that of the guidance bureau. In the latter the advancement and failures of the student are carefully recorded for future reference, whereas in the chaplain's office a record is never kept on file for use by others. Here the chaplain's opportunity is to help the student see the difficulty in which he has become involved from the point of view of his religion, and encourage him to face it boldly and make an intelligent decision that holds promise of leading him out of it. With a firm resolution on his part, the grace of God will do the rest. But the decision must be the student's own, not that of a counselor.

Non-directive Counseling

One of the most recent and most hopeful developments in the guidance movement is that of non-directive counseling. According to Father Charles Curran, who treated this topic at the Midwest Regional Meeting of the N.C.E.A. College and University Department in Chicago, 1949, we do not need the adjective "non-directive" if we understand what St. Thomas means by the virtue of counsel.

All counseling rightly understood is personal and unique, and, in that sense, is non-directive. It is the function of the person's own intellect surveying the means which he knows to be possible in reaching a given goal. He may take advice and guidance from others, but he alone can integrate that advice and act on that guidance. St. Thomas says that even if the guidance were absolutely correct and a man carried it out completely, such a man would still not be living a perfect life, because goodness as a virtue must come from himself on his own responsibility and not merely be dependent on the guidance of others.[5]

We all know the tendency to advise another with the words, "If I were in your place, . . ." But the fact we must face is that we can never be in the place of another. We have not had the experiences he has had, and we are never driven by precisely the same motives and emotional reactions which may impel him. How, then, can we put ourselves in his place? Nor need we do this. We are astonished at times by the knowledge, understanding, and even wisdom that students sometimes reveal in stating their problems. Often they see what they must do, but they do not see how to do it. Here is where counsel comes in. It means evaluating, integrating, and measuring the means available for the ends in view. But young people are so often disturbed by their emotional reactions and instincts that they do not see their way clear to make an intelligent decision. Then it is not advice that they need, but rather peace of mind and courage to face the facts, which they often receive from one who merely listens to their problem with a sympathetic ear. The great spiritual directors among the saints knew this fact and therefore declined to make the decisions for those who consulted them, limiting themselves to helping their clients see clearly the situation they were in and laying before them the various means available for extricating themselves from the difficulty. They promised to join with the troubled one in prayer for light and strength of will to act resolutely on their decision once it had been reached; but they did not make the decision. They realized the importance of one's making one's own decisions.

Father Curran concludes his paper with suggestions for teachers that merit careful consideration by all engaged in counseling young people on personal problems.

[5] Rev. Charles Curran, "The Virtue of Counsel" in the *College News Letter*, May, 1949, p. 4.

One of the dangers of classroom education of large groups at a time is that instead of being sensitive to the feelings of each student and the singular unique events in which each student's attitudes are formed and related to what is being taught, the teacher is concentrating on himself, his lecture plan and his own emotional needs to be accepted and successful. Such a teacher may give knowledge but he will miss many valuable opportunities to aid in the growth of the moral virtues, especially counsel and prudence. But a teacher who is sensitive to counseling and has acquired a non-directive skill in the classroom and in individual contacts with students is alert to the student's need to unfold his personal emotions about certain ideas or principles. Such a teacher is not forcing passive acquiescence, but is conscious of the student's acquiring personal integration if he is to be a responsible man of virtue.

In this way education is not centered only on the intellectual virtues of knowledge and understanding but also on the moral virtues that are essential to the formation of mature self-reliant character. This can only be done by each person for himself. The moral virtues are founded on prudence, and prudence, says St. Thomas, is an incommunicable knowledge. It *cannot be taught; it must be lived.* But since the virtue of counsel is basic to prudence, it is the way through which a prudent judgment is made and prudence can be facilitated by a counseling process. Counseling then enables a man to clarify and integrate the confused instinctive and emotional impulses that block him from taking responsible action on what he knows he should do. It is the final step in education by which a man is able to live by the principles he knows. In this sense we feel non-directive counseling could profitably be added to teaching and guidance to round out our educational program, so that we form not only large masses of students who know what they should do, but dynamic men of principle each of whom is a person conscious of his own responsibility and of his own views.[6]

[6] *Ibid.*, p. 13.

3. The College as a Community

This chapter completes our analysis of what the school can do for the student in terms of training in the virtues. In the college the direct attack is on the intellectual virtues through the program of study. The primary responsibility of the Church is the development of the theological virtues, while that of the home is the development of the moral virtues. Educators know that they are almost helpless in accomplishing their own task if no foundation for this has been laid in the lives of children by parents, other members of the family circle, and playmates before they ever enter school. But with a foundation in habits of obedience, docility, honesty, and so forth, the school can implant in the minds of the young reasons for living the moral virtues. Moreover, the school is also a community, and as a community it offers a rich opportunity for the practice of these virutes. For this reason many educators believe that the residential sectarian college is the ideal situation for older adolescents, since it is home, church, community, and school all integrated in one institution; and four years in such an institution, they say, is the best possible preparation for that transition from the home of their childhood to the home of their choice. This choice involves making that momentous decision of choosing a partner for life, of embracing a life of celibacy in the priesthood, or of becoming a member of the spiritual family of a religious community. This is the most important decision that they will ever make in their lives.

Active participation by all students in the liturgy of the Church and in the extracurricular activities of the campus together with the intellectual life of the classroom, lecture hall, library, laboratory, and study, creates a community conducive to the practice of all the virtues, and it should be the ambition of all college administrators and teaching staffs to make it a reality. The result hoped for from such a program is beautifully described in a sketch found in an old manor house on Gloucestershire, written and framed and hung over the mantelpiece of a tapestried sitting room.

Portrait of a True Gentleman

The true gentleman is God's servant, the world's master and his own; virtue is his business, study his recreation, contentment his rest and happiness his reward. The saints are his brethren and all that need him his friends; devotion is his chaplain, chastity his chamberlain, sobriety his butler, temperance his cook, hospitality his housekeeper, providence his steward, charity his treasurer, piety his mistress of the house and discretion his porter to let in or out as most fit. Thus is his whole family made up of virtues, and he is the true master of the house. He is necessitated to take the world on his way to Heaven, but he walks through it as fast as he can and all his business, by the way, is to make himself and others happy. Take him in two words,—

a Man and a Christian.

CHAPTER 11

THE CHALLENGE TO THE LIBERAL
COLLEGE

GLANCING back over the past century, during which almost all the Catholic colleges in the United States were established and have grown to maturity, we have some idea of the many significant changes that have taken place in both the content and method of their educational programs. Such changes were inevitable. The school as one of the great social institutions, always reflects the society it is serving; but the school as the agency of formal education, should also reform society, that is, strive to remake it according to the desire of those constituting the society which brought it into being. It fulfills this purpose by preparing the youth of today to become the constituent members of the society of tomorrow in a way that will make their society an improvement over that of their fathers. Sometimes it fails in this duty, and then we have regress instead of progress.

I. TWO GUIDING PRINCIPLES

In our efforts to evaluate the changes which have taken place and continue to take place within the American college, we look for certain principles which will guide us in deciding whether we should resist these changes now going on in the Catholic college, or whether in the case of some of them we should embrace the anticipated results as ideals to be aimed at, and direct our efforts toward planning procedures for their realization. We have two such principles to guide us, the principle of permanence and the principle of change. The first arises from the nature of man; the second, from the nature of society.

1. The Principle of Permanence

Man is a rational animal, and the purpose of education is to make him more rational and less like an animal; that is, to give his rationality control over his animality. But we are thus speaking from a purely natural point of view. All true humanists from ancient times to the present hold that man's nature is partly spiritual. But with the advent of Christianity as the predominant influence in Western civilization, a new concept comes to the fore: man has a supernatural destiny with supernatural means available to help him achieve that destiny. This concept contains two correlative ideas, original sin and the doctrine of grace, which are not recognized by the naturalists. But Pascal's comment on original sin—"without this mystery, the most incomprehensible of all, we are incomprehensible to ourselves"—gives a deeper insight into the nature of man. Created by God and endowed with gifts above what his nature called for, but by his rebellion fallen from that high estate, man is redeemed by Christ and called to live a supernatural life, wherefore he is offered the aid of divine grace. If he is faithful to that call, he will achieve his supernatural destiny.

The school, of course, has a part to play in helping man attain that eternal destiny; but this is the essential function of the Church. The distinction between "knowledge about" and "acquaintance with" helps us understand the function proper to the school in this area. As an intellectual agency it may offer its pupils a course in sacramental theology, through which they may acquire knowledge about their eternal destiny and the means to attain it; but it is only in its function as a community (a part of the parish community) that the school leads its pupils to a participation in the liturgy of the Church, which actually acquaints them with the sacraments, the channels through which grace flows to the faithful in abundance. For this reason, as we mentioned in the last chapter, many educators advocate the residential college as the ideal educational institution for older adolescents since it is home, church, and school integrated into one community. Life within such a community, they claim, is the students' best preparation for making the transition from the home of their childhood to the home of their choice, a transition which confronts most of them soon after they leave college.

But there are other fields of knowledge besides religious knowledge which every member of the community should possess if he is to play an intelligent part in forming the public opinion that governs the community. It is the thesis of general or liberal education that there is a common denominator of knowledge which in a democracy all should possess; on the college level it is commonly spoken of as the arts and sciences and represents one phase of the educative process, social transmission. The other phase, the individual development of each citizen's powers of thought and expression, is equally important. One is complementary to the other. They must proceed simultaneously if either is to achieve a high level of attainment. Powers of thought and expression cannot develop in a mental vacuum; hence we have both the sciences and the arts, the whole complex being called the liberal arts. It includes our knowledge of the three worlds in which man lives and the ability to think intelligently about them, together with the ability to communicate such ideas, so that all men may work together for the improvement of the society in which their lives are cast. All this follows from the nature of man as a rational being, and only pseudopsychologists can claim that they are going to remake that nature and change it into something different. As Norman Foerster has stated it, any student of the past should "recognize the fact that human nature is in all times and places of recorded history fundamentally the same and that it will not be changed tomorrow." [1]

2. The Principle of Change

An analysis of the nature of society reveals an entirely different situation. Beginning with the religious revolution of the sixteenth century, followed by the scientific and political revolutions of the seventeenth and eighteenth centuries and the industrial revolution in the United States in the nineteenth century, society has undergone many changes and is still undergoing transformation to such an extent that we may speak of the social revolution of the twentieth century. So many and so varied have been the advancements in transportation and communication during the past generation that we can literally say that we are living in a new age. We should not be surprised that these changes have had a marked influence on the school since, like the home, it is more responsive to social change than are the church and the state. The developments within the sciences, both natural and social, have had a direct effect in changing the curriculum of the school. Knowledge has expanded so rapidly in these fields and has divided into so many branches and become so highly specialized that the problem of the school today is the integration of this knowledge so that the student may have some idea how the sciences in their application have transformed the complex society of which he is a part.

In theory, at least, we have extended the period of universal education from eight to twelve years of schooling, and with the recommendations of the President's Commission on Higher Education, we are now extending it to fourteen years. This means extending education to the age of twenty. With the advance of technology, a very small part of this

[1] Norman Foerster, *The Future of the Liberal College,* pp. 75 f.; used by permission of Appleton-Century-Crofts, Inc.

time, even in the later years, need be devoted to occupational training. Vocational training is taking on a more general character in order that the skills developed may be applied in many occupations. As the report of the Fourth National Conference of Life Adjustment Education states it: "Every youth is entitled to common learnings and to vocational education *of a general character*. This philosophy is leading to the extension of free public education today beyond the twelfth grade." [2] We are reminded of Henry Ford's statement some years ago that he could foresee the time when all the workers in his factories would be college graduates working four hours a day, four days a week; but he added that they would not need their college education to operate the various machines at which they worked; the factory would teach them that in a day or so. Their general or liberal education would benefit them in the enjoyment of their increased leisure time and in carrying on effectively their responsibilities as citizens in a democratic society. This prediction emphasizes the obligation of the school, and particularly the college, to prepare young people for making our present complex social organization a society in which all men will have not merely life and liberty, but also the opportunity for the pursuit of happiness with some promise of success.

II. The Call to the Liberal College

The liberal college in America is called upon to give to its students that kind of education which, as the experience of centuries in our Western tradition has taught us, holds the best promise for turning out free men and free women who alone can preserve and improve a free society. With the universalization of high-school education, we used to say that there were more students in secondary education in the

[2] *School Life* (Washington: Office of Education), III, no. 3 (December, 1950), p. 45.

United States than in all the rest of the world together. We can say that no longer, for secondary education is now being widely extended in Europe, Latin America, and the rest of the world. The segregation of the old dual system is disappearing, and if the claim is true regarding education behind the "Iron Curtain," this segregation of the classes has already vanished in Soviet Russia. The movement in the Soviet Republics merits our special consideration. Apparently they also are universalizing secondary education if we interpret this phase to mean any education beyond the primary school, where fundamental facts and skills in the tools of education (the three R's) are the primary objective. Secondary education in Russia today does not place its primary emphasis on general or liberal education as those terms have been traditionally interpreted (the study of the arts and sciences with emphasis on the liberal arts) ; rather, the emphasis in Soviet education is on the useful arts—that is, technology—in order to bring about a rapid industrialization of the country and prepare it for war. Second in importance are the fine arts, particularly music and the dance, in which Russia has always been pre-eminent and which have always had a special appeal for arousing the passions of men. We can hardly expect that the phrase "liberal arts" would be used in a police state, since the very purpose of this form of government is to control man's powers of thought and expression and not to set them free.

In contrast, the life of a free society depends on the reception, by all members, of an education that merits the name liberal. We are encouraged, therefore, by the extension of liberal education that is now taking place throughout the world this side of the "Iron Curtain." The strength of our armed forces during the recent conflict was not due solely to our advance in technology and the industrial production of the machines of modern warfare. It has been pointed out that since 40 per cent of our youth in the armed forces were

high-school graduates, they had one remarkable characteristic that marked them off from any army the world had
ever known; and that characteristic was not their training
in the industrial arts in high school, enabling them to operate
the new machines of war, but rather their gift of having
learned how to learn, thus enabling them in a few months,
through intensive training, to become familiar with the basic
principles of the new machines and to rapidly develop skill
in their operation.

But another thing is necessary in a free society. The education its citizens receive must not only be such that they learn
how to learn; they must also learn how to live. Any liberal
education worthy of the name makes its greatest contribution
in this respect. In concentrating its efforts on the development
of the powers of thought and expression, it must impress upon
its students that the most concrete form of expression is
conduct in life. It must implant in the minds of youth ideals
by which they will live. The United Nations Educational,
Scientific and Cultural Organization (UNESCO) should not
exhaust its resources in its efforts to eliminate illiteracy
throughout the world and in similar projects. Rather, these
resources in this present emergency may better be spent in
helping to spread throughout the world an education that is
truly liberal in character. With such an education the free
citizens of free nations should know how to work together
to bring into being a free world. The following statement by
Father Guthrie, president of Georgetown University, is surely
idealistic, but it well merits consideration in this connection.

As things are today, we cannot appeal to religion to break
down the barriers which divide nation from nation, group from
group, and man from man. Unfortunately religion itself constitutes one of the most infrangible of barriers. If, then, a beginning
is made in our time toward a common brotherhood of man, an
inroad can be made only through that element of human nature

which constitutes its common and outstanding characteristic, *reason*. We must find a common, human and rational code of ethical or moral standards; we must restore the spirit to its dominant role in human affairs and return reason to its throne.

This is the awesome task of integrated liberal education today. . . . Quite independently of religion and answering the innermost urgencies of human reason, we have a set of human values, a code of moral standards, a naturally virtuous and a rationally sound system of education in the liberal arts. It is our duty as educators to re-examine the meaning of these courses, discover their profound riches, gain some understanding of their providential role in the education of man throughout history and perhaps learn much to our surprise that, despite the death knells that have been tolled over their effigy by modern psychologists and brisk, dynamic, sales-conscious educators, they are very much alive and constitute the only natural, rational hope for peace in the individual soul and a cultural bridge and basis of mutual understanding and concord between war-weary nations.[3]

But if these ends are to be attained through "education in the liberal arts," there is necessary what Robert Ulich calls an extended period of "incubation." The maturity of the college student makes possible more rapid and more extensive learning in a given time than is possible by the elementary or high-school student, since the latter is still maturing. But for college students there is real need for a period of reflective thinking—yes, of contemplation—if the student is to "absorb the beauty and depth that distinguish the great styles of thought from mere informational material." [4] The liberal college should provide for this reflective thinking as well as for formal training in the religious heritage of Western

[3] Hunter Guthrie, "An Important Contemporary Purpose of Catholic Education" in *Fifty Golden Years, Commemorating the Golden Jubilee of the College of Notre Dame of Maryland* (1946), p. 105.

[4] Robert Ulich, "The Meaning of Liberal Education" in *The Teaching of Religion in Higher Education*, ed. by Christian Gauss, p. 51.

civilization. The colleges are awakening to this fact, and in many institutions radical steps are being taken to remedy the situation that secularization has brought about.

III. The Call to the Catholic Liberal College

An appeal to reason alone could never satisfy the Catholic who sees human nature as a wounded nature with a darkened intellect and a weakened will. It is through this fallen nature alone that we can explain the tyrants of the past as well as the dictators of the present who apparently glory in the concentration camps and slave labor of their subject peoples. Disregarding God, they deify themselves and seek ruthlessly to add to their own power and prestige.

How can we talk about the brotherhood of man if we have no common Father, and how can we claim any rights for man if we question the truth of those ten famous words of our own Declaration of Independence: "All men are endowed by their Creator with inalienable rights"? Once these rights are denied, the law of the jungle, in which might is right, is supreme. The naturalists may invoke Rousseau's social contract or some more modern theory as a basis for a democratic society; but Rousseau's theory is nothing but a form of sublimated self-interest: "We will agree not to rob or kill each other so that we can help each other to a more abundant life." Natural law has a higher sanction than that conferred by social living. Morality has roots that are deeper than human reason. Newman thus states the matter in his usual penetrating style:

Knowledge is one thing, virtue is another; good sense is not conscience, refinement is not humility, nor is largeness and justness of view faith. Philosophy, however enlightened, however profound, gives no command over the passions, no influential motives, no vivifying principles. Liberal Education makes not the Christian, not the Catholic, but the gentleman. . . . Quarry the granite rock with razors, or moor the vessel with a thread of silk; then may you hope with such keen and delicate instruments as human knowledge and human reason to contend against those giants, the passion and the pride of man.[5]

There seems to be a general awakening now to the fact that "Liberal Education makes not the Christian, not the Catholic, but the gentleman." For several years now the Association of American Colleges has had not only a Commission on Liberal Education and one on International Cultural Relations, but also a Commission on Christian Higher Education, in which both Protestant and Catholic colleges and universities are working on the problem of making religion a vital force in the curriculum and in the campus life of their institutions. But even more: not only the denominational colleges but even the secular institutions of higher education are beginning to recognize that religious knowledge is a part of the spiritual inheritance of mankind that should be passed on to students as part of their general education. Among the state institutions Iowa University has taken the leadership by providing instructors in three faiths (Jewish, Protestant, and Catholic), who are fully recognized members of the faculty, teaching their faith not only to the members of their own persuasion, but to all students who care to take their courses.

In the Catholic college, of course, instruction in theology is not merely available; it is required of all Catholic students intending to graduate from the college. We have recommended above (pp. 164–73, 181 f.) that theology, as the social science par excellence, be the core of the curriculum by being made the core of the two-year course in the humanistic and philosophical sciences required of all students, and that theology be offered, moreover, as a field of concentration as well as an elective in the last two years of college. I am convinced that if theology were presented in this way to all stu-

[5] *Idea of a University*, Discourse V, p. 137.

dents, there would be a much greater prospect of really integrating it in their lives not only during their college days, but even after they leave school and become the mainstay of their parish. Then the comparatively few students who might choose theology as their field of concentration should become laymen and laywomen who would apply their knowledge of theology to their everyday lives in a way that would be an inspiration to those who did not have the same educational advantages. These would provide a leadership of thinkers, writers, and doers, in the training of whom the college would be making a tremendous contribution to the community. Integration of theology with life is surely more important than mere integration in the social studies, but the college that brings about both types of integration is the one that will most closely approach the ideal all should be striving for. The importance of this integration of theology in liberal education is thus expressed by Doctor Nutting of the University of Notre Dame:

This bringing about of a reasoned acceptance of the ideas of a Christian civilization is the job of the liberal higher education, and it is much the most important job in the whole educational field, much more important than professional training or scientific research. It is much more important than literacy itself. The creating of a scheme of liberal education that will be effective, therefore, is the most important task that we face now.[6]

[6] Willis D. Nutting, "Mark Hopkins, the Log and the Dollar" in *The Commonweal*, April 14, 1950, p. 9.

CHAPTER 12

THE LIBERAL COLLEGE OF THE FUTURE

IF WE will consider the fact that the American school system developed from an accumulation of heterogeneous institutions with varying purposes, we should not be surprised that it stands in need of serious reorganization. The eight-year elementary school was modeled on the Prussian *Volksschule*, or "Peasants' School," the purpose of which was terminal education for the peasant class.[1] There was need for such a school in this country during the rapid expansion of the frontier and the period of immigration, but it did not adequately provide for the education of scholars. That part of the German school system which prepared students for the university, the *Vorgymnasium* (three years) and *Gymnasium* (nine years), found no counterpart in the American system. Since the rapid development of the high school in the early years of this century, the eight-year elementary school is no longer a terminal institution, but a preparatory school for further study in the high school.

The modern high school developed from the academies and Latin Grammar Schools of colonial times,[2] which it gradually

[1] The ordinance of Frederick II explicitly designated the teacher "as an officer whose duty is to form good tenants for landlords" (F. F. Bunker, *Reorganization of the Public School System* [Washington: Government Printing Office, 1916], p. 28).

[2] This is our one indigenous institution, and we are proud of what we now call the American cosmopolitan high school: a school that takes in all the children of all the people. Cf. Edgar W. Knight, *Education in*

253

replaced during the last half of the nineteenth century. In the beginning the high school was a finishing school for the children of the people, with a practical curriculum modeled on that of the early academy; but early in its development it took over the function of a college preparatory school, as the academy once had done, and eventually became dominated by this new function. In their efforts to free themselves from this role, and aided by the passage of the Smith-Hughes Act in 1917, which gave federal aid for vocational training on a dollar per dollar basis, many high schools introduced curriculums in home economics and the industrial arts; later other occupational courses were introduced. Thus for the past several decades our high schools have been trying to fulfill the two functions of preparing early adolescents for advanced education in the college and university, and of providing a terminal general education which will prepare the non-academic group for life as citizens in a democracy. Since these two functions are so widely different, we can hardly expect our present system of high-school education to adequately satisfy both (or either) of these needs.

The American college has developed from another source. All colonial colleges were importations from England, both in their foundation and in the educational philosophies which guided their early development. In their conversion into universities, the German influence was paramount; but in the middle of the last century, the college had become so well established in American life that no foreign influence could disturb it. The educational tradition which the colonial colleges adopted from England, still inspires the American college and is thus described by Newman:

---

the United States, p. 385. A few educators challenge this claim: "probably copied originally from Edinburgh" (A. Ross Hill, "The Junior College Movement" in Educational Problems in College and University, ed. by John Lewis Brumm [Ann Arbor: University of Michigan Press, 1921], p. 197).

There are three great subjects in which human reason employs itself:—God, Nature, and Man: and Theology being put aside in the present argument, the physical and social worlds remain. These, when respectively subjected to Human Reason, form two books: the book of nature is called Science, the book of man is called Literature. Literature and Science, thus considered, nearly constitute the subject-matter of Liberal Education.[3]

But in its development the American college has become, like the high school, an institution designed to provide the culmination of general or liberal education for all its students and to prepare some for further study on the university or professional level.

I. THE DILEMMA OF DEMOCRATIC EDUCATION

This country was the first country in the world to set up a democratic school system, if by that we mean a system in which all the children of all the people are in the same school. But this single system, we have already seen, has created for us a variety of school situations that demand solution. Every society is confronted with the problem of making provision in its educational system for training those who are to be its leaders, and those who are to be the followers. Europe has traditionally met this problem by two separate school systems, one for the followers (like the *Volksschule* of old Germany) and one for the leaders (like the *Gymnasium*, preparatory to the university in that country). But such a system creates a social distinction between the classes, and the outcome is social stratification. The United States, with its single system, is aiming at mass education, which promotes group solidarity; but the development of superior minds is sadly neglected. The tendency of the single system is to gear the pace to the average student: a pace too slow for the fast

[3] *Idea of a University,* Discourse IX, "Duties of the Church toward Knowledge," p. 239.

learners, and too fast for the slow. Can we solve this dilemma, retaining our single system (the outstanding contribution of the United States to democratic education), and at the same time make provision for the slow, the average, and the superior minds, all within the same system? [4]

With this end in view, reconstruction of our system is already being attempted on all levels. Some form of ability grouping is being tried in the elementary school, the high school, and also in the college. Special plans are being tried on the different levels. The Winnetka Plan, on the elementary level, provides for one half of the school day being devoted to individual instruction in the tool subjects; the other half to group activities in the auditorium, the gymnasium, and classes in the social studies which all pupils carry together. The Dalton Laboratory Plan in high schools provides for students working on "contract" according to their interests and abilities, doing away with the "lockstep" of the ordinary school, yet all working together within the same "laboratories." Honor courses and the "honors and pass" degrees of the English and Canadian universities are suggested as the solution on the college level.

Some solution to the dilemma, whereby the slow, the average, and the superior students can all be kept working at capacity in the same system, is the challenge to the new science of education now developing in this country.[5] In the Catholic system one plan is now operating under the guidance of Msgr. Clarence Elwell, Superintendent of Catholic Schools in the Diocese of Cleveland. In this plan the fourth and seventh grades are called "review and preview grades"; that

[4] Cf. Nelson L. Bossing, *Principles of Secondary Education* (New York: Prentice-Hall, 1949), chap. 6, "In What Respects Are Our Secondary Schools Now Different from Those of Europe?" pp. 127–72; Germany's *Volksschule, Grundschule,* and *Oberstufe* are described on p. 151.

[5] Cf. W. F. Cunningham, *The Pivotal Problems of Education* (New York: Macmillan, 1940), chap. 11, "The Dilemma of Democratic Education," pp. 341–68.

Figure 10. THE DILEMMA OF DEMOCRATIC EDUCATION

School Systems	Social Outcomes	Makes Provision for:	Fails to Provide for:
Europe— Dual Systems (for leaders and led)	Social Stratification (class and mass)	Development of Different Groups (leaders and led)	Social Solidarity (as a nation)
United States— Single System (same for all)	Social Solidarity (one people, one nation)	National Solidarity	Development of Leaders

is, all the essentials are distributed over the other grades, and in the case of each pupil it is decided whether he should enter the fourth or seventh grade, in which he would review what he has already studied and anticipate the work in the grade to follow; or he may skip this review work and go forward to the next grade above. Thus some superior children save two years and others save one. When they enter high school as a group, the solidarity of this group saves them from isolation by the majority of slightly older students in their class.[6]

Other plans are being developed in some public-school systems. One of these allows the promotion of all pupils on the basis of a pupil's physical and social development with differentiated assignments for their academic development, in this way making provision for the brighter group to complete the work of the grades in less than eight years. These are the pupils who should enter high school and continue in college at a lower age than the average, but the high school and college must make provision for their rapid advancement also,

[6] Report of progress of the National Catholic Education Association Committee on the Reorganization of the School System (Bulletin no. 2), XI (November, 1943), p. 27.

since they are the ones most likely to continue their education in the graduate and professional schools unless prevented from doing so by economic handicaps. The only way to get around this last difficulty is a system of full scholarships from state and federal funds as well as from philanthropic organizations, making it possible for these potential leaders to develop their unusual gifts at an early age.

Another recent development in reorganization is the appearance of the community college. The Report of the President's Commission on Higher Education (1947) brought the community college to the fore with the following statement of its nature and functions: "Its purpose is educational service to the entire community, and this purpose requires of it a variety of functions and programs." The Report states further that "some community colleges may offer a full four years of college work, but most of them probably will stop at the end of the fourteenth grade." [7] According to Frasier, in this reorganization "the college is made up of grades 11 through 14. This plan is not common; it is used in some thirty school systems, many of which are in California." [8] The most prominent of these is in Pasadena, California, where the plan was inaugurated in 1929. The program developed in this system is one of the most hopeful indications that the movement toward reorganization is finally taking form in a way that holds much promise for the improvement of American education.[9] In fact, Leonard V. Koos, Professor of Secondary Education at Chicago University, in the Foreword to the book describing this program, when discussing what he feels "recommends itself as the most acceptable pattern of organization," namely the 6–4–4 plan, states that "all indications are that commitments to this pattern . . . will multiply at

[7] *Op. cit.*, p. 67.

[8] George Willard Frasier, *An Introduction to the Study of Education* (New York: Harper and Brothers), p. 156.

[9] John A. Sexson and John W. Harbeson, *The New American College* (New York: Harper and Brothers, 1946).

an accelerated rate." [10] In another work Koos tells the story of nine other institutions organized on this basis; [11] one of these is the college at his own institution.[12]

Roughly we may distinguish two types of curriculums planned to meet the needs of the unselected student body which the new college must serve, preparatory and terminal. Each of these types divides into two different groups. The preparatory curriculums are preparatory (1) to the upper years of the college as now organized and to continued education in the graduate school of arts and sciences, and (2) to the professional schools of the university. The two groups of terminal curriculums are (1) those that terminate general education for the ordinary citizen of the world today, and (2) those that are primarily concerned with occupational training. Pasadena offers a half dozen curriculums preparatory to continued education in the university, but it offers more than fifty different curriculums of the terminal variety, most of them occupational training with certain core subjects in general education urged upon all.[13]

Most of these plans for the reorganization of the American educational system are based on the conviction that most students by the time they are twelve years old are intellectually mature enough to begin secondary education, whereas at the present time most students do not enter high school until they are fourteen years old. I am convinced that in the system in general use at the present time, two years are wasted in primary education. I do not wish to be interpreted as saying that all the time spent in the seventh and eighth grades of the present elementary school is wasted. The point I am

[10] *Ibid.*, p. xiv.
[11] Leonard V. Koos, *Integrating High School and College* (New York: Harper and Brothers, 1946), "The Six-Four-Four Plan at Work."
[12] Cf. above, p. 82, for a brief discussion of the curriculum at Chicago University College.
[13] Cf. *ibid.*, Part IV, "The Offerings of the New American College," pp. 231–92.

making is that the activities of these years are secondary in character and should be recognized as such and incorporated into the first cycle of secondary schooling, the high school.

II. Growth and Maturation

Although the American educational system has four distinct steps, the elementary school, high school, college, and university, if we consider the high school and college as two cycles of secondary education, our system of education will correspond with the almost universally accepted threefold classification into primary, secondary, and higher education. On the basis of age, elementary education is presently concerned with the education of children from about six to fourteen years of age; secondary education, with the education of adolescents from about fourteen to twenty-two years of age; and higher education, with the education of students over twenty-two years of age. But the very ages here assigned to adolescence, the period of secondary education, indicate that this division of our educational system is faulty. The different divisions within our system should be determined, not by arbitrary age groups, but by the changes in growth and development which take place in young people through the experiences brought to them by the school's program of studies, both curricular and extracurricular.

1. The School for Childhood—Elementary Education

From this point of view, elementary education (or as almost all other countries call it, primary education) is concerned with developing within each pupil a command of the tools of education, the three R's. But these tools, we have previously observed, cannot function in a vacuum. Here is the school's opportunity to introduce the child to its social heritage. A child will be reading and writing, speaking and listening, counting and computing about the three worlds in which he lives, the world of nature, the human world of man in society, and the spiritual world in which God is supreme.

Once the child has achieved a command of the tools, once he can reflect as he reads and writes, he is in the second stage of his education, no matter what grade he may be in. Since the average child reaches this level of intellectual development before he is twelve, we maintain that the elementary school should extend only six years, not eight years as at present. Our present eight-year elementary school developed from the German *Volksschule*, which, we must remember, provided terminal education for the peasant class. But now since almost all of our students continue their education in high school, there is no advantage in delaying their secondary education once they have achieved command of the tools and begin reflective thinking.

2. Schools for Adolescents—Secondary Education

The secondary school shifts the emphasis from the command of the tools to the assimilation of the social inheritance through the use of the tools. The achieving of mastery in these tools is still important, especially in the first cycle of this second stage, the high school; but it is of secondary importance. It is more important at this time to become familiar with the arts and sciences which have made our civilization. Without this knowledge of the social inheritance one cannot become an educated person.

In the elementary school and in the first cycle of the secondary school, the organization and presentation of this great array of materials is psychological rather than logical, which means that it is presented to the child's mind in such a way that he can comprehend it. His needs and interests are dominant here. His needs determine the content of the curriculum; his interests determine the method of presentation. Although this principle applies to the first cycle of secondary education, we must remember that early adolescence is a period of transition. The early adolescent is rapidly maturing, and when he is about sixteen years of age, he should be ready for a new type of intellectual experience, the logical organization and presentation of subject matter; but this change should not be abrupt.

During the first cycle both content and method should gradually take on more of the characteristics of scientific organization; that is, the logical organization which arises out of the nature of the subject matter itself as viewed by the maturing mind of the student. In the second cycle, the college, the late adolescent craves the logical organization of the program of study for the simple reason that his mind has been maturing. Now he welcomes a challenge and feels ready to take on the job of an adult. During this second cycle of secondary-school experience, the logical gradually becomes also the psychological. On the university level, of course, the logical and the psychological are one. The period of transition is over, and finally we are dealing with mature minds. A student who has not reached this intellectual maturity is not ready to enter the university, no matter how old he may be.

With this brief description of the changes taking place in the mind of the average student, we can see the anomaly of the present organization of our school system in which secondary education does not begin until the ninth year of school. The junior high-school movement beginning about 1909 held out some hope for a while that reorganization was about to begin; but in practically all systems that adopted this nomenclature, it meant nothing more than a regrouping of the grades, the 6–3–3 plan and the 6–6 plan being the most common. But neither of these plans saves any time for the quick learners. With the four-year college of liberal arts following these twelve years, we have sixteen years devoted to general education. Nothing like this exists anywhere else in the world. Certainly the youth of the United States are not so intellectually retarded that they cannot be prepared for university work before reaching the age of twenty-two, whereas in the rest of the world the common age for entering the university is about nineteen years.

It is true that some students mature faster than others. But those educators who maintain that social maturation in such individuals does not keep pace with their physical and intellectual development, are not supported by what evidence our study of the problem has provided. Dr. Sidney L. Pressey of Ohio State University is quite specific with regard to the question whether fifteen- and sixteen-year-old youths are emotionally mature for college life. At this university he finds not only that "younger students average brighter in class" and make "better students" than those who enter later in life, but also that "contrary to common belief, the young students also appear to be best adjusted socially." [14] Studying that university's report on campus activities, he discovered that only 10 per cent of the younger group were not listed as active, whereas 34 per cent of the older group were "inactive." He also noted that more of the students graduating at twenty-one or younger held office in college.

Besides the time wasted in elementary schools and the consequent reduplication of courses in the high school, there is also some overlapping between high school and college. One college student told me that in his freshman year he had been required to take a course in the history of Western Europe which was identical, even to the textbook used, with one he had taken in high school. Instead of a high school sandwiched in between elementary and collegiate education, a closely knit and well-integrated primary and secondary system embracing the offerings of all three schools—elementary school, high school, and college—would eliminate most of the duplications existing in the present system, thus achieving in fourteen years what is presently accomplished in sixteen years.

Some readers may be surprised that we classify the college

[14] *Chicago Daily News,* Editorial, December 28, 1944.

as a phase of secondary education rather than as higher education. But the college is, as we have explained above, a stage of intellectual development preparing the student for the professional or specialized training of university work. A. Ross Hill, president of Missouri University, corroborates our position: "The American college was and in part still is a secondary school, suited to the educational needs of youth in the later teens, while the development of American universities with the college as the center and heart of their life and instruction instead of their preparatory division, has brought confusion of terms and standards into our higher education." [15] This statement confirms our thesis that the liberal college as the second cycle of secondary education is or should be the culmination of general or liberal education for all of its students in their later teens, and at the same time it is or should be the best possible preparation for those who will continue their work in the graduate or professional schools of the university.

3. The School for Mature Minds—Higher Education

As the highest intellectual agency of our society, the university is primarily concerned with knowledge. Its purpose is to assemble scholars and provide facilities for them to do their part in the advancement of knowledge and to train a highly selected group of the youth of the nation to carry forward this same endeavor. In the advancement of knowledge the university has three functions: the conservation of knowledge, the interpretation of knowledge, and the extension of knowledge. To these three functions we must add another: the transmission of knowledge to posterity; and in this respect the university is similar to the undergraduate college, but with this difference: whereas the undergraduate college is the culmination of the general or liberal education

[15] "The Junior College Movement" in *Educational Problems in College and University* (Ann Arbor: University of Michigan Press, 1921), p. 197.

that every educated American should have if he is to fulfill intelligently and successfully his role in a democratic society, the professional schools and research centers within the university provide specialized instruction in the professional knowledges and skills necessary for the welfare and advancement of civilization.

Since the problem of university studies is beyond the scope of this work, let us now see how the principles outlined in this section are to be applied to the educational system in the United States.

III. The 6–4–4 Plan in American Education

A recent book, *General Education in School and College,* seems to approach the problem of the reorganization of the educational system from the point of view of "vested interests." It concludes, however, with "A Seven Year Program" which saves one year for the brighter pupils; but the plan does not affect the seventh and eighth school years, where the duplications are worse than in any of the others. The authors say: "It is enough here to state our feelings that the traditional content of the 12th grade school course has little present justification and that the whole traditional school sequence should be reorganized." [16] I maintain that the system should be so reorganized that the elementary, high-school, and college courses can be completed in fourteen years. I wish to make it clear, however, that when I am advocating the 6–4–4 plan as the American system of the future, I am speaking for the average student, the middle 50% of our school population. Special provision should be made for the lower 25% and the upper 25%, giving more time for the former and less time for the latter if they are to be kept working at capacity to develope their God-given powers. More than half

[16] *General Education in School and College,* A Committee Report by Members of the Faculties of Andover, Exeter, Lawrenceville, Harvard, Princeton and Yale (Cambridge: Harvard University Press, 1952), p. 14.

of the upper quarter, by attending a summer session or two, should complete secondary education (that is, both high school and college) in seven years or less; and the upper 5% to 10% should complete each cycle in three years or less. Then these highly gifted students would be prepared for university work at the age of eighteen or nineteen instead of twenty-two, the common age for completing college today. This idea is thus stated by the president of Johns Hopkins University:

Freedom to participate in research as a way of life and learning as soon as a student is fitted for that freedom is an essential element of the faculty's proposal.

We believe that many young men and women are capable of benefitting from the freedom for intellectual development which characterizes graduate education without first completing eight long years of secondary school and college. [He does not mention the pupil's "eight long years" in the elementary school, which is worse.] As soon as he is fitted for such freedom we will offer to each student the advantages now granted only to graduate students.[17]

I realize that the reorganization I am advocating involves many difficult problems; but these problems are all problems of administration. There is no theoretical problem involved. If we admit that in our present system the brighter students are not kept working at capacity, we must take practical steps to remedy the situation by enabling them to progress more rapidly. If these students are to begin their life careers in their middle twenties so that they may establish their own homes at a reasonable age, they should begin their university training at an earlier age than is now the practice. The United States is now recognized as the leader in the management of industry and business. Cannot professional administrators of education display a similar ingenuity in the management of

[17] Detlev W. Bronk, *The Johns Hopkins Future* (Baltimore: The University Press, 1951), p. 7.

our schools to meet these problems of different abilities and of variant interests and needs? In *The Atlantic* for April, 1952, Edwin S. Burdell, president of the Cooper Union, New York City, and former Dean of the Humanities at M.I.T., concludes an article entitled "For a Faster Schooling" with these words:

> To meet the various problems of the second half of the twentieth century we need professionally trained specialists. . . . We also need a citizenry trained to recognize the values to be gained from exploring the humanities and the social sciences. To produce a nation of adults equipped in all three fields, educators face a challenge to their creative abilities. The task of building an effective system of education requires imagination, skill, knowledge, and courage.[18]

Assuming that administrators have the knowledge, skill, and imagination needed for this task, as the members of the new profession of industrial management had for theirs, what professional school administrators need is fortitude, or as Burdell says, "courage," to carry out a reorganization of education on all levels which will give us a system that will meet the needs of our heterogeneous student bodies. The diagram in Figure 11 is my conception of such a system. If by adolescence is understood the teen-age, this system fits admirably the 6–4–4 plan; but I have deliberately omitted years and grades in order not to suggest that any fixed number of years is required for any division of the program. Such a system, I believe, meets the demands of the situation in which we now find ourselves.

The 6–4–4 Plan in the Catholic System

The introduction of the 6–4–4 reorganization of schools into the Catholic system frightens some educators because

---

[18] Edwin S. Burdell, "For a Faster Schooling" in *The Atlantic*, vol. 189, no. 4, p. 65.

Figure 11. THE EDUCATIONAL SYSTEM OF A DEMOCRACY

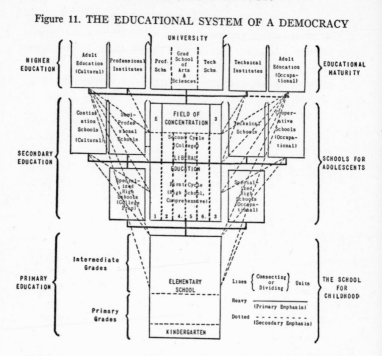

of the adaptations called for in present facilities and teaching staffs. Such an adaptation should not be so difficult as it appears at first sight. In the first place, it is a return to the Catholic tradition of Europe except that in this country it will be a single system instead of a dual system. Although the single system presents some problems, as described above, the solution of these problems is a challenge to American ingenuity and inventiveness, and not beyond our powers.

Some parishes, in the light of their resources, should be content with a six-year elementary school. With a continued increase in enrollment, an old eight-room school will soon be taxed to its capacity to accommodate a kindergarten and six grades. New buildings for the most part should be built for a high school composed of grades 7, 8, 9, and 10. Then the central high school serving several parishes will become a community college for grades 11, 12, 13, and 14. This plan provides for the development of boys' military high schools and girls' academies, setting up a two-cycle institution of high schools and colleges accommodating adolescents from about twelve to twenty years of age. Such institutions could give a new academic degree, the B.G.E., bachelor of general education, or something similar.[19] Even though the last two years may make some provision for occupational training, the emphasis throughout the eight-year continuous course of two cycles will always be general education as interpreted by the Catholic philosophy of education.

The Jesuit academies and colleges have a great opportunity here to revert to the principles of the *Ratio* reinterpreted in terms of the American scene. Father Henry S. Spalding, S.J., when telling what happened at Marquette Academy in Milwaukee before the turn of the century, made this statement:

At that time Marquette received young boys into the high school, or as it was then called, the Academic course, after the end of the sixth grade. The boys came at a time when their memories were quick, pliable and retentive; they were fully prepared to take up secondary work. As far as Marquette was concerned the arrangement was satisfactory and the sixth grade standard would have remained. . . . The Marquette authorities felt that the eight grade requirements for those boys who intended to go to high school and college were pedagogically unsound; yet they decided to submit to the force of circumstances and adopt a plan that was in harmony with the public and parish educational system of Wisconsin.[20]

[19] James Bryant Conant, President of Harvard University, in *Education in a Divided World*, recommends B.G.S., "bachelor of general studies," p. 201.

[20] Henry S. Spalding, *Proceedings, Report and Addresses of the Catholic Educational Association*, XVI (1919), no. 2, pp. 82 f.

Several years ago I thought a Benedictine school was to be the first Catholic American institution to inaugurate an eight-year system of secondary education; but after a visit to their famous "English Public School," Downside, the administration decided that the time was not yet ripe for its introduction into the community in which their institution was located. Here the difficulty of persuading parents that their boys should enter high school at the completion of the sixth grade, and the still greater difficulty of holding them through the fourteenth grade, made the plan impractical at that time. But with the gradual spread of the 6–4–4 organization throughout the country, these difficulties are slowly solving themselves.

Religious communities of women, however, have the greatest opportunity in this regard and also find in it their greatest challenge. If they really believe that the life of women calls for an education that is different from that of men, here is their opportunity to make provision for it. In those situations where the same community is conducting elementary schools, a girl's academy, and a women's college, the transition should be easy. In the upper cycle, of course, the institution would have to make adequate provision for those highly selected students who would go on to university training in graduate and professional schools, but it would be relieved of the great expense involved in conducting the upper two years of the four-year college as now organized, which commonly provide a kind of university specialization instead of a culmination of general education as urged in this study. The members of the community, however, who are to be trained as teachers in their various schools, should transfer to another institution of higher rank after being graduated by their own college, thus doing away with that intellectual inbreeding which is perhaps the worst feature of our present situation; and for these students this change of scene would be the most valuable educational experience of their lives, giving them new light and inspiration for their work when they return to the institutions of their own community.

We cannot say that the accrediting associations stand in the way of the reorganization of the school system advocated here; at least this is true of the largest of the regional associations, which operates in nineteen states of the middlewest, the North Central Association of Colleges and Secondary schools. For several years a new accrediting procedure has been in operation whereby institutions combining the upper years of high school and the lower years of college can be accredited as a single institution. The artificial separation whereby no teacher could teach in both divisions, has been done away with, and the Examiners Committee for an institution of this type is made up of representatives from both commissions, the Commission of Colleges and Universities and the Commission of Secondary Schools. Furthermore, the secretary of the former Commission is a professor of education at the University of Chicago, where the 6–4–4 organization of Laboratory Schools and Colleges has now been in operation for a number of years, awarding the A.B. degree at the completion of the fourteenth year. The fact, then, that a college is operating on this reorganized plan, instead of being a hindrance to its accreditation, would decidedly favor the institution as being progressive, provided the reorganization is intelligently planned and effectively carried out.

Our minor seminaries should consider this plan of reorganization. For most of them, admitting boys after two years of high school and taking them through a four-year curriculum in the arts and sciences, would seem to be the best possible preparation for the courses in philosophy and theology to be studied in the major seminary.

It may seem that we have been using this formula, the 6–4–4 plan, as if we considered it a fixed pattern to be imposed on all students. But we have no such idea in mind, for this would be a violation of one of the "Principles of

Operation" presented in chapter 7 (pp. 158 f.): every student should be kept working at capacity. This principle of variant capacity demands that administrative techniques provide for the upper quarter and lower quarter in any student body in regard to the number of courses to be carried and the time for the completion of the curriculum. We have illustrated how this can be done for students of both groups following a curriculum such as we have suggested in Figure 6 (see p. 166). The university colleges have a special opportunity and a special obligation here. As reported by the U.S. Office of Education, the average age of high school graduates in 1942 (the latest statistics available in 1951) was 18.10 for boys and 17.86 for girls. After the war this undoubtedly increased for boys on account of the influx of veterans; but for many years yet the colleges will be receiving freshmen with an average age of about eighteen years, and many of the brighter students will continue in the graduate and professional schools. These should have the opportunity to complete their college work in less than the traditional four years if their advanced study is not to be unduly prolonged. The argument that maturation requires time is all on the side of the economy of time. Some young people mature more rapidly than their fellows, and for that very reason they should not be held back to the pace of the average student. The only result of such retardation will be the cultivation of habits of sloth and indifference instead of a sense of obligation to make good use of the superior gifts with which they have been endowed.

A different but similar arrangement should be made for the slower students, who may be able to carry only three subjects adequately if we take into account all the other "activities" they commonly engage in. Therefore they should take more time to complete the curriculum. Their failures in certain courses will require repetition of these courses; hence they will need more time as well as a lightened load to continue the forward process of their education. We do not wish to lose a present-day Cure d'Ars by the application of a rigid scholastic standard which ignores those other qualities that make saints—the love of God and man and a devoted zeal in the performance of one's duties.

CONCLUSION

CHRISTOPHER Dawson tells us that for the last fifteen years he has been insisting "on the fundamental thesis that the crisis of Western civilization is due to the separation of our culture from its religious basis." [1] We do not believe that anyone acquainted with what has been going on in the Western world during the past century can question the validity of this thesis. When it comes to assigning causes for the development of this crisis, however, the matter is much more difficult. Secularization of our education is certainly one of them and possibly the most important of all. With more than two hundred different religious sects each jealous of its particular dogmas, the only compromise that seemed possible in the United States was to leave religious information to the church and home and exclude it from the school entirely. This was a stupid decision. But, as Dawson says, "The real evil of popular education was not so much its secularism, but its utilitarian character, which led to the progressive discarding of all non-secular elements and motives." [2] With the industrial revolution the profit motive became supreme for labor as well as for the capitalists, and this motive together with the drive for power has brought upon us two world wars and is now threatening a third.

[1] *Education and the Crisis of Christian Culture* (Chicago: Henry Regnery Company, 1949), p. 5.
[2] *Ibid.,* p. 6.

For the Catholic, the universalization of education which is now in progress all over the world, holds high hopes for the improvement of culture if it can be freed from the secularizing influences that have been its chief characteristics in many countries like our own. It fits in perfectly with the Catholic concept of the mystical body of Christ, which Dawson never mentions. St. Paul states the analogy of the body in the twelfth chapter of the First Epistle to the Corinthians in these words: "For as the body is one and hath many members; and all the members of the body, whereas they are many, yet are one body, so also is Christ. . . . Now you are the body of Christ, and members of member." [3] Msgr. Benson develops this analogy in terms of the latest scientific discoveries concerning cell life in living organisms.

We considered just now whether it was possible to speak of the life of the Church as identical with the life of Christ—of the identity, that is, of the myriad consciousness of Catholic Christians with that Divine consciousness of Christ; and we see that recent research supplies us with a parallel, exact, so far as we have considered it, with the entire Catholic claim on the point. We see how it is not only possible, but essential, for an organic body—that is, for the highest form of physical life with which we are acquainted—that it should consist from one point of view of a myriad infinitesimal lives that lose themselves, and yet save themselves, in the unity of the whole, and that the unity of the whole, while it transcends the sum of the individual cell-lives, is at once dependent on them and apart. If this is true of physical life, literally and actually, it is surely not unreasonable to expect that it should be true also of spiritual life; and the coincidence is the more remarkable when we remember that the science of cell-life is of very recent date. [4]

[3] I Cor. 12:12, 27.
[4] Robert Hugh Benson, *Christ in the Church* (St. Louis: Herder, 1911), p. 17.

To carry the analogy still further, we call attention to the fact that as the cells of the body need food for their nourishment that they may play their part in the activity of a vigorous organism, so too do the cells of the spiritual body of the Church need nourishment to play their part in the spiritual life of this corporate body. This nourishment is of two kinds, the supernatural food, which is divine grace streaming into the individual cells through the ministration of the Church and their own activity as members of the faithful, and the natural food for their spiritual lives, which is education truly so called.

We agree with Dawson when he says, "The real source of the evil is to be found not in the universalization of education, but in the destruction of the old hierarchy of Divinity, Humanity and Natural Science that was the tradition of European higher education." [5] Man must learn to know nature, man, and God in all their interrelations and understand this analysis of the natural, humanistic, and philosophical sciences together with man's works in these three worlds: the applied arts, the literary arts, and the fine arts—at least in the effects they have had in transforming the world in which we are living today. These form the basis for a general or liberal education that will train the youth of the land to develop their God-given capacities to the fullest. But the opportunity to do this must be extended to all the youth of the land, to each according to his capacities and his willingness to apply himself to their development. How else can they be prepared to play their part in the mystical body if they have little or no opportunity to grow and develop as vigorous cells in the corporate organism? If they do have this opportunity and make use of it, we have solid ground for hoping that the three qualities which we identified in the third chapter of this book—leadership, followership, and fel-

[5] *Op. cit.*, p. 6. Cf. the quotation from Newman, p. 255.

lowship—will characterize the youth of the land as they take over the world of tomorrow.

The special task of the liberal college is to develop the leadership needed; but the most important quality in a free society is fellowship. And this must be a fellowship in Christ, by which we are brothers one of another and sons of our common Father, God. If this is lacking, we will be turning our "graduates loose with simply an increased capacity to prey upon each other." [6]

[6] President Calvin Coolidge in an address at Phillips Academy.

SELECTED READINGS IN GENERAL EDUCATION

Bagley, Wm. C. *Educational Values*, New York: Macmillan, 1911.

Brooks, Robert C. *Readings for Honors at Swarthmore*, New York: Oxford University Press, 1927.

Brubacher, John S. *Modern Philosophies of Education*, New York: McGraw-Hill, 1939.

Bryson, Lyman (ed.). *Goals for American Education*, New York: Harper & Brothers, 1950.

Chalmers, Gordon K. *The Republic and the Person*, Chicago: Henry Regnery Co., 1952.

Chicago University College Faculty Members. *The Idea and Practise of General Education*, Chicago: Chicago University Press, 1950.

Cohen, I. Bernard, and Fletcher G. Watson (eds.). *General Education in Science*, Cambridge: Harvard University Press, 1952.

Committee on the Objectives of a General Education in a Free Society. *General Education in a Free Society: Report of the Harvard Committee*, Cambridge: Harvard University Press, 1945.

Conant, James Bryan. *Education in a Divided World*, Cambridge: Harvard University Press, 1948.

Cunningham, Wm. F. *The Pivotal Problems of Education*, New York: Macmillan Co., 1940.

Curran, Charles F. *Counseling in Catholic Life and Education*, New York: Macmillan Co., 1952.

Dewey, John. *Democracy and Education*, New York: Macmillan Co., 1946.

———. *Education Today*, New York: G. P. Putnam's Sons, 1940.

Demiashkevitch, Michael. *An Introduction to the Philosophy of Education*, New York: American Book Co., 1935.

Diekhoff, John S. *Democracy's College*, New York: Harper and Brothers, 1950.

Fitzpatrick, Edward A. *How to Educate Human Beings*, Milwaukee: Bruce Publishing Co., 1950.

Flexner, Abraham. *Universities, American, English and German*, New York: Oxford University Press, 1930.

Foerster, Norman. *The American State University*, Chapel Hill: University of North Carolina Press, 1937.

———. *The Future of the Liberal College*, New York: Appleton-Century-Crofts, 1938.

General Education in School and College, A Committee Report by Members of the Faculties of Andover, Exeter, Lawrenceville, Harvard, Princeton and Yale; Cambridge: Harvard University Press, 1952.

Gideon, Harry D. *The Higher Learning in a Democracy*, New York: Farrar & Rhinehart, 1937.

Good, Carter V. *Teaching in College and University*, Baltimore: Warwick and York, 1929.

Gray, William S. *General Education, Its Nature, Its Scope, and Essential Elements*, Chicago: Chicago University Press, 1934.

Greene, Theodore M., and others. *Liberal Education Reexamined: Its Role in a Democracy*, New York: Harper & Brothers, 1943.

Henry, Nelson B. (ed.). *Philosophies of Education, Forty-first Yearbook of the National Society for the Study of*

Education, Part I, Chicago: Chicago University Press, 1942.

Hopkins, L. T. *Integration*, New York: Appleton-Century, 1937.

Hutchins, Robert Maynard. *No Friendly Voice*, Chicago: Chicago University Press, 1936.

————. *The Higher Learning in America*, New Haven: Yale University Press, 1936.

Huxley, Thomas Henry. *Autobiography and Selected Essays*, Cambridge: Riverside Press, 1909.

Johnson, George. *Better Men for Better Times*, Washington: Catholic University Press, 1943.

Johnston, J. B. *The Liberal College in a Changing Society*, New York: Century Publishing Co., 1930.

Jones, Howard Mumford. *Education and World Tragedy*, Cambridge: Harvard University Press, 1940.

Kallen, Horace M. *The Education of Free Men*, New York: Farrar, Straus & Co., 1949.

Livingstone, Richard. *On Education*, Cambridge: Cambridge University Press, 1944.

————. *Education for a World Adrift*, Cambridge: Cambridge University Press, 1942.

Maritain, Jacques. *Education at the Crossroads*, New Haven: Yale University Press, 1943.

————. *True Humanism*, New York: Charles Scribner's Sons, 1938.

Martin, Everett Dean. *The Meaning of a Liberal Education*, New York: Morton & Co., 1926.

Mercier, Louis J. A. *American Humanism and the New Age*, Milwaukee: Bruce Publishing Co., 1948.

Millett, Fred B. *The Rebirth of Liberal Education*, New York: Harcourt, Brace & Co., 1945.

Newman, John Henry. *Idea of a University*, 1852.

————. *Sermons on Various Occasions* (Sermon I, "Intellect the Instrument of Religious Training").

Nock, Albert Jay. *The Theory of Education in the United States*, New York: Harcourt, Brace & Co., 1932.

Palmer, A. M. (ed.). *The Liberal Arts College Movement*, New York: J. J. Little and Ives Co., 1930.

President's Commission on Higher Education. *Higher Education for American Democracy*, New York: Harper & Brothers, 1949.

Redden, John D., and Francis A. Ryan. *A Catholic Philosophy of Education*, Milwaukee: Bruce Publishing Co., 1942.

Reeves, Floyd W., John Dale Russell, H. C. Gregg, A. J. Brumbaugh, L. E. Blauch. *The Liberal Arts College*, Chicago: Chicago University Press, 1932.

Richardson, Leon B. *A Study of the Liberal College*, Report to the President of Dartmouth College, Hanover: Dartmouth College Press, 1924.

Ryan, J. J. *The Idea of a Catholic College*, New York: Sheed and Ward, 1945.

Sexson, John A., and John W. Harbeson. *The New American College*, New York: Harper & Brothers, 1946.

Spafford, Ivol, and others. *Building a Curriculum for General Education* (University of Minnesota Studies of General Education), Minneapolis: University of Minnesota Press, 1943.

Stuart, Henry Waldgrave. *Liberal and Vocational Studies in the College*, California: Stanford University Publications, 1918.

Van Doren, Mark. *Liberal Education*, New York: Holt and Co., 1943.

Ward, Leo R. *Blueprint for a Catholic University*, St. Louis: Herder Book Co., 1949.

Wise, John E. *The Nature of the Liberal Arts*, Milwaukee: Bruce Publishing Co., 1947.

Wriston, Henry M. *The Nature of the Liberal College*, Wisconsin: Lawrence College Press, 1937.

Wynne, John P. *Philosophies of Education*, New York: Prentice-Hall, 1947.

———. *General Education in Theory and Practise*, New York: Bookman Associates Inc., 1952.

Publications of the Committee on the Cooperative Study in General Education of the American Council on Education, Washington, D.C.

McConnell, T. H. *A Design for General Education for Members of the Armed Forces*, 1945.

Cooperation in General Education: A Final Report of the Executive Committee, 1947.

Dunkel, H. Baker. *General Education in the Humanities*, 1947.

Levi, Albert Wm. *General Education in the Social Studies*, 1948.

Brouwer, Paul J. *Student Personnel Services in General Education*, 1949.

Proceedings of the workshops conducted by the Catholic University of America, edited by Roy J. Deferrari and published by the Catholic University of America Press, Washington, D.C.

College Organization and Administration, 1947.
The Philosophy of Catholic Higher Education, 1948.
Guidance in Catholic Colleges and Universities, 1949.
Integration in the Catholic College, 1950.
Discipline and Integration in the Catholic College, 1951.
The Curriculum of the Catholic College, 1952.
Theology, Philosophy and History as Integrating Discipline, 1953.

Series edited by E. J. McGrath (formerly Commissioner of Education and dean of the Liberal Arts College, State University of Iowa); Dubuque: William C. Brown Co.

Science in General Education, 1948.
Social Science in General Education, 1948.
The Humanities in General Education, 1949.
Communication in General Education, 1949.
Organization and Administration of General Education, 1951
(edited by Hugh Stickler).

Publications of the Commission on Secondary School Curriculum of the Progressive Education Association; New York: Appleton-Century-Crofts.

Science in General Education, 1938.
Language in General Education, 1940.
Mathematics in General Education, 1940.
The Social Studies in General Education, 1940.
The Visual Arts in General Education, 1940.

BIBLIOGRAPHIES

E. J. McGrath. "A Bibliography on General Education," *Education Record,* XXI (1940), 96–118.
W. N. Lyons. "A Further Bibliography on General Education," *The Journal of General Education,* IV (1949–1950), 72–80. (This is a continuation of the earlier bibliography by E. J. McGrath.)

REVIEWS

The Journal of General Education, Chicago: The University of Chicago Press.
Main Currents in Modern Thought. ed. by F. L. Kunz, New York: The Foundation for Integrated Education.

INDEX

American Cooperative Study in General Education, 155, 164, 168, 174
American Council on Education, 155, 169, 206
Apprenticeship, 201 f., 204 f.
Arts, the
  applied, 75-77, 100, 115, 221
  fine, 75, 78, 109-11, 155 f., 176 f.: discipline of the, 136, 139, 142-44; in Russia, 247
  liberal, 17 f., 77-80, 194 f., 244, 247
  of communication; see Language
  visual, 109, 176
Association of American Colleges, 205 f., 251
Augustine, St., 39, 59, 171

Bowman, Isaiah, 113, 146
Brown, J. Douglas, 60, 62, 64
Butler, Nicholas Murray, 67, 76, 133

Catholic colleges: design for, 23, 27, 109, 119 f., 154, 242; practices of, 156 f., 196, 198, 214, 222, 235; problems of, 175, 197, 213, 231, 236, 251; purpose of, 22, 25, 34
Catholic education, 44-46, 48-50, 71, 99, 102
Catholic University of America, 179-81, 185
Character, definition of, 48

Chicago University, 82, 157, 185, 220, 271
Childs, John, 90 f., 93
Columbia University, 82, 169, 172
Curran, Charles, 237 f.
Curriculum, 31, 73 ff., 100 ff., 155 ff., 259: in Greece and Rome, 20

Dawson, Christopher, 275-77
Democratic education, dilemma of, 97
Departmentalization, 81
Discipline, 130-33: intellectual, 133, 135 ff., 177; liberal, 196, 213

Education, 17, 31, 43 f., 121
  Catholic, 44-46, 48-50, 71, 99, 102
  definition of, 38, 50, 71
  for democracy, 29, 58
  professional, 19, 24-27, 125, 258, 264
  ultimate goals of, 90, 93, 114, 168
Elective system, 81, 156

Foerster, Norman, 26, 81, 148, 244

Gentleman, portrait of a, 241
Grace, 42, 49, 243 ff., 277
Graduate study, 121, 198 ff., 258 f., 265 f., 270
Grammar, definition of, 160

Harvard University, 83, 122, 157, 208, 220

285